The Nineteenth-Century French Short Story

The Nineteenth-Century French Short Story by eminent scholar, Allan H. Pasco, seeks to offer a more comprehensive view of the definition, capabilities, and aims of short stories. This book examines general instances of the genre specifically in nineteenth-century France by recognizing their cultural context, demonstrating how close analysis of texts effectively communicates their artistry, and arguing for a distinction between middling and great short stories. Where previous studies have examined the writers of short stories individually, this book takes a broader lens to the subject, and looks at short-story writers as they grapple with the artistic, ethical, and social concerns of their day. Making use of French short-story masterpieces, with reinforcing comparisons to works from other traditions, this book offers the possibility of a more adequate appreciation of the under-valued short-story genre.

Allan H. Pasco is the Hall Distinguished Professor of Nineteenth-Century Literature at the University of Kansas. Specializing in French culture, his critical and historical orientations are rooted in literature. *The Nineteenth-Century French Short Story* focuses on reasons for the power of the French short story, and follows his earlier consideration of novel forms, *Inner Workings of the Novel*. Professor Pasco has published ten books on Proust, Balzac, romanticism, allusion, concepts of affection, aesthetic forms, and the thoroughly revised, expanded second edition of his anthology of nineteenth-century short stories. His articles have appeared in such journals as *French Studies*, *Modern Language Review*, *PMLA*, *New Literary History*, and the *Revue d'Histoire Littéraire*. While serving on eight editorial boards, he was recognized with the Civilian Service Award by the US government, and has been listed both in the Marquis *Who's Who in America* since 1999 and, more recently, the Albert Nelson Marquis Lifetime Achievement Award. He has also been named a Chevalier in the *Ordre des Palmes Académiques* by the French government.

Routledge Studies in Nineteenth-Century Literature

43 **Women's Emancipation Writing at the Fin de Siècle**
Edited by Elena V. Shabliy, Dmitry Kurochkin, and Karen O'Donnell

44 **Dickens, Nicholas Nickleby and the Dance of Death**
Jeremy Tambling

45 **G. W. M. Reynolds and His Fiction**
The Man Who Outsold Dickens
Stephen Knight

46 **Arthur Morrison and the East End**
The Legacy of Slum Fictions
Eliza Cubitt

47 **Constructions of Agency in American Literature on the War of Independence**
War as Action, 1775–1860
Martin Holtz

48 **Neglected American Women Writers of the Long Nineteenth Century**
Progressive Pioneers
Edited by Verena Laschinger and Sirpa Salenius

49 **W.S. Gilbert and the History of Comedy**
The Progress of Fun
Richard Moore

50 **The Nineteenth-Century French Short Story**
Masterpieces in Miniature
Allan H. Pasco

For more information about this series, please visit: https://www.routledge.com

The Nineteenth-Century French Short Story
Masterpieces in Miniature

Allan H. Pasco

NEW YORK AND LONDON

First published 2020
by Routledge
52 Vanderbilt Avenue, New York, NY 10017

and by Routledge
2 Park Square, Milton Park, Abingdon, Oxon, OX14 4RN

Routledge is an imprint of the Taylor & Francis Group, an informa business

First issued in paperback 2021

© 2020 Taylor & Francis

The right of Allan H. Pasco to be identified as author of this work has been asserted by him in accordance with sections 77 and 78 of the Copyright, Designs and Patents Act 1988.

All rights reserved. No part of this book may be reprinted or reproduced or utilised in any form or by any electronic, mechanical, or other means, now known or hereafter invented, including photocopying and recording, or in any information storage or retrieval system, without permission in writing from the publishers.

Trademark notice: Product or corporate names may be trademarks or registered trademarks, and are used only for identification and explanation without intent to infringe.

Library of Congress Cataloging-in-Publication Data
A catalog record for this title has been requested

ISBN: 978-0-367-33271-6 (hbk)
ISBN: 978-1-03-209159-4 (pbk)
ISBN: 978-0-429 31900-6 (ebk)

Typeset in Sabon
by codeMantra

For Dallas

Contents

Preface	ix
1 On Defining Short Stories	1
2 Sequential Uncertainty in Vivant Denon's "Point de lendemain"	18
3 Huysmans and the Bifocal Dilemma	35
4 Sequence Denied in Barbey's "Don Juan" and "Le Dessous de cartes"	51
5 Sequence Framed in Mérimée's "Carmen"	72
6 Reforming Society and Genre in Hugo's "Claude Gueux"	90
7 Flaubert's Talking Heads in the Cyclical *Trois Contes*	110
8 The Power of Ambiguity in Balzac's Open Closures	131
9 Maupassant's Exploding Closures	147
10 Conclusion	164
Works Cited	179
Index	193

Preface

Despite their commercial popularity, short stories are underappreciated by critics, often mistakenly considering them as though they were abbreviated novels. More attentive examination should be paid to the discriminating qualities of brevity and artistry. Especially when short stories succeed in drawing the reader into the author's creative process, brevity affects short masterpieces on lexical, metaphoric, and generic levels; it has significant impact on the devices used to touch readers; and it compounds meaning by exerting pressure on the generic form. The following book's examples are chosen from a small group of masterpieces whose strategies provide coherence and revelation to highly engaged, informed and perceptive readers. The successive chapters consider how these works rise above the ordinary by analyzing metaphoric detail, image and sequential structures, allusions, frames, cycles, and open conclusions in well-known masterpieces by major authors, with close attention to the text. Contemporary guidelines develop as the devices are studied in examples that facilitate, indeed demand, optimal participation by short-story readers.

Short stories vary in quality, and as a number of masterpieces in this rather neglected genre are considered, I hope (1) to reinvigorate the close analysis of brief texts by emphasizing that they are embedded in their culture, (2) to demonstrate how close analysis of texts effectively communicates their artistry, (3) to show how generic distinctions are crucial to brevity's reformulation of detail, allusion, compression, implication, intensification, and context large and small, (4) to argue for a distinction between run-of-the-mill and great short stories as the reader is enticed into the creative process, and (5) to suggest approaches that will facilitate understanding. *The Nineteenth-Century French Short Story: Masterpieces in Miniature* also serves as a companion panel for my previous consideration of genre, *Inner Workings of the Novel: Studying a Genre* (2010).

By focusing on key devices, like brevity, and strategies like the ways in which outstanding writers attract readers into the creative process, I trust *The Nineteenth-Century French Short Story* will offer a more comprehensive view of what short stories are and what they can accomplish.

x *Preface*

It is not enough to propose a definition of the genre, though I consider one in the first chapter. A sense of the genre's potential is also required. Making use of French short-story masterpieces, with reinforcing comparisons to works from other traditions, I have offered the possibility of a more adequate appreciation of this under-valued genre.

Chapter 1—"On Defining Short Stories": while definitions change, have exceptions, and are only approximate, expectations nonetheless guide readers. A simple formula like *short stories are artistically designed, brief, prose fictions* has advantages of clarity and inclusiveness in dealing with the ancient genre. It says nothing about the aesthetic value of individual examples, however. For this reason, I shall deal with masterpieces, which share the most important traits of brevity and artistry. Although critics and scholars of the short-story genre frequently mention brevity (it even occurs in several titles), no one has as yet focused on how shortness both optimizes the compact format and determines the devices, strategies, and dominant features that give short stories their particular definition and vitality. Both brevity and artistry are, in addition, particularly adept at energizing the reader's creative role.

Chapter 2—"Sequential Uncertainty in Vivant Denon's 'Point de lendemain'": because of brevity, short-story authors must assume readers will forget nothing, which imposes a special economy, one that normally shuns amplification and redundancy in favor of allusion, implication, context, elision, compression, and intensification. Readers expect every element to serve the overall effect. While stories may be predominantly sequential or imagistic, the most common and the most commonly analyzed are sequential. Lilliane Louvel, Karen Blixen, Chekhov, Valery Shaw, B.M. Ejxenbaum, Gerlach, even Robert Louis Stevenson, and many others insist on narrative structures leading to a powerful conclusion, and I shall bow to them in this second chapter, though subsequently I turn to those critically neglected works where an image dominates structurally and whose meanings are often less perceptible, even frustratingly obscure. Brevity and sequential structure, the major issues of the chapter, are considered within an analysis of Vivant Denon's "Point de lendemain" ['No Tomorrow'].

Chapter 3—"Huysmans and the Bifocal Dilemma": authors regularly exploit vocabulary that comes to them laden with meaningful connotations, that is, ideas or feelings that extend beyond the basic, normal sense of a word's denotations, whether insinuations, implications, analogies, or allusions, few of which would be listed in standard dictionaries but which are nonetheless cultural associations that authors can bring into focus. There is no imperative for writers to do so. Proust, for example, often avoided traditional symbols. Instead, as I argued regarding Proust's color in *The Color-keys to "A la recherche perdu"*, he slowly built his own related connotations into particular hues by repeated use in similar contexts. Building associative significance is possible in

Preface xi

short stories, as well. Huysmans wrote in a period when symbolism was important. He exploited such meaningful images regularly in *A rebours* and *En rade*, while neglecting standard plots. In his short story, "Un Dilemme," he returned to traditional forms of literature and built a story on both denotative and connotative levels. He later called it "spiritualistic naturalism." One pattern of "Un Dilemme" exposes father and grandfather denigrating, manipulating, exploiting, and, finally, annihilating their dead son's mistress, who was carrying their only heir. At another level, sensitive readers perceive vulpine bourgeois secretly stalking and destroying innocent prey. Both image systems reveal the noisome abomination of the burgeoning bourgeoisie in startling detail, though the interacting denotations and connotations require close attention to the full context for the reader's appreciation.

Chapter 4—"Sequence Denied in Barbey's 'Don Juan' and 'Le Dessous de cartes'": the short story requires no specific device, not even plot, as legions of recent examples prove. Because short stories are put under pressure by shortness itself and by the writer's desire to deal with significant issues, they tend to use loaded language, thus innuendo, implication, and symbolism. Unlike the sequential narratives of "Point de lendemain" and "Un Dilemme," image (spatial or lyrical) structures dominate several of Barbey's stories (and, indeed, the entire *Les Diaboliques*, though I shall deal with such cycles in Chapter 7). I begin the analysis Barbey's stories by suggesting that writers have long been aware of the power arising from structuring their works to incite readers to provide what the text merely implies. Barbey d'Aurevilly's "Le Plus Bel Amour de Don Juan" ['Don Juan's Most Beautiful Love'] and "Le Dessous de cartes d'une partie de whist" ['Beneath the Cards in of a Game of Whist'], for example, depend on the legal peculiarities of the historic Civil Code, on the rules of whist, on the period's understanding of Sardanapalus, and on popular, religious traditions. Readers who can connect such cultural meanings to the various names and images not only appreciate these enigmatic stories, but also sense their power.

Chapter 5—"Sequence Framed in Mérimée's *Carmen*" turns to a device favored by Chaucer, Boccaccio, Marguerite de Navarre, and others. Ordinarily, the frame and the story establish parallels that support and illuminate major themes and images. Nineteenth- and twentieth-century writers were particularly skillful in setting their stories in frames emphasizing a background that reverberates to increase realism or illuminate one or more constituent elements. In *Carmen*, for example, Mérimée offers an engaging narration of eroticism, violence, and crime, then encloses it in a frame exposing the narrator as a coward tempted but terrified by Bohemia (Bizet took the story and character for his opera and ignored the frame).

Chapter 6—"Reforming Society and Genre in Hugo's 'Claude Gueux'" considers authors' inventiveness in taking full advantage of the genre's

xii *Preface*

apparent restriction of shortness. Hugo extended the inherent meaning of "Claude Gueux" by alluding to the structure of fables, which carry with them the knowledge that they are long lived and that their lessons are ageless. The story's coda insists powerfully on France's horrendous prison conditions. While the author based the main personage on a real recidivist criminal, he changed his character to one that elicits sympathy, since his crime was caused by society's penal system. Hugo then demands reform. The conclusion like those of fables allows him to insist repeatedly on his message and issue a clarion call for radical changes.

Chapter 7—"Flaubert's Talking Heads in the Cyclical *Trois Contes*" observes that frames may lead logically to cycles. Some volumes of short stories are so integrated that they develop across the whole, almost like chapters in a novel, while maintaining the independence of each narration. The unity of cycles often comes, not through devices of narration, but rather through association or development of images and themes. Authors, thus, circumvent the restriction of brevity and, yet, exploit the genre's compressed nature. Flaubert's *Trois Contes* ['Three Tales'] demonstrates the firm integration of three saints' tales into a unity that moves in a retrograde sequence from the present through the medieval period and back to the time of Christ, while simultaneously bringing the three stories together in a powerfully cohesive image of the religion of art.

Chapter 8—"The Power of Ambiguity in Balzac's Open Closures" focuses on Balzac's codas. In such stories as "Gobseck," their importance is signaled by the fact that they were added after the fact, suggesting that the author sought a more probing conclusion, but, in most cases, the stories are simply ended ambiguously. "Gillette" ['Le Chef-d'œuvre inconnu'] and its dramatization of Poussin's terrible conflict between love and art ends in confusion, until we remember that the story's Gillette does not appear in the painter's historical biography. Only then do we recognize, and regret, that love lost the battle for Poussin's heart. Outstanding stories regularly use terminal confusion to force readers to seek an underlying but unstated image in the open conclusions. "L'Auberge rouge" ['The Red Inn'] likewise builds a tangled pattern of multifaceted guilt until the reader seizes the terms of oxymoronic innocence and culpability to "write" a resolution.

Chapter 9—"Maupassant's Exploding Closures," deals with the way some conclusions annul sequences, and through incompletion insist on the possibility of an unexpected image, in order to focus not on the impulsive drive toward an end, but rather toward a unified vision. Maupassant would occasionally force his reader to view the story s/he has just read in a new way, with very different results. "Les Epingles" ['The Pins'] makes use of culturally determined connotations. It implies a judgment on the narrator and his mistresses, much to the benefit of the young women. In "Le Champ d'oliviers" ['The Field of Olive Trees'], the

Preface xiii

reader follows the horror raised by the priest's appalling son until by implication the priest sets the son up for appropriate punishment and, as a corollary, sacrifices himself. As an early variant confirmed, Maupassant is unquestionably calling on the reader to collaborate in creating the conclusion of this telling story.

Chapter 10—"Conclusion" reviews the lessons of the preceding pages. For outstanding writers, brevity is not a limitation, but rather an aesthetic constraint that acts in masterpieces as an incentive. In outstanding short fictions, brevity also encourages devices that impose economy in a plethora of applications. It becomes the short story's greatest glory when writers plumb and manipulate levels of language, technique, and form, thus exploiting private and cultural symbolism while arranging their stories in ways that go beyond shortness by making use of frames, cycles, and other genres. They thus meet the challenge of what might otherwise become a restriction and, in the process, encourage the reader to complete or, actually, to create an implied conclusion that extends, expands, and delves deeper into meanings of short stories.

The chapters are ordered according to the devices that short stories exploit rather than chronologically by author or date of publication. While I could undoubtedly have found examples of each device in whatever period I wished, I would not have been able to uncover the superb masterpieces that have seemed appropriate for the argument of the following pages. I ask for the reader's indulgence, hoping that it will be worth the read.

Before closing this "Preface" I would like to thank the Hall Family Foundation and the University of Kansas for their continued support. I am also very grateful to N. Dean Weaver, M.D., for sharing his medical knowledge about migraine headaches in regard to Frédéric Taillefer. Likewise, it was both helpful and kind for Professors D. L. Ashliman to be so generous with his research on lion/dog stories, for Maria Carlson with her quest of the possible sources of Tolstoy's fable, and for Kathryn M. Grossman with sharing her insight into *Les Misérables*. Perhaps especially important, I am grateful to Bradley Stephens for his generosity with his enormous background in Hugo. Finally, I want to express my very real gratitude to Corry Cropper, who helped me with the Mérimée bibliography. Several chapters make use of revised material that appeared earlier. I am very grateful to *Modern Language Review* for permission to re-edit the material on Hugo that appeared in their pages in 2016, to *Romance Studies* for the work on Barbey that they published in 2010, and to *New Literary History* for the analysis of short stories that originally appeared in 1991.

1 On Defining Short Stories

Compared to the novel, the short story has had remarkably little criticism devoted to it, and what theory exists reveals few definitive statements about its nature. During the last quarter of the twentieth century, critics neglected generic questions and turned to the consideration of narration or storyline or *récit*. They hedged on definitions, origins, major traits, and just about everything having to do with the short story as a genre. For them, the concept of genre was not important. I make this observation without censure, for one is doubtless wise to be circumspect with anything of unequaled antiquity and adaptability. I am less tolerant of post-structuralist claims that exceptions invalidate generic rules.[1] As Gullason, May, and many others have pointed out, the short story may be an "underrated art," but it remains remarkably hardy,[2] so much so that Mary Doyle Springer and Elisabeth Bowen have attempted to distinguish "modern" and "artistic" short stories of the last one hundred years from more antiquated, inartistic predecessors,[3] though the case is difficult to make. We remember, with H. E. Bates, that "the stories of Salome, Ruth, Judith, and Susannah are all examples of an art that was already old, civilized, and highly developed some thousands of years before the vogue of Pamela."[4] And while Geoffrey Brereton is quite right that the French have excelled in the short story or *nouvelle* since the sixteenth century, Clements and Gibaldi have argued convincingly that recent masterpieces continue in an age-old genre.[5] Indeed, without *parti pris* it is difficult to read certain Milesian tales or stories from the *Arabian Nights*, not to mention subsequent masterpieces by such writers as Marguerite de Navarre, Chaucer, or Boccaccio, without being struck by the modernity of these creations from long ago. The subject matter may be different, the devices at variance, but no substantive trait or quality distinguishes their tales from the products of nineteenth- and twentieth- or twenty-first century practitioners. I do not say there is no difference. I argue rather that, similar to archetypes, which have certain key elements that are combined with other traits specific to a given epoch and are thus reconstituted, the short-story genre has a central, identifiable set of characteristics most of which each age and each author deploy in different ways and with different variables. The result is

2 On Defining Short Stories

generically recognizable, allowing for parallel and oppositional play, but specific to the author, age, and culture.

Just as claims for the recent origin of the short story are difficult to defend, most of us would agree that we cannot be decisive about any suggested birthplace or time. It surely takes its source in the earliest days of civilization. We all know that, just as children tend to ask "Why?", so too do human beings tell stories in their idle moments, but we cannot explain why some individuals choose to write them down, or why certain epochs have more such individuals than others. We only note that it began occurring rather early.

It might help if we could agree on a definition for the short story. Unfortunately, every time critics and theoreticians reach a modicum of agreement, some writer apparently takes it as a challenge and invents a contradiction to disrupt our comfortable meeting of minds. Certain post-structuralists have used the lack of really stable definitions, the absence of universally accepted conventions, and the difficulty of firmly establishing an undeviating external reality to justify denying credence to all but the reader. In their hands, the texts, like other objectively verifiable truths, become mere pretexts of little ultimate importance. Genre, which has no physical existence, since it consists of a shared concept of a generalized collective, thus non-individualized reality, has fared even worse. A few recent reconsiderations may signal a change,[6] but, for the most part, critics continue to view the matter of fictional genres with indifference. In the words of Harry Steinhauer: "[T]here are tasks of greater substance to engage [members of the scholarly community] than the search for the phantom traits of the ideal novella."[7] Perhaps it is time to suggest that this position may make interesting theory, but it represents an extreme that is too far removed from the actual mechanics of reading literature. When readers are reading, they quite properly act as though conventions, language, texts, civilization itself do exist, and they manage rather well to reach an understanding within such contexts.

E. D. Hirsch, Jr. pointed to perhaps the most significant obstacle to defining genre:

> Aristotle was wrong to suppose that human productions can be classified in a definitive way like biological species. [... A] true class requires a set of distinguishing features which are inclusive within the class and exclusive outside it; it requires a *differentia specifica*. That, according to Aristotle, is the key to definition and to essence. But, in fact, nobody has ever so defined literature or any important genre within it.[8]

Hirsch's position raises several issues. Most important, despite an indiscriminate admiration of science and the scientific which unfortunately pervades humanistic studies, biological typology does not benefit from a *differentia specifica*. The distinctive features are distinctive only in their

On Defining Short Stories 3

plural congruence, when they function successfully to isolate—more or less and for the most part—a locus. As any good biologist knows, biological typology is rife with problems; every class has its own variation on the duck-billed platypus.

That said, I do suspect aesthetic genres are more problematic than biological species. In the latter case, only the definition is of human invention. The external referent may change, but that alteration is at worst very slow. In aesthetics, however, both the classification and the objects under study come from the creative hearth of man and are subject to constant, sometimes revolutionary change. Moreover, no aesthetic definition can be anything but retrospective, and it must be revised and updated to accommodate innovations. The old distinction between *novel* and *romance* on the basis of the presence of realistic or fantastic material is no longer helpful, for example, and current definitions of the novel need not, and indeed should not, take subject matter into account. The hope of contriving a definition of the short story that will remain useful until the end of time will be possible only when the short story dies as a genre. Although that has happened with the epic poem, it has not done so with the short story, and I shall be content to point to common ground. The indistinct, problematic outer edges of that defined area may be safely left for individual exploration.

Lexicographers are basically collectors. After gathering as many samples of usage as possible, and discarding the outliers, they compose a definition which comes as close to standard usage as possible. If the norm changes, adaptations or completely new formulations must be devised. Just as the reality referred to by linguistic signs is neither *ab ovo* nor *ad vitam aeternam*, so too definitions must shift, change, and adjust to reflect the reality circumscribed. Definitions are not God-carved and imposed from above. Rather, they reflect shifting, communal agreement. It may be unsettling that this accord is subject to change, has exceptions, and is seldom more than approximate, but it is a well understood and accepted fact of linguistics. It should not keep us from reaching that modicum of agreement necessary for perceiving and identifying almost any human and all social activity. Such accord is certainly a *sine qua non* of reading. On remembering Heinreich Wölfflin's magnificent effort, one might draw comfort from the realization that even topological failures may be helpful in understanding art. Though Wölfflin failed in his intention to categorize all art, he went far toward delineating both "classical" and "baroque."[9]

No generic definition of science or literature can hope to do more than draw attention to the dominant aspects of the system, which will inevitably include elements used elsewhere. As Tynjanov explains with particular reference to literature,

> Since a system is not an equal interaction of all elements but places a group of elements in the foreground—the "dominant"—and thus

4   On Defining Short Stories

involves the deformation of the remaining elements, a work enters into literature and takes on its own literary function through this dominant. Thus we correlate poems with the verse category, not with the prose category, not on the basis of all their characteristics, but only of some of them.[10]

The problems that cause difficulty in arriving at definitions of human creations should not cause us to join Leon Roudiez in concluding, "[T]he concept of genre is not as useful as it was in the past."[11] Acceptable definitions are even more needed these days, since most, though not all, of the generically controversial works (I think in particular of creations by Godard and Sollers) were *meant* to disrupt categories. To deny the existence of the novel genre, for example, deprives Sollers of the opportunity to attack bourgeois society by undermining one of its conceptual categories. Surely, part of the enjoyment of works which fall on the edge of—or between—well-established generic boundaries comes from their problematic nature as genre.[12]

There comes a time when human cleverness, on the one hand, and stubborn ineptitude, on the other, must be reckoned with. It may be impossible to define a genre, but readers do it all the time, and they use their own definitions as guides. That such readers are consequently led astray on occasion does not impede their behavior in the slightest. A reader may not know a lesson of the ancients and of modern psychology: that we see only what we are prepared for; we understand only what is within our ken. Nonetheless—however unconsciously—readers look for congruences with what they know. History is replete with the disasters caused by those whose expectations did not correspond with their experience and who nonetheless clung to their misconceptions. As just one example, we might remember the bizarre misreadings that several centuries of readers accorded Boccaccio's tenth tale of the tenth day about Griselda, because they did not know the story of Job.[13] Perhaps such misreadings are unimportant. Perhaps. I would rather conclude that there may be wisdom in laying groundwork which aids perception and understanding. Not only does it lead to communication, thus civilization rather than the jungle, in art it can lead to the enjoyment of great beauty.

The work of defining a genre succeeds when the definition corresponds to general practice and understanding, when it includes the samples generally present, and excludes those normally left out, when its categories do not erroneously focus on elements that cause misapprehensions. No one element will ever serve as a discretionary touchstone. One hopes that the various traits together will provide a means of discrimination. The fact that both flies and snakes are cold-blooded, for example, does not prevent using "cold-blooded" in definitions of both. There will be problem cases which present intentional or unintentional difficulties, but until such exceptions become commonplace, they should be appreciated

On Defining Short Stories   5

for the significance raised by their very deviations. They should not be allowed to negate existing definitions and certainly not the possibility of arriving at an accord.

If, then, one is justified in distinguishing short stories from the vast sea of narrations, the following definition might be advanced: a short story is an *artistically designed, short, prose fiction*. At first glance, such a formula seems uncontroversial, but whether it proves useful depends upon what it truly means, for, at second remove, one realizes that every one of the definition's four key terms covers a library of controversy. I leave the more important problem of assessing value for later. Here I wish only to distinguish the short story from other genres. The Dick and Jane primary text readers may exploit the short story, for example, but they constitute a pathetically inartistic example of the genre, however useful they may be pedagogically. Likewise, hundreds of short stories populate literary reviews, commercial magazines, anthologies, and even the collections of oral storytellers. While everyone may reveal the intent to make art, there may not be one single work of aesthetic excellence in the lot. Masterpieces are rare. Those devices and tactics that raise the occasional work of superior art above its generic contemporaries are the focus of the following chapters, where I center on the short story that came of age in France of the nineteenth century. I have attempted to choose examples that are masterpieces, extraordinary works of art and artistry. There are many definitions of the word "masterpiece," which grows from an apprentice's work to create something near perfection to prove his appropriateness for membership in the guild. I mean something more than that. I found my favorite definition in a study by Thomas E. Peterson: a masterpiece is "a crystallization of human 'genius,' a timely or prophetic validation of the human spirit."[14] The stories that I analyze below are of this nature.

Returning to the terms that define the short story in general, the concept of "fiction," for example, has challenged our best minds and elicited volumes of commentary, perhaps justifying a certain wary caution in dealing with it. For the purposes of discrimination, I pay particular attention to fiction's linguistic referent. Though it may be propositionally true, it "deals in untrue specificities, untrue facts," as Thomas J. Roberts would have it,[15] and it explicitly or implicitly warns the reader of this state of affairs. Consequently, the primary creation of fiction—be it pattern, plot, or world—cannot be verified externally. The whole point of the writings of scientists, sociologists, and historians is that they can be verified and replicated; however well organized and abstract they may be, they are open to the control of objective validation, both in totality and in detail. Of course, current or historical events may be present in fiction without changing its primary thrust of creating an unverifiable complex in a reader's mind. Likewise, the occurrence of a lie or two, for example, in Rousseau's *Les Confessions* (1781, 1788), does not fiction

6 On Defining Short Stories

make, for Rousseau explicitly intended his work to present the general, rather than specific truth of his character. Conversely, Jesus' parable of the prodigal son exists for the most part in that focused image created by the words of the parable. There will be extremely problematic instances. One famous example, though in the realm of the novel, is the *Lettres de la religieuse portugaise* (1669). "Are they authentic?" asks Philippe Van Tieghem. "It seems that we cannot doubt it."[16] In fact, many scholars have doubted their authenticity. Are they indeed actual love letters from the nun, Maria Alcoforado, or do we owe them to the literary skill of someone like Guilleragues? They seem just too well done, their haunting lyricism too unflawed for non-fiction. But in truth, we do not know. Furthermore, the potential problem of illusion in conflict with reality does not seriously afflict the short story. This genre, most of us would agree, includes factual history only incidentally; it is fiction. While it is calumnious to doubt the virtuous Marguerite de Navarre's insistence on the truth of her stories, their artistry (in line with what I shall suggest farther on) has raised them above mere reality. They are short-story masterpieces. All art is reality raised to a new reality.

The term "fiction" does, however, cover a difficulty of considerable magnitude. Most considerations of the short story insist upon the "story," for the causally and chronologically constructed narrative sequence is generally viewed as central. I have argued at some length elsewhere that Balzac, in story and novel, often subordinated narration to description, that he was interested in painting the portrait of an age and a civilization, rather than telling the events in the life of a fictional Gobseck or Father Goriot. Fiction's tendency toward the dominance of image is anything but rare after the early nineteenth century. It appears in an emphasis on what Joseph Frank has called "spatial form," what I have called "image structure," what others call tone, or mood, or focus, or theme (as in Frank O'Connor's "loneliness").[17] Whoever thinks that the events leading up to the moment when the Prussians leave the mad woman to die alone in the snowy woods are the main thrust of Maupassant's "La Folle" ['The Crazy Woman'] (1882) has missed the point and been drawn to the negligible plot rather than to the central focus on man's brutish pride and his resultant inability to communicate, likewise for "Minuet" (1883), the touching portrait of two delicate remnants of former days, and for dozens of other tales by Maupassant and Daudet. In these and an increasing number of stories in the twentieth and twenty-first centuries—whether Todorov's single change in state or Prince's three or more conjoined events[18]—plot has the undoubted importance that it has in Robbe-Grillet's "La Plage" ['The Beach'] (1962), where three children walk along leaving imprints in the sand which, the reader understands, will shortly be effaced by the timeless sea's tide. Of course, for most short stories, plot or sequence is not a negligible item. I could cite a plethora of examples, from the discovery and punishment of the fornicating monks of the thirty-second tale in the *Cent Nouvelles Nouvelles* (1462) to the progressive discovery of the hero's past as he falls from the Empire State

On Defining Short Stories 7

Building to become "a red medusa on the asphalt on Fifth Avenue" in Boris Vian's "Le Rappel" (1962). The term "fiction," in *artistically designed, short, prose fiction*, may cover stories that are predominantly narration or description, sequence or image. It is truly unfortunate that the English label "short story" includes the term "story" that suggests the sequence of narration, while in fact "short fiction" would be a more appropriate term for these creations that increasingly turn around static images rather than sequential developments.

Some have wanted to reserve the term "short story" for rather specific subject matter. Murray Sachs feels, for example, that for the "educated," *conte* or tale "has a strong flavor of the unreal or the supernatural. [...T]he French word *nouvelle* [short story] is sometimes confined because of etymology to narratives which have the character of real events (or 'news'), and is felt to be inapplicable to stories of the fantastic or the improbable."[19] Alfred G. Engstrom is similarly exclusive. For him, "supernatural narrations (fairy tales, legends of demons, saints, gods, and the like) and the tales of outright wizardry" are generally to be excluded from the *conte*, thus from the short story.[20] This distinction is, of course, similar to the old separation between the novel and the romance, concentrating on subject matter rather than formal elements. While I might interject that francophone *nouvelle* seems to be used primarily in English as a generic term to cover such sub-categories as conte, tale, anecdote, etc., and that *conte* maintains a strong association with its oral roots, I think all such discussions miss the point.[21] Ian Reid is right to be disturbed by the distinction, however much he accepts it. As Reid recognizes,

> *Exempla* about tediously saintly figures, snippets of legend about marvels and eerie occurrences: such things differ quite patently from those tales that are imaginatively cohesive even when fantastic and elliptical, or from tales that explore a mental and moral dimension by evoking the preternatural, as in Hawthorne's "Young Goodman Brown" with its symbols of devilry and witchcraft.[22]

Still, the key is not whether or not a myth, legend, or mythological story is recounted, it is whether it is done artistically in a brief compass.[23]

Although I would not wish to question the artistry of Charles Dickens' short stories, I do not agree with his understanding of what they entail. For him, the short story's "construction" differed from that of the novel, though it was a matter of "detail in the working out of character within [...] limits" or, elsewhere, the "elaboration of detail, in the working out of character."[24] If art is important to the short story, one would think that the shortness of the fiction would and should function as a major aesthetic feature. Great short stories—even good or decent short stories—*use* brevity, whether by Dickens or anyone else. Of course, there is such a thing as poor quality in any genre, but those stories that are worth reading have focus, a quality that cannot be over-emphasized. When Dickens

8 On Defining Short Stories

regrets that his stories are constrained by a pre-determined length, he is seeing them as truncated novels, while they should be much more than that.[25]

Artistry constitutes a given of any definition of aesthetic genres. It need to be neither intended nor understood—to take into account Northrop Frye's compelling argument that Thucydides' *History of the Peloponnesian War* (424?–404? BC) could now be appropriately taken, not as history, but as art. Of course, "artistry," as a generic touchstone leaves much to be desired, for one thinks of the shallow or failed art that graces certain popular magazines. Still, even such regrettable exemplars show a desire to touch readers aesthetically. One might then include some stories published, for example, in *Women's Day*, though one would doubtless exclude most tales catalogued in the Stith Thompson Index. Few would deny that Perrault's version of "Tom Thumb" (1696), Flaubert's "La Légende de Saint Julien l'Hospitalier" (1877), or Anatole France's "Le Jongleur de Notre-Dame" (1892) are excellent short stories. The short story is open to any topic, any material. Whether one admits a particular work—say, one of the legends in Jacobus de Voragine's *Legenda aurea* (1255–56)—to the short-story category is open to discussion, but the deciding factor is usually not the presence or absence of a saint or supernatural events, rather the creative use of the four terms in my definition as essential elements in the reality whose existence depends primarily upon the text in question. Masterpieces demonstrate the potential of the genre, and are thus the material considered by this book.

When I suggested that a short story is an *artistically designed, short, prose fiction*, I meant only that the creation must be artistically fashioned, with the apparent intention of making something beautiful. How one determines the existence of such an intention is, of course, debatable especially in specific instances. For our purposes, here, this is less important than establishing that there must be artistry for the short story to exist. While the problem is not often posed in these terms, short-story criticism makes it clear that the story's implicit aesthetic goal is, though perhaps unstated, accepted. Certainly, the particular cast to the creation has been an important consideration for many interested in prescriptive theory. Ludwig Tieck emphasizes the importance of the narrative crux, that moment where things change, as does Ruth J. Kilchenmann, though she makes a much bigger point of the plot rising to and falling from that crisis.[26] Others, like Ellery Sedgewick, stress the importance of the ending—"A story is like a horse race. It is the start and finish that count most"—while for Chekhov neither beginning nor end really matters.[27] Brander Matthews attempted to turn Edgar Allan Poe's less than precise comments into a rigid *Ars poetica*, and numerous writers and critics have held up O. Henry's trick endings as a model (May, *New* 4–5). Some insist on highly developed character,

On Defining Short Stories   9

others on a unique, unilinear plot, and others on one device or another. I would rather say simply that the preferred devices and vehicles are varied through the ages without changing the short story from its primary thrust—whether real, intentional, or merely perceived—of making an aesthetic unit.

Aesthetic canons change to some degree from individual to individual and to a large degree from age to age and culture to culture. The pre-Renaissance *Novellinos*, for example, were extremely short (one to two pages) and concentrated on the moment of revelation or resolution, on a wise judgment, a noble deed, or a clever retort. When Boccaccio expanded the anecdote, exploiting a situation, elaborating on the circumstances leading to the resolution, the aesthetic value shifts from appreciation of vigorous effects to the skill in revealing the subtleties as they played one against the other. Had Gobineau written his expertly narrated short stories during the eighteenth century, when it was common in short and long fiction to string episodes onto a protagonist's perambulations, they would have been far more successful than they were in the mid-nineteenth century, when intensity and focus were prized. Still, in all periods, though the values may change, though the concept of artistry may diverge, the impulse to make art is usually discernible. Neglecting the specific aesthetic criteria of a specific age for the purposes of conceptualizing the genre as a whole does not, of course, prevent one from concentrating on a particular period and its values or, from another point of view, from doing a history of the genre where changing values and techniques are stressed. As René Wellek pointed out, relating an individual reality to a general value does not necessarily degrade the individual to a mere specimen of a general concept. It may, in fact, give significance to the individual, by providing a backdrop which adds depth of meaning to the example under consideration.[28]

To suggest that short stories are "prose" seems at first glance the least contentious claim possible. Of all the assumptions prevalent in anthologies and critical theory, this is surely the most commonly understood. Still, all one need do is bring attention to bear on the issue and one remembers fictional, indeed narrational, works of verse. I think, for example, of Pushkin's *Eugen Onegin* (1833). (Verse is simply a written language organized primarily by a meter, which makes prose that written language where metrical rhythm exists only incidentally.) Few would wish to exclude *fabliaux*, those marvelous verse-tales of the Middle Ages, even though they rely heavily on assonance and rhythm. Of course, in an age that prides itself on its tolerance, it is difficult to approve of any exclusivity. Unlike the color line in a Birmingham bus depot during the Civil Rights movement, however, no harm comes from refusing *fabliaux* the status of short story. To the contrary, it does considerable good, for it emphasizes an essential but neglected characteristic. In the original versions (as opposed to prose translations), one understands how

10   *On Defining Short Stories*

important the rhythm is to these medieval creations. Without it, they are much impoverished. The question is not whether the text contains a marked rhythm, for many fine novels and short stories do, but whether that rhythm constitutes a dominant element. As Victor Erlich explains in regard to the Russian Formalists,

> [T]he differentia of verse [is] not in the mere presence of an element— in this case, a regular or semi-regular ordering of the sound-pattern—but in its status. In "practical" language, it was argued, in ordinary speech or in scientific discourse, rhythm is a secondary phenomenon—a physiological expedient or a by-product of syntax; in poetry it is a primary and "self-valuable" quality.[29]

As with the other issues I have discussed, there will be cases where judicious application of the touchstone remains difficult or impossible. I think of Dylan Thomas' "stories" or "fictions" or whatever, whose lush and rhythmical verbal palate "was not easily confined to literary categories and prescribed lengths," as stated in an anonymous "Note" to *Adventures in the Skin Trade and Other Stories.*[30] Some might even wish to raise the issue of Edwin Arlington Robinson's storied poetry. For myself, though "Richard Cory" or "Miniver Cheevy" or "Old King Cole" would doubtless add luster of a certain sort to the short story, it would change the cast of the particular luminescence we all recognize. But the matter is open to disagreement, and there they are bound to be ambiguities in particular examples. As said before, definitions in aesthetic matters are never definitive; they are guidelines *or* baffles that may at any point be abandoned by either readers or writers.

"Short," the most difficult touchstone of *artistically designed, short, prose fiction* remains. No one disputes the necessity of brevity to the short story, though there has been considerable discussion about the precise meaning of the trait. Many feel 6,000–8,000 words are suitable, though not everyone agrees.[31] German critics retained the word *Novelle* for fictions of intermediate length and coined a new term for the very short: *Kurzgeschichte.* Should one instead follow E. M. Forster and separate short stories from novels at 50,000 words?[32] It is easy to quibble with that figure, for it would include as short stories such works as *L'Immoraliste, L'Etranger,* and many others generally considered novels. While, as said before, inclusion or exclusion from a genre does not affect the quality of a work, it may encourage readers to read with inappropriate expectations. Arbitrariness is not in itself wrong, but at some point distinctions must be made, at least for the purpose of examination and discussion, even in the physical realm. While everyone would, for example, agree that red is the color produced by rather long light waves (33,000 could be fitted into an inch), it is not easy to tell precisely where

On Defining Short Stories 11

red becomes orange and orange yellow. The gradations seem infinite, though perhaps not as numerous as in literature. Whatever categories be established, they should at least give an impression of reasonableness, and, for me at least, Forster's 50,000 words is simply too long for a successful short story.

Perhaps because of the discomfit caused by an arbitrary figure, be it 8,000 words or 50,000 words, most critics have felt more at home with Poe's claim that one should be able to read a short story at one sitting. The problem with the distinction is obvious, though William Saroyan is credited with pointing it out: some people can sit for longer periods than others (Reid 9). Bookmarks may be for quitters, but they are not for short stories. There is a good deal to be said for Poe's stance, however. Most importantly, it emphasizes the absolute impossibility of extreme arbitrariness, without denying the necessity of shortness, however it be defined. Conceptions of brevity are affected by particular conditions, by individual idiosyncrasies, and, as Paul Zumthor has said, by culture.[33] What seems short on an ocean cruise is impossibly long on a lunch break. As should be evident, however, I am not attempting to impose rigid rules. Excellent short stories of less than 1,000 words exist (I think, for example, of Maupassant's "Le Lit"—1882), as do those of over 30,000 words (like Gautier's "Jettatura"—1856). Rather, I wish to take up the provocative suggestion that brevity imposes particular forms: "Brevity is never aleatory, but rather *it constitutes a formalizing model*,"[34] as Zumthor has pithily stated. I would not be quite so quick to categorize the way this formalizing function is actualized, but it seems to me that this insight, in combination with the other generic markers already discussed, goes far in allowing the proposed definition to be discrete. As Lilliane Louvel says, "In its enunciation, the short story has to say less to say more."[35]

Edgar Allan Poe's insistence on "one pre-established design" has been roundly condemned as having led to an abuse of formulas and formula writing. Nonetheless, the limitations of Poe's imitators do not impugn the wisdom of Poe's original intuition:

> A skillful literary artist has constructed a tale. If wise, he has not fashioned his thoughts to accommodate his incidents; but having conceived, with deliberate care, a certain unique or single *effect* to be wrought out, he then invents such incidents—he then combines such events as may best aid him in establishing this preconceived effect. If his very initial sentence tend not to the outbringing of this effect, then he has failed in his first step. In the whole composition there should be no word written, of which the tendency, direct or indirect, is not to the one pre-established design. [...] Undue brevity is just as exceptionable here as in the poem; but undue length is yet more to be avoided.[36]

12   On Defining Short Stories

Chekhov's famous dictum—that, if one introduces a revolver or a shotgun in the early part of a story, it must go off before the end—similarly stresses the short story's need for economy. Because of brevity, the short story remains as foreign to loosely motivated detail as it does to amplification. For precisely the same reasons that we become annoyed if even a good lecture goes beyond the allotted time, readers begin to fidget when a "short" story begins to drag on, when one suspects that the main point is being dissipated or lost. Where many of the most telling effects of Proust's lengthy *A la recherche du temps perdu* come from the rediscovery only possible after having forgotten, readers of short stories have everything present. They may of course be inattentive, but writers cannot count on it, and, most importantly, authors of short fiction especially must assume that their readers will pay attention, and will remember what they read. Katherine Anne Porter poses the requirement somewhat differently, though for all art "nothing can be accidental" ("On Writing" 440). In the context of a short story, readers will have less patience with repetition, which in one form or another is fundamental to most of the devices used to give form to all literature. I do not wish to suggest that there will be no reiteration, only that it must be done with great discretion to avoid setting up the kinds of rhythm that turn prose into poetry, on the one hand, or, on the other, effects that seem overly obvious and thus heavy-handed or pedestrian.[37]

For similar reasons, the short story is usually single rather than multivalent. Both *Doppelgänger* and subplot do occur, though in nowhere near the frequency of longer fiction. There is, in fact, a marked tendency toward unity. Complexity comes more frequently from depth or implication than from obvious repetition or multiplicity. Even where doubling occurs, there is a particular simplicity about it which distinguishes it from the novel. Take, for example, Maupassant's "Ce Cochon de Morin" ['The Pig, Morin' 1882], where the humor depends on watching Morin's charges be dismissed only because his friend is a more successful pig. One's attention is constantly directed to the poetic injustice of it all, and the doubling is kept singular in effect. The plurality that serves a novel to emphasize, nuance, or countervail runs the risk of appearing redundant and distracting, if not disruptive, in the short story.

Equally, because of the need for brevity, the short story tends toward the general. Even when detail is rife, readers expect the vocabulary to bear more than its usual significance and are, I suspect, more prone than with the novel to universalize. Not only does every word carry a full weight of meaning, short stories also make frequent use of ellipsis and implication. Readers expect to generalize, to read in depth and between the lines. With due regard for Robbe-Grillet's insistence on neutral creations that permit the reader to invent his own meaning, "La Plage" ['The Beach'] would not have anywhere near its power if the children were crossing a park to answer their mother's or nature's call. Instead,

On Defining Short Stories 13

because of the sand and sea, we view the ephemeral children before a timeless—because cyclical—universe.

A discussion of the ways brevity marks and indeed forms the short story could go on and on without exhausting the subject. Authors' inventiveness is unlimited, which is the nature of creation. The point, however, is not an enumeration of the particular procedures and devices which might be listed under a rarified term like brachylogy, but to suggest the importance of those qualities that distinguish a short story from all other prose fiction. I would suggest that brevity and artistry constitute the most significant traits of the particular short-story genre. In large measure, they determine the devices used and the effects achieved. Certainly, they constitute the short story's greatest limitation. For a short story to succeed, the author must overcome the restraints of limited length and communicate not a segment, a tattered fragment, but an aesthetically pleasing or, at least, touching world. In a National Public Radio interview by Jennifer Kerrigan (October 1, 2017), Jeffrey Eugenides called short stories "difficult, maddening little puzzles. [...] There's no space; I mean, they're very short. That's the problem with a short story: you get it going, and then you have to shut it down. [...] You're trying to boil experience down into a very small precipitant." Eugenides' insight leads me to another requirement for the following chapters. I am primarily interested in masterpieces, that is, those stories that surpass the run-of-the-mill to become truly outstanding and, especially, those that go beyond the limits of brevity. They paradoxically maximize the potential of brevity to expand beyond it.

Shortness has often been considered a weakness, a flaw, a disappointing measure of competence if not excellence. The best exemplars of the genre exploit all manner of devices and techniques to expand the bounds of their brevity. These devices, ranging from ellipsis to implication, from circularity to allusion, from reference to analogy, from generic assimilation to openness, such strategies draw the reader into the creative process. Henry James calls it "trying for the more," "the large in a small dose, the smaller form put on its mettle and trying to do—by sharp selection, composition, presentation and the sacrifice of verbiage—what the longer alone is mostly supposed capable of." This is the point, James says, "when art comes in."[38]

By suggesting that one might view the short story as an *artistically designed, short, prose fiction*, I have been only secondarily interested in providing a definition, and certainly not a formula. It is rather the defense of such a definition which might be most helpful. The discussion of the constituent elements of a short story, while falling far short of a touchstone useful in all cases and for all time, may help readers have productive rather than destructive expectations when they pick up a representative example. Once one has settled on a definition, there are numerous subcategories that can serve for whatever purpose in view. The recent work

14   *On Defining Short Stories*

of Concepción Palacios and Pedro Méndez delves into historical short stories. Other categories also come to mind. Repertories can easily be produced that are limited to topics like the fantastic, crime, science fiction, adventure, romance, or to such periods as the classical or the *belle époque*, or to gender and the author's orientation, though they do not in essence differ from other short stories. The possibilities of sub-topics within genres are virtually limitless. Or to go further afield, however impressed one might be by those who would avoid the problem of literary genres by denying them, it is indisputable that most readers are firmly conscious of genre and use their preconceptions to guide their reading. The more adequate the preconception, the more chance there is of an satisfactory reading which recognizes the true significance of the story, whether it be in line with or in revolt against that particular cluster of traits that I have treated here and that most of us recognize as a short story. At this point, then, it is necessary to look at examples of the best of short stories, in the attempt to understand what fine writers can do with them.

Notes

1 Allan H. Pasco, "The Short Story: The Short of It," *Style* 27.3 (1993): 242–44.
2 Charles E. May, "Introduction: A Survey of Short Story Criticism in America," in his edition, *Short Story Theories* (Athens: Ohio UP, 1976) 3–12; Thomas A. Gullason, "The Short Story: An Underrated Art," in May's *Short Story Theories* 13–31.
3 Mary Doyle Springer, *Forms of the Modern Novella* (Chicago, IL: U of Chicago P, 1976) 17; Elizabeth Bowen, "The Faber Book of Modern Short Stories," in May's *Short Story Theories* 152–58.
4 H. E. Bates, *The Modern Short Story: A Critical Survey* (Boston: The Writer, 1972) 13. Katherine Anne Porter is even more definite:

> [T]hat painting, that statue, that music, that kind of writing, that way of thinking and feeling, that revolution, that political doctrine—is it really New? The answer is simply no, and if you are really in a perverse belligerent mood, you may add a half-truth—no, and it never was— "Reflections on Willa Cather." *The Collected Essays and Occasional Writings of Katherine Anne Porter* (New York: Delacorte, 1970) 34

5 Geoffrey Brereton, *A Short History of French Literature* (London: Casell, 1954) 108; Robert J. Clements and Joseph Gibaldi, *Anatomy of the Novella: The European Tale Collection from Boccaccio and Chaucer to Cervantes* (New York: New York UP, 1977); see also, for example, Warren S. Walker, "From Raconteur to Writer: Oral Roots and Printed Leaves of Short Fiction," in *The Teller and the Tale: Aspects of the Short Story*, Proceedings, Comparative Literature Symposium, 23–25 Jan. 1980 (Lubboch: Texas Tech P, 1982) 14.
6 For example, Gérard Genette, "Genres, 'types,' modes," *Poétique* 32 (Nov. 1977): 389–421; Jean-Marie Schaeffer, *Qu'est-ce qu'un genre littéraire?* (Paris: Seuil, 1989); Austin M. Wright, "On Defining the Short Story: The Genre Question," *Short Story Theory at a Crossroads*, ed. Susan Lohafer and Jo Ellyn Clarey (Baton Rouge: Louisiana State UP, 1989) 46–53.

On Defining Short Stories 15

7 Harry Steinhauer, "Towards a Definition of the Novella," *Seminar* 6 (1970): 174.

8 E. D. Hirsch, Jr., *The Aims of Interpretation* (Chicago, IL: U of Chicago P, 1976) 120–21. As Norman Friedman says, "Trying to particularize the definition of a genre on the basis of a single and general *differentia*, which is all too common, is doomed to failure from the start. What is needed instead is a set of multiple *differentiae*"—"Recent Short Story Theories," *Short Story Theory at a Crossroads*, ed. Lohafer and Clarey 17–18.

9 Heinrich Wölfflin, *Principles of Art History: The Problem of the Development of Style in Later Art*, tr. from the 7th ed. (1929) by M. D. Hottinger (New York: Dover, n.d.).

10 Jurij Tynjanov, "On Literary Evolution" (1927), *Readings in Russian Poetics: Formalist and Structuralist Views*, eds. Ladislav Matejka and Krystyna Pomorska (Cambridge, MA: MIT P, 1971) 72–73.

11 Leon S. Roudiez, *French Fiction Today: A New Direction* (New Brunswick: Rutgers UP, 1972) 6.

12 See Douglas Hesse's analysis of what he calls a "boundary zone": "A Boundary Zone: First-Person Short Stories and Narrative Essays," *Short Story Theory at a Crossroads*, ed. Lohafer and Clarey, 85–105.

13 See Enrico de Negri, "The Legendary Style of the *Decameron*," *Romanic Review* 43 (1952): 166–89.

14 Thomas E. Peterson, "'Le Dernier Coup de pinceau': Perception and Generality in 'Le Chef-d'Œuvre Inconnu'." *Romanic Review* 88.3 (1997): 385–86.

15 Thomas J. Roberts, *When Is Something Fiction?* (Carbondale: Southern Illinois UP, 1972) 11. See also René Wellek and Austin Warren, *Theory of Literature* (New York: Harcourt, Brace, 1949) 15–16, 221–22; Monroe C. Beardsley, *Aesthetics: Problems in the Philosophy of Criticism* (New York: Harcourt, Brace, 1958) 419–37; and Michel Butor, *Répertoire /1/* (Paris: Minuit, 1960) 7–8.

16 Philippe Van Tieghem, "Les Prosateurs du XVIIe siècle," *Encyclopédie de la Pléiade*, ed. Raymond Queneau, Vol. 3 (Paris: Gallimard, 1958) 429.

17 The distinction is crucial, though described in different ways. Henry James explained,

> "The short tale [...] may be, like the long one, mainly of two sorts: the chain of items, figures in a kind of sum [...] or else it may be an effort preferably pictorial, a portrait of conditions, an attempt to summarize and compress for purposes of presentation, to 'render' even if possible, for purposes of expression"—"Introduction." *Hubert Crackanthorpe: Last Studies* (London: William Heinemann, 1897) xviii–xix, or James, "The Story-Teller at Large: Mr. Henry Harland," rpt. in James, *The American Essays*, ed. Leon Edel (New York: Vintage 1956) 190

See also Joseph Frank, *The Widening Gyre: Crisis and Mastery in Modern Literature*, Midland Book (1963; rpt. Bloomington: Indiana UP, 1968); Allan H. Pasco, *Novel Configurations: A Study of French Fiction*, 2nd ed. (Birmingham: Summa, 1994) 51–71. Suzanne Hunter Brown prefers the terms "configurations" and "successive structures [paradigmatic rather than metonymic]." She reminds us that "[t]his proposition is in accord with the common insistence of short story writers that their genre 'works' more like poetry than like the novel. [...]*Temporal* is often equated with *succession* and is then opposed to *spatial*"—"Discourse Analysis and the Short Story," *Short Story Theory at a Crossroads*, ed. Lohafer and Clarey 234. For "tone," see Robert Pinget, "Pseudo-Principes d'esthétique," in *Nouveau roman: Hier, aujourd'hui*, ed. Jean Ricardou, Françoise van Rossum-Guyon,

16   On Defining Short Stories

2 vols. (Paris; 10/18, 1972) 2.311–24; for "mood," see Georg Lukacs, *The Theory of the Novel* (Cambridge, MA.: MIT P, 1971) 51–52, or Eileen Baldeshwiler, "The Lyric Short Story: The Sketch of a History" (1969), in May's *Short Story Theories* 202–13; for "focus," see Mordecai Marcus, "What is an Initiation Story?" (1960), May's *Short Story Theories* 189–201; for "theme," see Frank O'Connor (pseud. Michael O'Donovan), *The Lonely Voice: A Study of the Short Story* (Cleveland: World Publishing, 1963).

18 Tzvetan Todorov, "La Grammaire du récit," *Langages*, No. 12 (1968) 96; Gerald Prince, *A Grammar of Stories* (The Hague: Mouton, 1973) 31.

19 Murray Sachs, "Introduction," *The French Short Story in the Nineteenth Century* (New York: Oxford UP, 1969) 13. This point of view is, of course, not shared by all. See below, n20.

20 Alfred G. Engstrom, "The Formal Short Story in France and Its Development Before 1850," *Studies in Philology*, 42 (1945): 631.

21 I have by no means exhausted the controversies surrounding "conte" and "nouvelle." See, for example, Jeanne Demers, "Nouvelle et conte: des frontières à établir," *La Nouvelle: écriture(s) et lecture(s)*, ed. Agnès Whitfield and Jacques Cotnam (Montréal: GREF, 1993) 63–71; and Bill Solomon, "The Novel in Distress," *Novel: A Forum on Fiction* 43.1 (2010): 124–31. One other position, which has had considerable mileage, might be mentioned: "Meanwhile [in the first half of the nineteenth century], the word *conte* was assuming a meaning that differentiated it from *nouvelle*, the former accepted as more concentrated, with one major episode, the latter more complex and consisting of several scenes"—Albert J. George, *Short Fiction in France: 1800–1850* (Syracuse: Syracuse UP, 1964) 234. The example of the *conte de fées* or fairy tale immediately points to the problems with such a distinction, for these tales are often remarkably complex and, indeed, aesthetic.

22 Ian Reid, *The Short Story*, Critical Idiom, No. 37 (London: Methuen, 1977) 8–9.

23 As John Cheever says, "With a short story, you have to be in there on every word; every verb has to be lambent and strong. It's a fairly exhausting task, I think"—"Is the Short Story Necessary?" ed. May, *Short Story Theories* 102.

24 The first quotation comes from the "Preface to the first cheap edition" and the second from the "Preface to the 'Charles Dickens' edition," both published in the author's *A Christmas Carol and Other Christmas Writings*, ed. Michael Slater (London: Penguin, 2003) 265. Cf., Adrian Hunter, *The Cambridge Introduction to the Short Story in English* (Cambridge: Cambridge UP, 2007) 10–15.

25 Zola was even more explicit, when he remarked that Maupassant would have to produce a novel, "une œuvre de longue haleine," in order to fulfill the promise shown in his first collection of stories—*Œuvres complètes*, ed. Henri Mittérand, 14 (1966) 623.

26 Quoted from Reid 12–13.

27 Quoted from Bates 17. A character in Richard Powers's novel *Galatea 2.2* says, simply, "Maybe the only universally valid generalization about stories: they end"—(New York: Farrar, 1995) 219, quoted by Michael Wood, "The Last Night of All," *PMLA* 122.5 (2007): 1395.

28 See René Wellek, "Literary History," *Literary Scholarship: Its Aims and Methods*, ed. Normon Foerster, et al. (Chapel Hill, NC, 1941) 124.

29 Victor Erlich, *Russian Formalism: History—Doctrine*, 3d ed. (Paris: Mouton, 1969) 213. For another point of view on whether *fabliaux* constitute short stories, see Roger Dubuis, "Le Mot 'nouvelle' au moyen âge: De la nébuleuse au terme générique," *La Nouvelle: Définitions, transformations*, ed. Bernard Alluin and François Suard (Lille: PU de Lille, 1990) 13–26.

On Defining Short Stories   17

30 Anonymous editor, *Adventures in the Skin Trade and Other Stories*, by Dylan Thomas (New York: Signet, 1956) vii.

31 Henry James—"The Lesson of the Master," *Critical Prefaces*, ed. R. P. Blackmur (New York: Charles Scribner's Sons, 1934) 231—for example, disagreed with the "hard-and-fast rule of the 'from six to eight thousand words'" ("Lesson" 220). His love of "the shapely *nouvelle*" (ibid.) is well known. Still, he wished for a certain amount of latitude and praised Henry Harland's "indifference to the arbitrary limit of length" (219).

32 E. M. Forster, *Aspects of the Novel*, Harvest Books (1927; rpt. New York: Harcourt, Brace, 1954) 5–6.

33 Paul Zumthor, "La Brièveté comme forme," *La Nouvelle: Formation, codification et rayonnement d'un genre médiéval* (Actes du Colloque International de Montréal—McGill University, 14–16 October 1982), ed. Michelangelo Picone, et al. (Montreal: Plato Academic Press, 1983) 4.

34 I quote Zumthor—"Brièveté" 4—though, of course, the idea that form is content and that in their relationship the one is governed by the other implicit in Aristotle. Nor is the thought that brevity may structure short stories new—see, for example, Edward D. Sullivan, *Maupassant: The Short Stories* (London: Edward Arnold, 1962). Zumthor's contribution resides in his attempt to go beyond the "form equals content" truism and to show *how*, specifically, the quality of being short affects the form at every level. See also Zumthor's *Essai de poétique médiéval* (Paris: Seuil, 1972) 339–404. I attempt to carry the analysis further.

35 Lilliane Louvel, "'Silence will speak'—Encoding the Short Story: for Brevity's Sake," *Tale, Novella, Short Story: Currents in Short Fiction*, ed. Wolfgang Görtschacher, Holger Klein (Tübingen: Stauffenburg Verlag, 2004) 249.

36 Edgar Allan Poe, Rev. of *Twice-Told Tales*, May 47–48.

37 See Suzanne Hunter Brown, "Discourse Analysis and the Short Story," *Short Story Theory at a Crossroads*, ed. Lohafer and Clarey 217–48.

38 Henry James, "The Story-Teller at Large: Mr. Henry Harland," *The American Essays*, ed. Leon Edel (New York: Vintage, 1956) 190.

2 Sequential Uncertainty in Vivant Denon's "Point de lendemain"

The epigrammatic *pointe* was long considered desirable, even essential, to the short story. At its worst, it was the "surprise" ending, for example, of Maupassant's "Le Mariage du lieutenant Laré" ['Lieutenant Laré's Marriage'] (1878) or one of O'Henry's less successful tales, where the revelation has only minor significance and does not encourage the reader to reinterpret what he has read. At its best, however, as in Villiers de l'Isle-Adam's "L'Enjeu" ['The Stake'] (1888) or Anatole France's "Le Procurateur de Judée" ['The Public Prosecutor of Judea'] (1892), the conclusion throws a startling new light on the preceding fiction and, in according profundity to what had seemed shallow, invites reassessment. Despite the frequency of stories that draw to a conclusion where exclamation points seem appropriate, not all short stories do. Similar to Ronsard developing sonnets which manage successfully to turn around a center, rather than lead to a terminal epigram, so many stories end when the portrait, or the tone, or the concept has been completed. As just one of many examples, one might think of Borges's "La Lotería de Babilonia" ['The Babylonian Lottery'] (1944), where the conclusion arrives when the potential of the permutations is evident.

For critics like Zumthor, short texts are particularly oriented toward the present.[1] He justifies his position by referring to the particular weight that language has when the real time of the reading is short. He goes on to consider another trait:

> [T]he cohesion of a text of some length is perceived progressively as the reading proceeds: a moment comes when the indications of this cohesiveness appears, then is organized in the reader's imagination as an ideal system of rules of combination, an interpretive hypothesis, confirmed or invalidated by what follows. The cohesion of a brief message is of another nature, at least tangentially: it is given at the beginning, empirically, sensorially, as a global certitude whose eventual consequences are deduced in the course of the brief reading or brief audition. (ibid.)

Such brief works appear to overpower the narration; the sequence, whether chronological or causal, then has less impact than the unit of

Uncertainty in "Point de lendemain" 19

perception or meaning that one grasps as a whole. It is often true that the short story, in particular, has a noticeable affinity for the epigrammatic, the formulistic, the epitome, the essential truth or idea or image which rises above time and either negates or amplifies whatever chronological progression the work possesses. Even in stories where change is of the essence, say, for example, Hemingway's "The Short Happy Life of Francis Macomber" (1936), one remembers Macomber's apotheosis as a "man," rather than his previous cowardice that leads up to the final scene. The crux, however, is not always the most important factor. For Maupassant's "Le Horla" (1887), it is the crescendo of fear rather than the fear itself which draws us, or, for one more example, Camus's "La Pierre qui pousse" ['The Growing Stone'] (1957) centers on d'Arrast as he progressively finds kingdom in exile. In short-story masterworks, there exists a subsurface message of enormous importance that constitutes the primary significance of the work.

I have asked many people who have admitted to a love for the short story why they like particular examples of the genre. Most often the response has to do with a "rip-roaring" story. A similar answer could be elicited in regard to a television program or series, but in both cases it would leave a person with "literary competence" dissatisfied. Jonathan Culler's analogy of literary competence with a "native informant" is helpful. People who are well-read and who know those conventions that govern great literature are energized only by masterpieces, only by those works capable of bringing a depth of meaning that can attract, detain, entertain, and indeed provide a reward that will attract an audience. Not that such readers do not enjoy a well-turned story or a powerful character or a vivid tableau, they certainly do, but it is only the masterwork that satisfies the need for greater understanding of ourselves, humanity, history, the future, or, simply, of the conception that has filled the mind of a great writer. As a story attains artistry, and is revealed as a masterful presentation, it comes closer to establishing a powerful relationship with what we are as human beings.

Definitions of the genres that literary works exploit are useful, since readers usually want a more or less approximate understanding of what they are about to begin. The qualities of prose or poetry can most often be sorted out early in the reading without difficulty. If one is about to enter into the reading of a short story—*an artistically designed, short, prose fiction*—it remains, however, to determine whether it is a question of high artistic expression or something more pedestrian. Brown is perhaps a bit hasty when she pronounces, "Regardless of the short story's oral antecedents, it is no longer a 'popular' form, but an art form."[2] The vast majority of short stories are scarcely worth the trouble to read, in that if there was any attempt to make fine art, they are obvious failures. Collections of "short stories" made for children, for example, may have pedagogical value, but little artistry is expected. The distinction is important, for artistic value raises the work above the level of simple

20   Uncertainty in "Point de lendemain"

narrative with minimal levels of meaning to a higher plane of expanded literary significance and pleasure. As the reader takes part in the work, suggestive denotations join to one another, and the connotations come alive, thus challenging the participant reading the text to create the masterpiece. Hemingway discusses those depths of knowledge with a memorable comparison, "The dignity of movement of an ice-berg is due to only one eight of it being above water."[3] For him, the meaning of art occurs only in the less than obvious implications, or connotations, that accompany denotations.

Even after the reader has come to a decision as to whether the work in hand has aesthetic value, it remains to make a further distinction. Short stories, like novels, poems, and other works of art, may be organized either sequentially or as an image. This insight constitutes a widely understood reality of cognition and of the structures of works of art. Critics use several terms to describe the formal arrangements, but at base they are simply separating metonymic relationships from the paradigmatic.[4] I shall refer to the prototypes as sequences, on the one hand, and image structures on the other.

This chapter turns around a masterpiece of a sequential nature: Vivant Denon's "Point de lendemain" ['No Tomorrow'] (1777, 1812). Many feel that short stories must be grounded in sequences, that it is the only possible structure. Ejxenbaum, for example, stated, "By its very essence, the story, just as the anecdote, amasses its whole weight *toward the ending.* [...] Short story is a term referring exclusively to plot, one assuming a combination of two conditions: *small size* and *plot impact* on the ending."[5] As insightful as Ejxenbaum is, he may have been too precipitate. I think of the Henry James story, "The Lesson of the Master," which like a Ronsard masterpiece turns around the long conversation that the narrator, Paul Overt, had with Henry St. George toward the middle of the account concerning commitment, the absolute commitment required to produce great art. Although chronological and although it moves toward the narrator's awareness of the sacrifice he has made in abandoning a woman he loved, Marion Fancourt, during the two years away focused on his art, there is no question that everything moves not toward a finale, but back to the middle truth and the way it joins the whole. For James simply being a great artist requires the sacrifice of family, children, and indeed love; in short, normal human relations must often be set aside for the sake of art. However much Henry James' Paul resents the cost of his sacrifice, he has apparently succeeded in creating something truly outstanding.

The great majority of stories are nonetheless governed by movement toward a conclusion, which often occurs at the end. The very word "narration" suggests movement, a sequential development that generally continues until the end, where it is resolved. "Point de lendemain," which was written at the turn from the eighteenth century to the nineteenth

Uncertainty in "Point de lendemain" 21

century, reveals the terrifying reality of a society that was out of control. Unlike most short stories, it depends principally on denotations rather than connotations. By denotation, I mean simply a term that refers to the primary meaning, usually a reality that could in the material world be present. Of course, most words carry connotations or secondary associations or analogies with them. The distinction is seldom total, though the significant, direct meaning can scarcely be confused. In this case, Denon has created a story that directly reflects the reality of his day. The radical social movements and cultural changes that embroiled French society in the last quarter of the eighteenth century culminated from seeds that were sown long before, and sensitive writers and thinkers were depicting the accompanying fear and anxiety prior to the major issues of the century blossoming into revolutionary violence. Vivant Denon also recognized the resulting insecurity that permeated the land in 1777, when he first penned *Point de lendemain*, as in 1812 when he revised it.[6] Indeed, uncertainty is a key feature of the charming tale. It is easy to understand why there was such widespread social malaise. Family, the Catholic Church, and government, the major supporting institutions of the country, had incontrovertibly demonstrated their weakness. None of the three was capable any longer of fulfilling its traditional function of providing stability and of guaranteeing a future in which the people could have any degree of confidence. The aristocracy, like the monarchy, like the Church had lost the respect of the people and was thus incapable of assuring the rule of law, which had been undermined by tumultuous mobs screaming in the streets. As individuals felt increasingly helpless, some suspected that there might be no basis for ethics, and ethical standards began to shift. Financial upheaval in banking, trade, and commerce disrupted economies, and the need for employment scattered families across Europe.

Marriage itself came under attack. The revolutionary Legislative Assembly declared that marriage was not guaranteed by God; it was a contract like any other contract and could therefore be altered or broken. Although in comparison with today there were very few divorces, the number seemed horrifyingly extreme to people of the period. How could a family raise children, protect property, and form useful alliances if the permanence of marriage could not be assured? For many individuals, divorce was at least as important and disruptive to the social fabric as the Revolution, perhaps more so.[7] Revolutionary warfare was, of course, a significant cause for anxiety, for it loomed, a roiling menace, in the background of the whole of France. Still, while relatively few people were directly involved in the civil strife, all were aware that its careening course could unpredictably affect them and their families. Tension increased to such a degree that in the early nineteenth century there was talk of burgeoning suicide rates being an epidemic. Migration, war, employment uncertainties due to the incipient Industrial Revolution, widespread malnutrition, disease, and other factors have been mentioned as

22 *Uncertainty in "Point de lendemain"*

possible causes for this society-wide anguish that resulted in the morbid appeal of Romanticism in the arts and its accompanying political, social, and aesthetic revolutions. Progressive breakdown of social systems was clearly in evidence, and people apparently felt lost. Certainly, one could no longer count on anything.

Many writers mirrored the uncertainty of the period's anxiety. Restif de La Bretonne's Cunégonde states unequivocally that there is "nothing stable in this world" (1.222), and "B," one of the prescient Diderot's interlocutors in the *Supplément au voyage de Bougainville*, considers two lovers in nature and notes "the instability of everything that surrounds them!"[8] A plethora of rhetorical promises of a glorious future from aspiring demagogues did little to render the gray reality of everyday life more acceptable, and random explosions of street violence only added to the anguish. In short, the public of revolutionary France was, and long remained, in the throes of disquiet, ready in 1779 to discard a king, relieved in 1802 to greet a despot promising order, and delighted in 1815 to push an emperor out of the way, so as to welcome back the Bourbon monarchy. After Napoleon's defeat at Waterloo, many politically alert people changed sides so often that they were known as *Girouettes* (Weathervanes). No one could doubt the reality of uncertainty in the interval embraced by the two major versions of "Point de lendemain." There were many indications of significant change, even of a social and artistic paradigm shift.

Today, after two centuries, although historical statistics only dimly reflect how the public felt about the events of the day, literature fleshes out what history tells us of the actual life of French people in the late eighteenth and early nineteenth centuries and paints a surprisingly consistent picture of this turbulent world. The Revolution seemed to be destroying the comfortable, trustworthy relationships, traditions, and movements that allowed people to prepare peacefully for the future. The past appeared increasingly distant and disconnected from the present. Problems might be real or only imagined, but whether real or anticipatory, fear of an uncertain future increased social anxiety. Today, we can see that although few of the larger historical movements were arrested by the Revolution, most people lived day to day, afraid of a sudden explosion of change and disruption. Providence had previously been in charge, and though a person might not understand the course of events, at least one could be certain that there was a reasonable power in control. Now, however, the fear that the events of the world had been abandoned to chance was common. It seemed that human life had lost its moorings and become subject to random fields of force with neither defining nor causative principles.

The *Encyclopédie* reveals two different views about *"Hazard"* (CHANCE). One is not particularly threatening: Diderot explains that in speaking of "pure chance," we should understand that we have in mind

Uncertainty in "Point de lendemain" 23

something "whose cause, being completely independent of us could and can act very differently from what we desire, without our having any reason to complain [...]. Chance is outside of our control."[9] In other words, while we may not see the cause, and though we may or may not understand what it might be, a cause does exist (8.74). The thought of a causal universe is theologically championed, and rather comforting. In such a world, it matters little that we discern the cause, regardless of whether things work out as we would like, for if there are providential causes, purpose, plans, it is at least possible that we may be able to influence or predict the outcome of future events. It is considerably more threatening, however, to contemplate the possibility that there might not be a cause, that events might occur in a realm of unfettered chance, without design, intent, or sequence. The difference between the possibilities of control by an external force (a god) or a situation with unlimited, random outcomes without any limits whatsoever is, of course, important. It projected a very different context for assessing personal risk and expectations. The alternatives could not be discussed openly or at any length, and, for fear of the censor and a long prison sentence, little written record for these terrors exists outside of passing comments. The possibility of a reality lacking causality is, nonetheless, touched on fleetingly in the article just cited and in such literature as "Point de lendemain." The possibility of "chance" (*hazard*) being a "term that is used to discuss events to indicate that they happen without a cause" (8.74) is very real. The *philosophes* were well aware of the possibility of a universe without divine control, a world governed by *hazard*, with nothing more stable than the odds of throwing dice. In considering the possibility, they had to recognize that they were left in a state of "INCERTITUDE" (UNCERTAINTY), a term that the Chevalier de Jaucourt defined as a "state of the indecision of the soul" (8.645). This background uncertainty was an important part of the literature of the day.

As is common in times of distress and disturbance, the theatre of Paris produced legions of comedies. Even if it was only temporary, people yearned to forget their troubles and fears. They needed the relief of laughter. And writers struggled to satisfy the public's demand for levity. After all, as Rabelais put it in the "Prologue" to *Gargantua*, "Laughter characterizes human beings."[10] Laugh citizens did. Even the most distressing subjects, like divorce, inspired numerous comedies, for example, the long-running *Le Divorce* by Desfontaines (Year 2 [1794]) or *Les Mœurs* by Pigault-Lebrun (Year 3 [1795]), and others. While popular writers kept busy in their attempt to lighten the mood of the public, rarely did their comedies have sufficient depth to establish and integrate aesthetic and social complexities, as would those penned by the greatest comic writers. Beaumarchais' comedy of 1794, *Le Mariage de Figaro*, was one of those masterworks. Though in a different genre, Denon's short story, "Point de lendemain," is another. Both show an astute

24 Uncertainty in "Point de lendemain"

consciousness of society's distressing realities and an ability to turn them into objects of humor.

On the surface, "Point de lendemain" is nothing but the story of an ingenuous young man thrust into a bewildering adventure, but the comedy grows from the author's clear awareness of the most basic fears of this society and the writers' skill in the use of such pervasive attitudes to induce laughter. Ambiguous roles, events whose meaning changes, unclear motivations, and surprising outcomes mark the tale. The male protagonist, an unnamed younger version of the narrator, simply does not know whether the events are by design, due to random chance, or growing from some combination of both, and he becomes the plaything of random happenings or, perhaps, of the beautiful Madame de T***.

The story opens at the opera, introducing the principal characters, who are regularly said to be playing roles, and thus establishing the themes of theatrical illusion, chance, and uncertainty. While hints that superficial appearances hide a completely different reality recur throughout the story, indications of illusion are repeated only implicitly until the end, where they are emphatically foregrounded. Unlike most operas, where the audience is the most important spectator, Denon's readers are invited to watch the adventures of several spectators who are included in the comedy. As Madame de T*** and the narrator spin out their fantastic mirage ("I was far from expecting how much this meeting would be extraordinary and fantastic" [385]), the actors—husband, lover, protagonist, and perhaps even Madame de T***—watch each other while trying to evaluate the others' thoughts and, even, discover what is going on.

We are told virtually nothing about the two protagonists, only what is essential. The young narrator is wealthy, relatively innocent, and available. His hostess has a broken marriage and at least one love affair in her past, but otherwise, she is "charming," "ravishing," and, in moments of passion, "abandoned" (393). From the soft murmur of the river (393) to the moonlight, to the gardens that seem to lean sensuously against a mountain leading down to the Seine's multiple sinuosities (388), to the obscurity of the pavilion, to dark corridors (396), the narration's descriptions serve to emphasize their passion and places apparently made for love.[11] Readers are at the outset offered the vision of conflict between the narrator's uncertainty before various possible explanations of events. "Are you by chance busy this evening?" Madame de T*** asks the naïve hero (385). She is acquainted with the narrator and with his mistress, the countess, and while she possibly knew that the countess did not intend to join him at the opera, it is at least as likely that Madame de T*** demonstrates serendipity in exploiting the accidental meeting and the countess' delayed arrival. For the young narrator, who complacently allows himself to be whisked away to the country, the meeting undoubtedly appears to be the result of chance, an important theme, as Thomas Kavanagh points out.[12] Soon they are off in Madame de T***'s carriage

Uncertainty in "Point de lendemain" 25

to her husband's chateau. The carriage lurches, and consequently, "by incredible chance," she ends up in his arms. She questions his intention. Did he mean for this to happen? No, he insists, it is "chance, a surprise" and, in words of extreme importance for Madame de T***, "that is forgivable" (385), since it is unintentional. It is a matter of point of view. A "forgivable" accident may be pardoned in a woman like Madame de T***, who is guided by "principles of decency" (385). Neither the reader nor the narrator knows whether the latter's mistress meant to stand him up and whether Madame de T*** knew it. Neither the reader nor the narrator can be sure that the physical contact they experienced during the trip was uniquely due to the "chance" of a sudden roll of their carriage (389). Chance is subjected to uncertainty.

In a later instance, Madame de T*** clearly does not know that her previously estranged husband has had his apartment torn down or that he has for the last three years been on a milk diet. She can hardly have predicted his early bedtime, which has the effect of leaving her alone with the narrator. However possible it may be that Monsieur de T***'s early retirement is due to his complacent willingness to allow his newly reconciled wife to spend one last night with the man who gives every appearance of being her lover, the result is that she and the narrator are left to their own devices for the evening. The uncertainty continues. One is never quite sure of how much Madame de T*** has orchestrated events, or, indeed, whether she is seducer or seduced, and whether one or the other or both of the characters are in the grip of passionate forces beyond their control. Frequently she *seems* in charge. It is she who arranges for him to go to the country with her. Later she forces ("força") him to leave the terrace and move toward the house, before changing her mind and leading him to the pavilion. "I do not know, at least, I did not know whether she had suddenly imposed this course of action on herself, whether it was a carefully decided resolution, or whether she shared the same chagrin that I felt" (389). After they embrace in the carriage while on the way to the chateau, she even accuses *him* of having planned all this. Can he really determine their relationship? He does not feel as though he is in charge. Clearly, he remains uncertain about his role. In fact, he has no understanding of what is happening.

To what degree are events due to Madame de T***'s sophisticated ability to create an amorous fantasy as she seduces the young narrator? To what degree is she seduced by circumstances, having been caught up in moonlight and an attractive young man? "The night's mysterious torch" (386) and the several references to the night insist on the mystery. Because of her well-known "inclination" for her official lover, the Marquis, the narrator early on refuses to believe that he will "be fortunate" (386) with his beautiful companion, and he wards off any presumptuous ideas (386). Clever readers will remember that they met at the opera, a place of theatrical make-believe, however, and suspect that the entire

26 *Uncertainty in "Point de lendemain"*

adventure represents an illusion created by the fine, perhaps serendipitous, perhaps knowing, but certainly masterful hand of Madame de T***.

The carriage taking the couple off to the husband's chateau establishes a travel motif. The first destination is the chateau and dinner with Madame de T***'s newly reconciled husband. Initially, the narrator and his companion merely seem to wish to pass time and enjoy the night in each other's company, a desire that remains after the husband has gone to bed. When they find themselves alone, their new destination takes shape in a leisurely fashion. On one of the terraces near the chateau, they share confidences and embrace repeatedly. "It is the same with kisses as with personal secrets: they attract more, that come faster and faster, warming each other as they come" (389). Unwilling to end the evening by going indoors and proceeding to their separate rooms, they eventually find themselves moving toward the pavilion. They walk without his noticing which direction they are taking (390). By this time, Madame de T*** unquestionably knows their destination, but the protagonist remains less sure.

She decides to open his eyes to his situation regarding his absent mistress, the countess:

> When she took you, it was to distract two overly imprudent rivals who were at the point of causing a scandal [...]. [S]he brought you onstage, occupied them with your attentions, caused them to look further into the matter, left you in despair, felt sorry for you, consoled you, and all four of you were happy. (391)

Madame de T*** sighs about the power the perfidious countess wields over her young companion: "Oh! How an adroit woman controls you! And how happy she is when she seems completely caught up in the game without getting very involved personally!" (391). The young hero feels as though he has had a sudden illumination: that Madame de T*** has provided him with the truth that his mistress was toying with him, though his older counterpart knows better when he much later tells the story: "It was the master stroke," says the more mature and knowing narrator. "I felt as through blinders had been removed, and didn't see the one being applied" (391). Of course, although in the new light that the young man has been given about his mistress, she seems irremediably false (391), Madame de T*** has just described what is happening in their own case. We may wonder how aware Madame de T*** is of the similarities. From this point on, one suspects that Madame de T*** is the director of the play, though one can never be quite sure. As they approach the pavilion, she regrets that she has no key (392). The fact that the door is actually unlocked might make one suspect that the entire "illusion" was from start to finish planned and prepared. They enter into the pavilion

Uncertainty in "Point de lendemain" 27

as the moon goes down. "The moon set, and the last of its rays soon carried off the veil of modesty that interfered. Everything mingled in the shadows" (392). The blindfolded hero continues unaware of his companion's machinations, long and perhaps forever remaining in the dark.

Many equivocal hints concerned with intentionality, on the one hand, and contingency, on the other, sprinkle their path. Early on, as already mentioned, the narrator has previously recognized that Madame de T*** "seemed to have some plans for my person" (385). Several actions are moreover never explained: what, for example, does Madame de T*** whisper in her servant's ear at the opera? Out loud, she tells the narrator to inform his servants that he will not return that night. We later learn that at some point during the evening she sent a message to her official lover, the Marquis, telling him to come to the chateau the next day. Perhaps additional, *sotto voce* instructions were to get permission from the countess to borrow the narrator? The reader does not know, though it is appropriate to wonder. But other explanations are equally plausible. Is she telling another friend or lover not to join her? Is she warning the servants at her husband's chateau that she is bringing a companion? We are, like the narrator, lost in murky possibilities. When he meets Madame de T***'s official lover the next morning as the sun comes up, "[h]e made sense of the previous evening's mystery, and gave me the key to the rest" (399). And he admits: "I did not know that all this was a play" (399). Of course, this is not the first time he has thought that he understood everything, and readers are justified in wondering whether he is any more correct this time. The ambiguous nature of the succeeding revelations allows the narrator and his one-night stand to be swept aside in the seeming reality of love at first sight, a *coup de foudre*. Or is Madame de T***, as Javorek believes,[13] simply jealous of the narrator's sometime mistress, the countess? Only afterwards, however, do we suspect the sincerity of Madame de T***'s seemingly overwhelming passion. We are left to float with the narrator "in these uncertainties" (399).

The voyage motif is explicitly related to "the broad way of sentiment" (392) and connects each of the five important segments. Whether at the opera, or on the terrace, or in the pavilion, or in the secret apartment (which itself has three compartments), or before the final unwinding of the play in the apparent revelation at sunrise, the narrator is on a spiritual and physical voyage. After arriving at the unlocked pavilion and indulging their passion, ardor fades and fatigue sets in. Madame de T*** leads him from the building, claiming that it is a dangerous place (393). She then stage-manages a new seduction. After forbidding him to continue their love play and claiming that there is no longer anything to desire from her, she reminds him that they will never be able to see each other again. Her husband would find their friendship suspect (395). She then raises his hopes for a new and even more seductive alcove, which, if he promises to be good, she says, she might show him (395). The activities

28   *Uncertainty in "Point de lendemain"*

in the pavilion have, however, diminished his energy. "I have to admit, I did not feel all the fervor, all the devotion that was necessary to visit *this* new temple, but I was very curious" (396).

Despite his weariness, she and the alcove create prospects of renewed amorous conquest and a new secret place to rekindle his desires and the possibility of a new victory for him. In truth, the entire chateau is designed to revive flagging energies. "The master of the house [...] had studied the process of reanimating physical resources" (387). From nature, Madame de T*** and the narrator have unquestionably moved into the creation of art (Diaconoff 264). Pierre Naudin has moreover argued that each of the major scenes of the story is arranged for spectators.[14] Madame de T*** understands that "[n]ovelty stimulates" (395) and that, just as her husband used to need "artificial resources [...] to strengthen his sentiment" (395), so may the narrator require a stimulant. From the opera, to the chateau, to the terrace, to the pavilion, to the secret hide-away, "[a]ll that seemed like an initiation. [...] My heart beat like a young proselyte's experiencing the celebration of great mysteries" (397). Within the chateau, she shows him through labyrinthine passages ("un dédale" 396) into her own apartment and then into a room lit as though by magic. His forces renewed, they move past the representation of the mysterious god of love into an obscure grotto consecrated to passion, and he begins in good faith to believe in enchantment (397). In the midst of their adoring engagement, a trusted servant comes to warn them. The sun has risen and the chateau is beginning to awaken.

Completely bemused, unable to find his room, the protagonist flees outside to await the outcome of these nocturnal, disjointed events that defy his comprehension. From the very beginning, the narrator insists that though Madame de T*** is a woman of great passions (386), she is committed to her official lover, the Marquis de ***, and is in addition the friend of the young man's own mistress. The further fact that Madame de T*** and her husband have been reconciled leaves her companion in a state of absolute confusion. Was it truly by accident when Madame de T*** tumbles into her companion's arms, only to repulse him as she wonders about "the imprudence of my actions" (387)? Implicitly, given her "dignity" and "decency," if the whole adventure was an accident, if she was seduced by the charm of the night and her companion, then everything can be forgiven. The reader is left to wonder about the contrary possibility that she may have organized the entire outing, if not from start to finish, then as she opportunistically makes the most of the possibilities. To what degree has Madame de T*** created the illusion of chance as a means of rendering herself innocent or, in her terms, "decent"?

In the end, a second, metaphorical curtain is raised and the narrator retrospectively views the "play" (399). With the apparent knowledge of Madame de T***'s other lover, the Marquis (though we are not sure

Uncertainty in "Point de lendemain" 29

whether the narrator was specifically chosen over any other passing male), the narrator was given a "role" (400) designed to trick the husband into distrusting the narrator, thus allowing her paramour, the Marquis, to remain as a trusted friend of the renewed household (400). The narrator listens as the Marquis extols Madame de T***'s faithfulness and complains of her lack of passion: "[S]he does not feel anything, she is made of marble" (400). Only Madame de T*** understands, if indeed she "was playing all of us, without losing the dignity of her character" (402). If it was an accident that he was chosen as a beard, and rewarded with a night of love, she maintains she is not to blame, for chance or accident implies innocence, while conscious control indicates an immoral intention. Uncertainty paints chance with an ambiguous brush. What is the young man's role? Is he simply there for the husband to blame, throw out, and unknowingly open the door for the regular visits of the Marquis, who has for some time been Madame de T***'s lover?

As the narrator tries to understand the ramifications of the play in which he has a role, so the reader is invited to try as well. The words *moral/morale* occur three times. The first occurrence instructs the narrator not to be in a bad mood, to stop sermonizing: "Oh! I beg you. No moralizing; you are failing to live up to your purpose. You are supposed to amuse me, distract me, and not preach at me" (386). Later, they laughingly try to separate any moral qualities from love and insist on the quality of pleasure (394). And finally he unsuccessfully tries to discover some kind of moral lesson ("la morale") in what has happened (402). The relatively innocent love play on the bench suggests the possible frustration of a lonely bed, while encouraging readers to glimpse a hint of the satisfaction that would come from making love. Not all short stories (or *contes*) have such extensive narrations. Many recent examples of the genre center on an epiphany, or image, or character with little or no story. But when a plot is central to the structure, that plot is at some point either subsumed to a core image or, as in this case, the plot leads to a terminal resolution that dramatically enhances the whole. Occasionally, it may encourage the reader to reconsider the story in the light of the new material that dramatically changes its meaning. To end the story with the satiety the lovers eventually feel in the pavilion would have lost much of the bloom of the moment by bringing the conclusion in the midst of fatigue. That might have been appropriate for the representation of profligate, dissolute persons, such as those painted in Villiers de l'Isle-Adam's "L'Enjeu," but it would have cost Denon's story its charming freshness. Far better to create a new, future goal, that will revive the narrator's flagging energies, take them to the secret room, and bring the affair to an end in the midst of a continuing climax, a *narratio interrupta*. At each step, we wonder whether the players are programmed or subject to chance. At each step, we look forward to a complete revelation that escapes us even at the very end.

30   *Uncertainty in "Point de lendemain"*

Though it is often claimed that short stories are not merely concise, but rather compressed or condensed,[15] it would be difficult to apply any of these terms to "Point de lendemain." The tale's "one-night stand" seems rather a subject made for the short story, since it is wonderfully appropriate in its brevity. The whole adventure is completed in only one night. Anything could, I suppose, be extended, but much extension would have ruined this particularly jewel-like creation, for it would have diluted the finely tuned vector taking the reader straight to the conclusion. Although the plot has some importance, as Madame de T*** leads the narrator from the opera, to the chateau, to the bench, to the pavilion, to the secret room, and to the concluding revelation, each pause on what in retrospect seems a straightforward path insists on the progression. The conclusion depends on the speed and focus of what precedes. The sentimental trip, pausing briefly at a number of important points, must be communicated without noticeable retardation. Otherwise, the reader might begin to doubt the accidental nature of the whole interlude. Every incident is designed to advance the seduction and to leave both narrator and reader uncertain. When Madame de T*** warns the narrator that she may never be able to see him again (394), the sincerity of her love is not impugned, but there is all the more reason to exploit the moment. Like the narrator, we readers find it impossible to "make out the end of the trip" (392). We are then susceptible to the allusion to Psyche and Amour (393), which raises the possibility of a durable and true rather than a transient love. There are few certainties. One might argue that it is the complexity itself that saves the story, for our interest is maintained to the very end when at least one explanation is apparent.

The reader rapidly arrives at the *grande finale* where everyone comes into the bright light of a curtain call that reveals all the actors for what they are, or, at least, what they may be. Although, as Michel Delon states, "Love is reduced to a desire and decency to a worldly code" (7), there are no judgments made. Madame de T*** is neither better nor worse than anyone else. She simply takes advantage of, or is seduced by, an opportunity for a cost-free night of sexual delight. The betrayals are without repercussion. As Madame de T*** tells the narrator in the end: "I certainly owe you many pleasures, but I paid you with a beautiful dream" (402). Indeed, as the narrator concludes, there seems to be no deep meaning or moral. The ambiguity of the roles, events, motives, outcome, and meaning is total.

Madame de T***'s unknowingly betrayed lover claims at the conclusion of the adventure that the hero did not have "a good role," for it was "comic" (400). He assumes that the narrator is an Arnolphe. He is, of course, mistaken, and has by a perfectly delightful twist on the allusion Cannet rightly attributes to Molière (Cusset 729) become the butt of the joke. Madame de T***'s cuckolded lover, who is, in fact, one of the two unquestionable Arnolphes, quotes the playwright's Horace speaking to

Uncertainty in "Point de lendemain"   31

Arnolphe: "But you do not laugh enough, it seems to me. You do not extract all the comic from your role" (400; cf. *L'Ecole des femmes* 3.4). The deluded "official" lover would like to believe that the hero has stood in for the frustrated Arnolphe, whereas the truth is quite the opposite. Will the protagonist now be her official lover? he wonders at one point (398). Or is he "without consequence" (386). "I did not know whether I was still dreaming. I doubted it. Then I was persuaded of it, convinced, and then I did not believe anything [...] I floated in these uncertainties" (399). The story ends, having powerfully and economically played out its moment. Our inability to ascertain whether Madame de T*** was a puppeteer, or the willing accomplice of chance, or a victim merely increases the mysterious charm of the moment.

The criticism of the story and its frequent republication leave no doubt that readers arrive at the end of *Point de lendemain* delighted, even charmed, by the shifting paradigm of possibilities offered. The fact that their contemporaries' lives were in serious jeopardy, if not because of the Revolution, then because of the numerous changes that were taking place in this society, makes it perhaps surprising that they would be attracted by a work that plays on uncertainty. They were worried about what was to come. They must have wondered whether they would have a *lendemain*. Their inability to count on a future with any assurance marks a significant reflection of the social mood of late eighteenth-century France and rendered an immediate recognition of the undefined context of the story. Legions of literary works make this uncertainty clear: literary personages and, by extension, French people were acutely aware of an inability to prepare for subsequent events. "Point de lendemain," as well, reflects this insecurity, but it does so in a way that induces smiles if not laughter, ending with a comforting conclusion that assures the reader of a mysterious cause that explains much, if not all of the preceding story. Whether the entire subterfuge was planned from the beginning or not, there is no question that Madame de T*** was sufficiently alert to recognize an opportunity for a night of pleasure without consequences, while protecting her relationship with both her lover and her husband. All literature reflects some aspect of reality, of course, but the image is often reversed, allowing comedy where there was once distress. By playing on the theme of "uncertainty," Denon succeeds in masking the anguish of the day by making it delightful, though perhaps only for a moment.

The story's ambiguity is for the most part resolved in the conclusion, and readers have a fair idea that the narrator's reward will not be repeated and that the official lover will be welcomed into Madame de T***'s château as a continuing sop to her willingness to return home, if not to resolve her marital issues. The evening has served to set up the narrator to play the role of a visitor who would do nothing but continue M. de T***'s cuckoldry, an unwelcome prospect for most men. He has

32 Uncertainty in "Point de lendemain"

then been shown the door, which left the way free for the wife's deluded lover. Although the latter mocks the narrator for having been used as a substitute Arnolphe, he has in fact himself filled Arnolphe's role, and the narrator moves off into his own future with a secret Mme de T*** begs him to keep.

"Point de lendemain" is an undoubted masterpiece. It is also a story that is as purely denotative as possible. The references I have made to the social context cannot be ignored, but Denon made use of neither symbols nor allusions to overcome the generic limitations of his tale. Instead he used the simple language of the day to paint a picture of a tantalizing but brief love affair. The story does include a conversational reference to Molière and the hint of a possible allusion to Psyche and Amour, but there the references to another level of meanings stop. Denon makes full use of the themes of travel, night, theatrical spectacle, and love, however, doubling each in ways that bring the entire text more closely into a whole. The surprising conclusion is simply an added bonus for readers who have been fully involved in gathering the enigmatic details of a passing love affair.

Notes

1 Paul Zumthor, *Essai de poétique médiéval* (Paris: Seuil, 1972) 339–404.
2 Susan Hunter Brown, "Discourse Analysis and the Short Story," *Short Story Theory at a Crossroads*, ed. Susan Lohafer and Jo Ellyn Clarey (Baron Rouge: Louisiana State UP, 1989) 242.
3 Ernest Hemingway, *Death in the Afternoon* (1932; New York: Scribner's, 1960) 192.
4 See, above, chapter 1n17.
5 B. M. Ejxenbaum, "O. Henry and the Theory of the Short Story," *The New Short Story Theories*, ed. Charles E. May (Athens: Ohio UP, 1994) 81. Of course, Ejxenbaum is not alone. Robert Louis Stevenson views the conclusion as the culmination of every preceding element. "Make another end to it? Ah yes, but that's not the way I write; the whole tale is implied [...]. To make another end, that is to make the beginning all wrong."—Letter of Sept. 1891 to Sidney Colvin, *The Letters of Robert Louis Stevenson*, ed. Sidney Colvin, Vol. 3 (New York: Charles Scribner's Sons, 1911) 335–36. See also John Gerlach's excellent book, *Toward the End: Closure and Structure in the America Short Story* (University AL: U of Alabama P, 1985), and many others.
6 With the exception of several instances in this note, I use the text that Denon revised in 1812: "Point de lendemain," *Romanciers du XVIIIe siècle*, ed. René Etiemble, Vol. 2, Bibliothèque de la Pléiade (1812; Paris: Gallimard, 1965) 383–402. I do so because the changes he made streamline the text and make it read both more rapidly and more inexorably, leaving the reader considerably less certain as to the intentions of Madame de T***. Most notably, Denon changed the protagonist's age and experience. Deleting the seasoned twenty-five-year old Damon of 1777, he gave his now anonymous hero of 1812 only twenty years, which make the latter's hesitations and confusion seem more realistic and invite the reader to identify with his adventure.

Uncertainty in "Point de lendemain" 33

In 1777, the countess de *** had broken with the rakish Damon. "[I]n order to get even better, I capriciously had her again" and, when the countess had committed herself, to break with her once more—*Point de lendemain* (1777; Paris: Jacques Haumont, 1941) 9. The "ingénue" of 1812 would have been incapable of such rakehelly behavior. And where Madame de T... of 1777 is presented ironically as a libertine on the prowl, with specific designs on Damon, in 1812 we are left without assurance about her character. She only "*seemed* to have designs on my person"—385; my italics. Furthermore, the lurching carriage that threw them into each other's arms resulted in a "kiss surprised [...] by chance" in 1777, but in 1812 only their faces touch. These few emendations change the earlier version's libertinism into what may potentially be nothing, but amorous play that goes out of control. In short, what in 1777 was clear-cut eroticism loses its blunt contours and certainty in 1812. As Michel Delon correctly understands, "Passion replaces cynicism, the demi-teints nuance the darkness of the first tableau"—"Préface," "Point de lendemain" *suivi de* Jean-François de Bastide, "La Petite Maison," Coll. Folio (Paris: Gallimard, 1995) 27.

7 Roderick Phillips, *Family Breakdown in Late Eighteenth-Century France: Divorces in Rouen 1792–1803* (Oxford: Clarendon Press, 1980) and Elaine M. Kruse, "Divorce in Paris 1792–1804: Window on a Society in Crisis," diss. U of Iowa, 1983, are essential for the consideration of revolutionary divorce. See also my, "Literature as Historical Archive: Reading Divorce in Mme de Staël's *Delphine* and Other Revolutionary Literature," *EMF: Studies in Early Modern France* 7 (2001): 163–200. A library of material supports the historical summary of the rest of this paragraph. See, as just one example, Alexis de Toqueville, *The Old Regime and the French Revolution*, trans. Stuart Gilbert (Garden City, NY: Doubleday, 1955).

8 Nicolas-Edme Restif de La Bretonne, *Le Palais royal*, 3 vols. (1790; rpt. Geneva: Slatkine, 1988) 1.222. Denis Diderot, *Supplément au voyage de Bougainville ou Dialogue entre A et B, Œuvres*, Bibliothèque de la Pléiade (Paris: Gallimard, 1951) 995. The *Supplément* was written in 1772 and revised at least twice, once in 1773 and then again in 1780, four years before the author's death.

9 Denis Diderot, *Encyclopédie, ou dictionnaire raisonné des sciences, des arts et des métiers*, 17 vols. (Paris: Briasson, 1751–65) 3.86.

10 François Rabelais, "A très illustre prince et révérendissime Monseigneur Odet, Cardinal de Chastillon" and "Aux lecteurs," *Œuvres complètes*, Bibliothèque de la Pléiade (Paris: Gallimard, 1955) 517 and 2, respectively. I am grateful to Daniela Teodorescu for reminding me of these passages.

11 See, for example, Sjef Houppermans, "La Description dans *Point de lendemain*," *Description-Ecriture-Peinture*, ed. Yvette Went-Daoust (Groningen, 1987) 36–47; Dominique Maingueneau, "Signification du décor: L'Exemple de *Carmen*," *Romantisme* 12.38 (1982): 87–91; Byron R. Wells, "Objet/ Volupté: Vivant Denon's *Point de lendemain*," *Romance Notes* 29.3 (1989): 203–08; John Patrick Greene, "Decor and Decorum in Vivant Denon's *Point de lendemain*," *Dalhousie French Studies* 39–40 (Summer-Fall 1997): 59–68.

12 Thomas M. Kavanagh, *Enlightenment and the Shadows of Chance: The Novel and the Culture of Gambling in Eighteenth-Century France* (Baltimore, MD: Johns Hopkins UP, 1993) 185–97, uses the story to illustrate chance, a discussion that Catherine Cusset usefully expands in, "A Lesson of Decency: Pleasure and Reality in Vivant Denon's *No Tomorrow*," *The Libertine Reader: Eroticism and Enlightenment in Eighteenth-Century France*,

34   Uncertainty in "Point de lendemain"

ed. Michel Feher (New York: Zone Books, 1997) 722–31. Gillian B. Pierce is content to call such key moments mysteries—"'Point de lendemain': Milan Kundera and the French Libertine Tradition," *Literature Interpretation Theory* 26.4 (2015): 305. doi:1i0.1080/10436928.2015.1092852. I differ from these critics in that I am interested in the way "uncertainty" subsumes the opposition between "contingency" and "intentionality," between chance and the possibility of a carefully executed seduction.

13 Henriette Javorek, "Vivant Denon's *Point de lendemain,*" *Chimères* 23.1–2 (1996–97): 39–40.

14 Pierre Naudin, "L'Architecte et le romancier au siècle de Le Camus de Mézières et de Vivant Denon," *Travaux de littérature: Architectes et architecture dans la littérature française* 12 (1999): 63–70.

15 See, for example, Forest L. Ingram, who defines a short story as a "condensed fictional narrative in prose"— *Representative Short Story Cycles of the Twentieth Century: Studies in a Literary Genre* (The Hague: Mouton, 1971) 15n8. Wallace Stegner believes that all short stories "demand an intense concision and economy"—"Teaching the Short Story," *Davis Publications in English* 2 (Fall 1965): 11; and Baudelaire notes that the short story is "tighter, more condensed" than the novel—"Théophile Gautier" (1859), *Œuvres complètes*, Bibliothèque de la Pléiade (Paris: Gallimard, 1961) 691. Paul Bourget wrote that the novel "procedes by development, the Short Story by concentration"—"Mérimée nouvelliste," *Revue des Deux Mondes* 90 (15 September 1920): 263.

3 Huysmans and the Bifocal Dilemma

Unquestionably, Huysmans was a prodigious literary technician engaged in significant experimentation. I previously suggested that he was the Mallarmé of the novel, recasting the form of that genre as Mallarmé did of poetry.[1] In the "Préface" written twenty years after the initial publication of *A rebours* [*Against Nature* 1884], Huysmans recalls admitting to Zola that he wanted to "suppress the traditional plot, truly even suppress passion, women, concentrating on a single character with a light brush; at any price, I yearned to do something new."[2] The statement summarizes what he actually accomplished in *A vau-l'eau* [*Drifting* 1882], the novella that tells the story of M. Folantin, a pathetic husk of a man trailing across one inexpensive restaurant after another, desperately trying to find decent food. There is a narrative, and the reader, who is dragged through a series of eateries by exquisite style and an amazing collection of synonyms describing appalling restaurants, recognizes the sequence. The point, of course, is that there is nothing special about the main character, and his quest requires a most compassionate reader to care about him and what he was doing, rather than simply to share in Huysmans' bleak humor. In short, Huysmans did not suppress the narration in this work; it is simply so trivial as to stagger belief that it could attract, much less hold readers. Only on keeping in mind the task Huysmans set himself in this period can one truly appreciate "Un Dilemme" (1884).

The plots of Huysmans' day help understand what he was determined to accomplish. He was focusing on narrative as it existed in most novels: stories of heroes prevailing in tales of passion, adultery, rags to riches, adventure, and so on, made banal by their commonplace multiplicity. Most of this fiction depended for its unity on a sequence of episodes highlighting a single character. Even in the case of a brilliant novelist like Zola, it always concerned something exceptional: a strike that became an open revolt against the established power, as in *Germinal* (1885), a prostitute whose infectious sexuality was contaminating society, as in *Nana* (1880), or even a war to destroy France, the great nation, as in *La Débacle* (1892). Huysmans turned away from such flamboyant narrations to an unimpressive little man with stomach troubles, who

36   *Huysmans and the Bifocal Dilemma*

optimistically, yet erroneously, thought that it was possible to find palatable food in modestly priced Parisian restaurants. The result, *A vau-l'eau*, tells a story of no importance whatsoever. On reading the text, it seems probable that even Huysmans' mentor, Zola, was bored. There is no evidence that he laughed.

Huysmans' auctorial goals of divesting himself of extravagant plot and heroic characters become clearer in the postdated "preface" he wrote for *A rebours*, where he told that, on reading the work, Zola recognized his disciple's growing independence. Huysmans denies having had any program: "I had no fixed plan [...]. *A rebours* is a perfectly unconscious work, imagined without preconceived ideas, without intentions reserved for the future, without anything at all" ("Préface," *A rebours* 54). As my *Inner Workings of the Novel* argued some years ago, when read carefully with a firm grasp of the symbols that became enormously important in fin-de-siècle literature, and in focusing not on what the main character, des Esseintes, does but on what he thinks, *A rebours* offers a tightly constructed albeit unusual novel. It reinforces Zola's recognition that Huysmans had slipped away from the naturalist camp (Pasco, *Inner Workings* 63–88).

Despite Huysmans' twenty-year post-facto denial that he had any purposeful intention in composing *A rebours*, with this 1884 masterpiece he turned his back on well-established aesthetic traditions. His "introductory" (but a generation tardy) remarks are important, especially because they give a good overview of his thoughts as he moved toward breaking with the naturalist group. As he explained in this after-the-fact "Préface" to *A rebours*, while a disciple of Zola and included with the writers published in the *Soirées de Médan* (1880), he felt a

> need [...] to open the windows, to flee a milieu where I was being stifled; then the desire took hold of me to shake off prejudices, to break the limits of the novel, [...] not to use it any more, in short, except as a form like a frame in which to insert more serious work. Suppressing traditional plot was especially what occupied me in that period. ("Préface," *A rebours* 62)

Of course, although such intentions are aesthetically revolutionary, Huysmans did not manage to suppress the sequence of episodes we call plot in *A rebours*. One might argue, however, that he virtually did away with what he called *traditional* plot, a series of more or less exceptional actions. He worked out a different kind of plot in *A rebours* and the later *En rade* [*Stranded* 1887]. The stories of the gradual disintegration of des Esseintes' inner self in *A rebours* (what he called his soul) and, as well, Jacques Marles' regeneration in *En rade*[3] are told in the dominate connotative narrations. Both novels are constructed of a sequence of episodes taking place primarily in the minds of the main characters. It is

Huysmans and the Bifocal Dilemma 37

precisely this kind of analogical story that Mallarmé tells in his poetry. Certainly, neither of Huysmans' novels imitates a normal biography. They do not begin with the birth of the hero, whether des Esseintes or Jacques Marles, or end with their deaths or a culmination of actions, as did most biographies and a good many novels. The real adventure has to be read on a level that has almost nothing to do with the usual "narration" recounting the progression of a main character's physical activity in a material world.

In his novel *Là-bas* [*Down There* 1891], Huysmans explained his intention and practice more clearly and more reliably, since he was still deeply engaged in breaking new ground in the creation of prose fiction. While he wished to retain the verity of the document, exact detail, and both the depth and complexity of Realism, whether on the level of vocabulary or vision, he also wanted to explore the spirit or "soul" of man, though without limiting his investigations to pathological illnesses, as did the Naturalists. Novels could and should be divided into two connected parts, he thought: the one concerned with material reality and the other with the spirit. "It would be necessary, in a word, to follow the wide road that Zola so profoundly established, but we would also have to trace a parallel path, another route, so as to reach what was on the other side and afterwards to create, in a word, a spiritualistic naturalism."[4] The explanation sheds light on his intentions for *Là-bas*, and as well for *A vau l'eau, A rebours*, and *En rade*. These four fictions were "spiritual" histories, and they reject traditional sequences of action that were standard fare in most novels. Huysmans did, however, decide to establish his descriptions according to connotations of alterations in the physical, neurological, mental, and spiritual entities of the main characters.

Though Huysmans provided a sort of plot, and did not reject narration with its attendant personage, they exist in these works only as they focus on the radical changes taking place in the main character's psychology. The reader need only accept the level of associations on which Huysmans has chosen to tell his analogical story to sense the progression of the narration. His emphasis on rare vocabulary attests to his concern for exact meaning in his choice of words that bear with them several levels of significance. The word "flower," for example, carries the denotative significance of a plant's blossom and its life span. Just as the word's precision depends on its modifiers and, more expansively, on its context, so its ramifications can easily expand to include the joy of a marriage and the distress of a funeral, the youth and beauty of a girl or her fading glory, the rainbow colors of a spring garden, or the winter of decay. The word's connected attributes or connotations can carry the base meaning as well. Almost at random, I open one of Gyp's novels to read the description of Madame Dampyré: "Thirty years of age. Beautiful, but not fresh" (*Les Femmes du colonel* 3). It certainly is not necessary to consult

38   *Huysmans and the Bifocal Dilemma*

a dictionary to understand that Mme Dampyré has passed beyond the most attractive years of her youth. It may be worth mentioning that we have moved into the realm of flowers, without mentioning them directly. A new set of rhizocarpean associations is then established, at the center of which is "not fresh," "faded," perhaps even "wilted," and, indeed, not even a flower, but rather a new portrait of Mme Dampyré. The reader is expected to sense the series of traits that define her.

Curiously, though nineteenth-century fiction was particularly successful at creating masterpieces that knowingly exploit connotations, it is known for its "Realism," for its mimetic attempt to reproduce the experience of a fast changing, confusing, disturbing society. In fact, a number of writers were not only mixing genres, but also attempting to go beyond the Aristotelian categories of plot, character, and narration to argue on the level of theme, image, symbolism, analogy, or allusion for a deeper understanding of reality that could not be expressed in simple terms. When Proust's young protagonist wanted to express his joy at being free to walk in the midst of a glorious nature, for instance, he found language incapable of expressing his feelings and was reduced to "My, my, my, my" ['*Zut, zut, zut, zut*']. But at the same time, the narrator goes on to say, "I felt that my duty would have been to stop using these opaque words and to try to see my delight more clearly."[5] Like his predecessors who struggled to find a way of expressing truth that went well beyond palpable reality, in later volumes the narrator learned to put language in contexts that would allow it to be more fully communicative.

Huysmans' creations of the 1880s offer important examples of the literary experimentation that was rife through the beginning of World War I. As Realism and Naturalism weakened, losing their ability to touch and inspire France's artists and readers, Symbolism became a school capable of influencing the most important writers of the first half of the twentieth century. Some of these young esthetes gathered regularly on the *rue de* Rome to sit at the feet of the superb poetic innovator, Mallarmé.[6] Authors like Henry Céard, Léon Bloy, Lucien Descaves, Léon Hennique, and Jean Richepin also broke the mold and moved on to new subjects and techniques, as did Valéry, Breton, Claudel, and Proust. And among all these innovative authors, Huysmans plays a prominent role.

For most critics, the problem with Huysmans seems to be that *A rebours* and *En rade* lack a story line. And as is clear from the chapter below on Flaubert's *Trois contes*, where there is no reappearing character acting out his or her particular destiny, something else must tie the various parts together. In other creations of this period, it may be a series of reappearing themes or images; it may be a particular setting that evolves; it may be a character that develops or is filled in and rounded out; it may simply be a reiterated narrative armature. Nonetheless, however fascinating a character who refuses the standards of society in a kaleidoscope

Huysmans and the Bifocal Dilemma 39

of chapters, readers still find it disturbing if there is no main character doing something important in the tangle of luxuriant description. And, in truth, des Esseintes exists in a novel that has almost no denotative narration.

Shortly after finishing *A rebours*, Huysmans returned to the experimentation that was driving his aesthetics and wrote "Un Dilemme," choosing to use the short story once again to further his efforts. He created an undeniable plot, accompanied rather than replaced (as in *A rebours* and *En rade*) by a series of connotations that illustrate the significance of the tale. Robert Baldick suggests that "Un Dilemme" was a "matter-of-fact antidote to the extravagant fantasy of *A rebours*."[7] In effect, given that Huysmans was disappointed by the poor sales of *A rebours*, as he would be with *En rade*,[8] one wonders whether he attributed the novels' marketing failure to their minimal use of traditional plots. He certainly was aware that he had scarcely exploited such sequences in either *A rebours* of 1884 or *En rade* of 1887, while such narrations do recur in "Un Dilemme" of 1884, "La Retraite de Monsieur Bougran" of 1888, *Là-Bas* of 1891, and subsequently. The uproar surrounding the appearance of *A rebours* unquestionably set him to thinking about what he was attempting to accomplish with fiction.

In "Un Dilemme," Huysmans takes two characters of the same detestable type as many other bourgeois who inhabit Naturalist literature.[9] He has them evacuate a young woman's humanity, thus devaluing her and making it seem acceptable for them to destroy her. The story opens with Maître Le Ponsart, a notary in Beauchamp, and his son-in-law, Monsieur Lambois, a retired hosier, folding their napkins prior to coffee. They are about to discuss their dead offspring Jules' pregnant mistress. The young man's father, M. Lambois, had planned to arrange a prefecture for himself and a sub-prefecture for his son, as soon as the latter finished his education, but, since Jules has recently died, he will have to be satisfied with his son's inheritance, a sum of 100,000 francs.[10] (Grojnowski estimates that in 2007 the amount would be something like 300,000 euros.[11]) Clearly, M. Lambois would have felt great personal satisfaction on arranging the sub-prefect position, though there is no indication that this feeling would have been stimulated by fatherly love. The appointment would have been a personal triumph. Given that the now dead young man can no longer offer his father this achievement, the two old men seem happy to settle for the inheritance left by law to the father and grandfather at the boy's death.

They act almost as though they see nothing unethical about adding the inheritance to their own wealth. Jules' pregnant mistress has requested support for herself and Jules' baby, whom she carries, but she has no rights according to the code if he died intestate, as his father and grandfather hope, for the couple was not married. Jules' inheritance would then flow legally to his father and grandfather, his only living

40   *Huysmans and the Bifocal Dilemma*

relatives. Their wives have passed (prostitutes are substituted), as now has Jules, and with the eventual demise of the latter's mistress and their unborn child, so is their line. They are well aware that the pregnant Sophie Mouveau is a young woman who lovingly cared for their son during his mortal illness and who carries within her their only hope for an heir, but the possibility of pecuniary gain by inheritance overshadows any concern for her welfare or their progeny. The story then contrasts the statutes of the official code that the young man's relatives impose on Sophie with a higher, ethical standard. Their interest in her and their grandchild is considerably less than that in their offspring's one hundred thousand francs. It is a nice sum that they could devote to their appetitive indulgences or the pleasure of a growing fortune. "In short, [Maître Le Ponsart's] carnal needs were alone strong enough to impede piling up additional savings" (151). The ethics of the matter are unambiguous. To choose cognac, cigars, and prostitutes over their only possible heir is to choose the flesh over spiritual values and against life. As Jérôme Solal concludes, the old men represent death.[12]

From early in the story, Jules' relatives recognize that their neighbors in Beauchamp would not approve of the decision they have made to disregard their descendant, as they have by preferring, indeed, replacing family with money. Huysmans does not leave the reader in the dark about the nefarious traits of the father and grandfather, who will be at work in depriving Sophie and her child of any but negligible funds. Sophie's friend, Mme Champagne, may be ridiculous, but her judgment rings true. The men are "heartless" (176, 179) and "pitiless" (193), a condemnation emphasized when Jules' grandfather, Maître Le Ponsart, brags that he has the necessary skills to defeat the young woman (147).

From the very first paragraph, Huysmans masterfully sets the story to highlight Maître Le Ponsart and M. Lambert's lack of compassion. Careful not to be overheard by the maid, they discuss the possibilities of splitting Jules' small fortune between them, while having coffee beneath a portrait of M. Thiers, the Third Republic Prime Minister who was abominated by sophisticated esthetes like Huymans and his friends. As Castries says, "The work of Thiers did not include a single social law. On this point, he was truly a bourgeois of the 19th century, insensitive to the miseries of the working classes and not hesitant to open fire on the masses when the public order was threatened."[13] The highlighted picture marks the two old men as similar: bourgeois, self-centered, deaf to the cries of the poor and less powerful members of the society. Lambois' son, Jules, as well, had hung a photograph of Thiers in his apartment (162). One wonders whether Villiers de l'Isle-Adam was not correct to suggest that Jules "takes after his father by instinctively and in a sublime gesture of obscure atavism neglecting to leave a last will and testament."[14] His neglect destroyed the lower-class woman who loved him.

Huysmans and the Bifocal Dilemma 41

From the first few moments of their conversation after dinner, the dead young man's father and grandfather plan to help themselves to Jules' money, something they do not wish noised about. And the crux of the matter is revealed. By their self-serving assumption that Jules' destitute mistress, who has written them for help, was living with her lover only because of his wealth and her greed, they justify their use of the law to bludgeon their access to the inheritance. But they recognize that appropriating the funds without tainting their reputation in their hometown needs secrecy to succeed, an evident strategy that exposes their vile natures in neglecting the importance of civilized ethics to satisfy their greed.

The story provides only meager background for Jules' father, M. Lambois. Once a hosier, he is now retired, having made his fortune. Given his son's death, he has abandoned his plan for a prefecture and now hopes to be named to the General Counsel. He continues to be avid for success, and follows the advice of his father-in-law closely. The role of the father-in-law as his mentor seems problematic, since the text reports numerous rumors about Maître Le Ponsart's dishonesty. The narrator mentions that the notary observed considerable perfidy while younger and working for a Parisian lawyer. Years later in Beauchamp, his priorities are limited to observing the letter though not the spirit of the code in order to pile up more money. He already has a fortune, but he is not satisfied. While the reader gains enough information to question the notary's uprightness, he appears on the surface to be a law-abiding citizen. He enjoys gossip, while remaining careful to maintain attorney-client privilege, and he has considerable pleasure in one-upmanship, taking great delight in feeling superior to his acquaintances. Still, while his love of good food is well known, his other carnal needs require clandestine trips to Parisian prostitutes.

It is after convincing himself that Jules' mistress deserved nothing that he reveals his true colors. The pregnant girl was not legally married while living with Jules, and although he is well aware of the care Sophie gave his grandson, he shows her no pity at all. Indeed, he treated her much worse than the prostitute who cheated him. The receipt he insists that the girl sign, agreeing to accept a few francs as a maid's salary through the end of the normal term of employment and ending her legal relationship to his family, is but one example. He goes further, needlessly insisting that Sophie move out of Jules' apartment immediately, and he confiscates all the furniture. But after his disappointing experience with the prostitute, who refused to do as he wished and paid for—"No, cut it out. You wear me out," she said (188)—he thinks happily that he "can freely get even with Sophie for all the unpleasantness women's greed caused" (188).

Huysmans sets the tone with Sophie's name, Mouveau. "Mou" is what a French cow says, as a child might put it, while a "veau" is, of course,

42   Huysmans and the Bifocal Dilemma

a calf. An accident of the girl's heredity has, in the author's hands, given her a family name that begins the work of reducing Jules' mistress to prey (and reminds readers of Emma Bovary's bovine name).[15] The way Le Ponsart and his son Lambois talk of Jules' mistress indicates what they have in mind. She will be reduced to the level of an animal, with no rights whatsoever. The story reports only three times that she is directly addressed (165, 166, 171), and it should be noticed that the notary either patronizes her or calls her "Mademoiselle" (161, 166), thus emphasizing her unmarried state. Otherwise, almost without exception, they refer to her in disparaging ways. Even when using such relatively empty words as "the woman" and "this woman," the context turns them into insults (e.g. 156, 164, 165, 166, 182). They plan to deny support for both herself and her baby. At first, she is almost anonymous: a "certain person" (146), though very soon they term her "this creature" (146), before she becomes a "hussy" (146), "this false maid" (147), and a dozen other terms that might be summarized with the vituperative "chippy" (156), "bitch" (163), and "slattern" (163).[16] They make a great deal of the fact that they know nothing of her background. As Jules' father and grandfather refuse to use her real name, giving her others instead, their maledictions degrade her importance and humanity, thus permitting and, to their minds, justifying their treatment of her. Nonetheless, despite his regularly proclaimed confidence in his ability to dominate the girl, he has been sufficiently concerned to talk to a Parisian police commissioner, in case she should pose a difficulty and need to be intimidated. However sly she might prove to be, he claims to have several tricks up his sleeve that will make her ineffective if she causes trouble (147).

Though determined to collect the money, Jules' relatives are equally aware that their heartless behavior would bring social condemnation from their fellow Beauchampois. No one must know what they are doing. Especially given that Sophie has made no coercive threats, one has to wonder whether she might actually have certain rights. She has written to ask for help because, she explains, she is pregnant. Certainly she has no standing before the law, and she requests nothing but the help one might expect of a family member. While the reader is told that she comes from difficult circumstances, she has just the kind of personality that pleased Jules: kind, retiring, loving. His father and grandfather judge her letter as uneducated, which was a common condition for women at the end of the nineteenth century. The letter demonstrates, however, that she has learned to write. They wonder where Jules landed her (*qu'il a péchée où?* 148), as though she were a consumable product. Full of a rich dinner, and enjoying cigars and cognac, Lambois stops thinking about his gouty toe, and the two men seemingly relish the thought that they have no worries. Their lips wet and their bald heads glowing, they begin to talk of sex. Le Ponsart likes his women short and with some meat on

Huysmans and the Bifocal Dilemma 43

them, Lambois prefers them quite thin, as long as they behave in a rather refined way and do not act like a plank in bed (149).

Le Ponsart is delighted to go to Paris, where his sexual pleasures can be tallied up far from the gossips at home. "In his eyes, only good food and sex were worth what they cost" (150). Otherwise, he pinched every penny and enjoyed increasing his fortune. What stamps him as a vacuous bumpkin, however, is the fact that he is committing Molière's *Le Bourgeois gentilhomme* to verse (153). Worse yet, ignorant of his inadequacies, he transfers Molière's thought word for word, and subjects his acquaintances to his occasional poems. In short, "A pure provincial, he was a gossip, a glutton, and riven with greed. Setting aside the sensual instincts that he could not satisfy without shame in Beauchamp" (155), he gave dinners, while skimping on cigars and lighting. Highly regarded in provincial Beauchamp, the notary feels nonetheless vulnerable. He and his son wonder what family weaknesses Jules could have revealed to Sophie.

Maître Le Ponsart is pleased that Sophie has no legal card to play. Jules left no last will and testament, no lease, no money, nothing, and the grandfather celebrates with a good meal after searching her apartment, while looking forward to more carnal enjoyments later. Despite his sixty-five years he continues to want to satisfy his lechery. "He thought of the festival of the rump, a sweet treat of lips, a special desert of breasts, going over and over the details until everything melted into a whole, into the woman herself, erotically naked" (157). He even imagines the grandson's mistress sexually, though that thought dissipates as he waits before barging in on her unannounced. He pictures his visit as a military attack: before her guns were mounted, he would destroy them (161–63). Although the military / love analogy had appeared in previous literature, in Stendhal's *Le Rouge et le noir*, for example, the context is completely different. Julien Sorel is only a peasant boy, who hopes to work up Napoleon's courage to demonstrate his aborning passion for the aristocratic Madame de Rênal. In "Un Dilemme," Maître Ponsart plans a greedy and destructive attack that will yield booty from a defenseless person.

Maître Le Ponsart is an old man with no understanding of human love. He wants merely to dominate his grandson's mistress, so that he may destroy her. His visits go as expected. Sophie is innocent and un-sophisticated, "just a poor girl [...] in a dishonorable situation, with no excuses" (182). Jules did not prepare her for a future without him, and she allows Le Ponsart free access to her apartment. He finds nothing of value, thus assuring himself of her vulnerable poverty. "He admitted to himself that he was perhaps cruel to push a woman onto the pavement in just a few hours" (169). Consequently, he probes for more information and succeeds in discovering that Jules was not the first man she had sex with (though it was a rape). He then suggests that she contributed to

44   Huysmans and the Bifocal Dilemma

Jules' illness by having intercourse with him. For less than fifty francs in expenses, as he had promised his son, the notary successfully routes the mother of his future great grandchild and brings himself and Lambois an inheritance of 50,000 francs each.

Words always trail "clouds of glory," as Wordsworth would have it. They emphasize particular associations and contexts for the reader's understanding and appreciation. Huysmans made Sophie's grief and Madame Champagne's outrage come alive. Sophie was raped, then beaten by her father and forced to flee. Her subsequent bourgeois employer starved her. Lambert and Le Ponsart dehumanize her by referring to her contemptuously, thus brutalizing and negating her. Reduced to virtual silence (e.g. 168, 170), she is easy prey. She is forced out of her home, and treated like a stray dog (177, 199) until she dies (198). The lovely girl has been dehumanized, pursued ("chassée" 167, 179, 182), and killed.

While highlighting Sophie's horrendous destruction, Huysmans follows two despicable men as they savor their cognac and cigars while, in effect, violating a young woman who had been loving and kind to their offspring. As they hide their avaricious plans from the maid and their neighbors, they arrange to intimidate Sophie, who had loved their son / grandson and cared for him as he died of typhoid fever. The swollen, gouty toe that Lambois coddles beneath the portrait of the bourgeois hero, Thiers, is but the beginning of a series of analogies that illuminate their revolting characters. Greedy, lustful, egotistical, and cruel, Le Ponsart and Lambois' love of money is explained by their determination to build their fortunes and satisfy their appetitive desires. In Huysmans' hands, it is perfectly believable for Le Ponsart to spend everything he had with him, for a brief interlude with a prostitute and, then, the next day to refuse to pay the mother of his grandson enough for her to find a position and care for the child. The implications of the choice are sufficient to condemn Jules' father and grandfather. For both men, the pleasures of the flesh are their most important value. Even money is but a means to that end, and its accumulation perhaps comforts them with the thought of continuing sensual pleasures.

Le Ponsart brags that "[t]he chickie [*poulette*] would have to have big teeth to take a bite out of an old fox like me" (147). Lambois describes her as "A brunette with the eyes of a wild animal (*fauve*) and straight teeth; she speaks little and impresses me with her ingenuous, reserved air as an expert, dangerous person" (147), and we understand that he and his son are vulpine animals stalking the girl, who has become prey. Simultaneously, with each decision, with each action they sink further into bestiality. In short, lacking empathy, they become bourgeois. As for Sophie, "since that morning she had been haunted by the thought of herself prowling, without money, without a home, thrown out like a dog" (177). When the girl says, "So, [...] you evict me [*vous me chassez*] with no money, with a child that I'm going to have" (167, 179, 182), the

Huysmans and the Bifocal Dilemma 45

obvious meaning of "chasser" within the context is "to evict," but the other meaning suggested by the analogical system that Huysmans has slowly constructed throughout the story is "hunted." The characters have by cruel behavior and constant denigration in their discussions evacuated both their own and Sophie's humanity. Interwoven with the denotative account of their grandson's tragedy, there exists a connotative system. The two bourgeois are animals tracking an innocent girl who carries their offspring. Le Ponsart points out that she is "too brown" (168), not fair skinned like most French people, but dark like a wild creature, like a Mouveau. Like the bestial creatures they are, they intend and do destroy her. Her name and her retiring personality leave her little hope.

Most interesting in this story is the way Huysmans surrounds his characters with implications that the reader is encouraged to interpret, thus revealing the very essences of Sophie, Mme Champagne, and Jules' relatives. The author has gone beyond the denotative puzzle that Denon spells out for the reader in the conclusion of "Point de lendemain" and moved to a connotative level. Huysmans' insistent indications of another system of meaning encourage the readers to sense an analogical pattern that allows them to understand the greater truth, the vile essence of the bourgeoisie. In the case of Madame Champagne, the author's narrator briefly describes her as a ridiculous but generous person. She "was, in fact, providential for the poor, frequently finding employment for them from important French people" (172). Similarly, we are explicitly told what we should think of the landlord and the movers. But in the case of Sophie, her suggestive given and family names and the few facts of her biography are enough to give her a special glow as she is clumsily victimized by Maître Le Ponsart. Abused, poorly educated, quiet, unassuming, and evincing a certain beauty, we understand how Jules could have loved her, and we perceive her unassertive virtues, if only because the connotations emanating from Lambois and Le Ponsart are so negative. The father and grandfather's characterizations slowly fill in and illuminate their selfishness, their greed, their cruelty, their shameless willingness to persecute an innocent young woman like Sophie to the detriment of their own flesh and blood grandchild. They are doing wrong, and their neighbors in Beauchamp would judge them harshly. Huysmans exploits his understanding of the connotations that can dominate physical actions and material objects. By forcing the reader to go beyond denotation to the implications the text brings to bear on this tragic account of exploitation, the story opens to become a powerful condemnation of the bourgeoisie of nineteenth-century France.

When Le Ponsart confronts Sophie with her choices—that she either move out and receive nothing or that she move out and receive almost nothing—he says proudly, though under his breath, "And that is called a dilemma, or I don't know what I'm talking about" (171). The notary is in fact misinterpreting the terms of his own argument. Not surprisingly,

46   *Huysmans and the Bifocal Dilemma*

given what we have already learned of this cruel, lustful man, he is also of limited intelligence. The concept of a dilemma, which has literary and philosophical precedents, and has been recognized at least since Plato,[17] is simply a syllogism, in which a person is forced to make a decision between two choices that are either equally desirable or undesirable. William Styron's *Sophie's Choice* (1979) named the quandary after Saint Sophia. It seems likely that Huysmans also knew the terrible legend of the saint, who had three daughters that attracted the emperor Hadrian's attention. One by one, the emperor offered them membership in his family and phenomenal riches to abjure their Christian faith and kneel to Artemis. Urged on by their mother who stood by them, they refused and suffered horrendous tortures before being beheaded and allowed to go to heaven with their Lord. The mother was likewise accorded a martyr's reward for her faithfulness in supporting her three daughters and her faith. Each of the daughters confronted the same dilemma: they could become apostates laden with riches and die in the eternal fires of hell, or they could die in the hands of Hadrian and go to Paradise. They had no other alternatives. Like Balzac's El Verdugo or Styron's Sophie, they faced a true dilemma, with no other possibilities but to accept death.

Le Ponsart's false dilemma can only succeed if Sophie and her friend and neighbor, Madame Champagne, believe that they have no other options. Terrified of being found out by his provincial neighbors—"the fear that she [Sophie] would come and scandalize Beauchamp by her presence never left him" (189)—his feelings of guilt leave no doubt that she had other possibilities, if she could leverage social pressure. Mme Champagne threatens, "I will go myself to your area, even if I have to go on foot, and I'll turn everything upside down [...]. I'll bring you the baby and I'll tell everyone whose it is; I'll say that you didn't even have the heart to help bring this child into the world..."[18] Madame Champagne and Sophie might have spent a few days in jail, but it would have been temporary. "Despite the principles that [the notary] paraded publicly, he regretted that there were no longer any *lettres de cachet* that allowed incarcerating people in the Bastille" (156), thus guaranteeing their silence. Le Ponsart and Lambois mention explicitly, several times, that the girl could try to blackmail them. They could moreover be compromised if she were to come to Beauchamp. The possibility of such public embarrassment is their vulnerable point, their "Achilles' heel," as the notary recognizes repeatedly.[19] Given persistence, Sophie would doubtless have succeeded in gaining financial help. Ignorant, pretentious, asthmatic, overweight, and ridiculous, Madame Champagne and her ward Sophie are in the right: "[I]t is infamous, cowardly, sir, a theft" (194). Unfortunately for Sophie and Mme Champagne, Le Ponsart successfully bluffs, and the hapless women are blinded by circumstance, inexperience, and a lack of education to believe they have no hope. At worst, the women need knowledgeable advice, and they have none that is sufficient to bring the bullying Le Ponsart to heel.

The titular "dilemma" is actually bifocal, one alternative false and the other real. Unlike Saint Sophia and her daughters, Sophie's potential choices are not even a dilemma in nineteenth-century France, for they are not limited to Le Ponsart's half-baked alternatives. He offers her not so much a dilemma but rather several possibilities. If she admits that she was Jules' mistress, before the law she has no rights. If she agrees that she was the young man's maid, she can claim thirty-three francs and seventy-five centimes, essentially a few weeks' pay. Furthermore, she cannot expect back salary, since no one would believe that a maid would work without regular pay (194). In either case, Le Ponsart announces that she is being evicted without further support and will be on the street the next day.

Madame Champagne, despite her ignorance and poor taste, represents the voice of conscience that abrogates the "dilemma" of which Le Ponsart is so proud and emphasizes the true dilemma that confronts him and Jules' father. The old men can no more avoid the terms of their dilemma than could Saint Sophia. Indeed, Le Ponsart does *not* "know what he is talking about." As a rapacious, brutish bourgeois, he faces terrible alternatives. Saint Sophia could not elect Artemis, since it would cost her eternal life in heaven, just as the heartless Le Ponsart (176, 179) cannot choose his grandson, since it would cost him 100,000 francs. He must decide for money and the flesh over any other value, even though it will bring the extinction of his family. The titular dilemma is then bifocal. Sophie could have ignored the alternatives Le Ponsart offers. Her choices function primarily to point the reader to the true dilemma confronting Le Ponsart. Like La Fontaine's scorpion that killed the frog carrying it to salvation on the other side of the river, choosing the grandchild would be in opposition to their true natures as bourgeois. Le Ponsart does not pose a dilemma, he confronts one. He and his son choose death.

While establishing a false dilemma and using Madame Champagne's blaring voice to suggest the call of virtue, Huysmans describes the essence of the evil and vents his wrath on the bourgeois society of his day. Technically, Huysmans includes a clear-cut, traditional plot in "Un Dilemme," a denotative plot that exists but minimally in *A rebours* and *En rade*, while also including the connotative sequence that condemns Jules' mean-spirited, bourgeois relatives. This combination may be the "spiritualistic naturalism" to which *Là-bas* refers. The result is significant, for it takes what is otherwise no more than a fair to good naturalistic short story and raises it to another level. Perceptive readers are encouraged to see Sophie's death as an appalling attack on an innocent girl who is treated like prey by vile men who are even worse than carnivorous beasts. Lambois and Le Ponsart confront their dilemma and turn their backs on civilized values for the financial means to enjoy passing physical pleasures. While Sophie was true to her core identity and prioritized values, so were Jules' father and grandfather. Like Saint Sophia, she stood up selflessly for her child and her God. They stood selfishly for money and the bourgeoisie.

48   *Huysmans and the Bifocal Dilemma*

Like the majority of short stories, "Le Dilemme" is structured chronologically. Such sequential narrations can exhibit considerable astute artistry and perceptivity, as "Sans lendemain" and "Le Dilemme" demonstrate. Sequential structures are the most common variety, and I could easily fill the remainder of the present book's pages with masterful gems of this variety. There is, however, an abundant minority of works that fall outside of dominant sequences, and they deserve examination, as well. Though frequently neglected by critics, these image structures make use of many patterns, including the subordination of sequences, to form the tableau or vision that they represent. Such stories often seem overly complex, overly subtle, requiring extraordinary care in interpreting their reality, but they indicate the wide range of possibilities available to the short-story genre and demonstrate why some of the greatest writers of France were willing to exploit their potential. All successful stories utilize a variety of literary devices, techniques and approaches, even occasional deception, and need to raise curiosity, encourage author / reader interchange, and satisfy the demands of shared aesthetic invention. Nonetheless, perhaps because readers expect prose to be constructed from first to last in a serial order, dominated by a story line, the increasingly common but essentially static organizations that I call image structures may defy understanding and seem truncated, fragmentary, non-contextual, even confused. They certainly contravene the serial order of the words themselves. If for no other reason than the reader's frustrated expectations, such stories may require more cooperation in the participatory, mental involvement required to recreate the author's creation. They almost always force special attention to ferreting out the significance of detailed aspects of the construction. Throughout the remainder of this book, I shall then focus on a variety of works organized around more static images, whether tableaus or concepts.

Notes

1 Allan H. Pasco, "Remaking the Novel," *Inner Workings of the Novel: Studying a Genre* (New York: Palgrave Macmillan, 2010) 87.
2 Joris-Karl Huysmans, "Préface écrite vingt ans après le roman," *A rebours*, ed. Rose Fortassier, Lettres françaises (Paris: Imprimerie Nationale, 1981) 62.
3 Allan H. Pasco, "Negative Representation in Huysmans' *En rade*," Novel *Configurations: A Study of French Fiction*, 2nd ed. (Birmingham, AL: Summa Publications, 1994) 123–50.
4 Joris-Karl Huysmans, *Là-bas*, *Œuvres complètes*, 18 vols. (Paris: Slatkine, 1972) 12*.10–11.
5 Marcel Proust, *A la recherche du temps perdu*, ed. Jean-Yves Tadié, 4 vols., Bibliothèque de la Pléiade (Paris: Gallimard, 1987–89) 1.152.
6 See Allan H. Pasco, "From Decadence in Huysmans and Barbey to Regeneration in Gide and Proust," *Dix-Neuf* 21.2–3 (2017): 192–203. doi:10.1080/14787318.2017.1386884.

Huysmans and the Bifocal Dilemma 49

7 Robert Baldick, *The Life of J.-K. Huysmans* (1955; Sawtry: Dedalus, 2006) 140. Ziegler goes further, suggesting that "[e]ven before Durtal commented in *Là-bas* that naturalism had run its course and literature had reached an impasse, Huysmans had already explored most of the familiar terrain of fiction, feeling that he had exhausted all the material that physical and psychic reality could furnish [...]. Yet before implementing his theory of spiritual naturalism, Huysmans produced two short narratives ('Un Dilemme' and 'La Retraite de Monsieur Bougran'), whose subject was their characters' destructively coercive language" (181).

8 Baldick 104; Michael Issacharoff, *J.-K. Huysmans devant la critique en France (1874–1960)* (Paris: Klincksieck, 1970) 16–18, 67.

9 Although I am convinced that Huysmans slowly developed his technological skills through the course of his career, there is no question that he carried with him a number of the Naturalists' attitudes, as has been pointed out by both Marc Smeets, *Huysmans l'inchangé: Histoire d'une conversion* (Amsterdam: Rodopi, 2003), and Bertrand Bourgeois, "Quatre Ans seulement et pourtant: la distante proximité des deux versions d' 'Un Dilemme' de Huysmans," *Australian Journal of French Studies* 53.1–2 (2016): 23–24. Smeets has, as well, concluded: "Huysmans does not change his conception of literature or, if you like, of style" (85, cf. 87). Ignoring the experimental nature of "Un Dilemme" when mentioning it to Zola, Huysmans called it "a simple little tale intended to show once again the unalterable filth of the bourgeoisie"—31 March 1884, Letter 39, *Lettres inédites à Emile Zola*, ed. Pierre Lambert (Geneva: Droz, 1953) 102. He wrote much the same to Villiers: "This little window onto the blood red soul of a bourgeois"—Huysmans, dedication, *Lettres: Correspondance à trois*, ed. Daniel Habrekorn (Vanves: Thot, 1980) 270. For Prins, he said simply: "It is a dull gray short story" [11 Nov. 1887], letter 44, *Lettres inédites à Arij Prins (1885–1907)*, ed. Louis Gillet (Geneve: Droz, 1977) 99.

10 J.-K. Huysmans, "Un Dilemme," *Nouvelles: Sac au dos, A vau-l'eau, Un Dilemme, La Retraite de Monsieur Bougran*, ed. Daniel Grojnowski (Paris: GF Flammarion, 2007) 150–53, which uses the definitive version of "Un Dilemme" published in 1887 and subsequently, to which I shall refer. While first published in 1884, after the publication of *A rebours*, though before that of *En rade*—"Un Dilemme," *Revue Indépendante* 1 (1888): 371–98, 469–501—the story was reworked for the definitive edition, produced separately as *Un Dilemme* by Tresse et Stock in 1887. Though there are relatively few emendations, Bertrand Bourgeois, who has studied the issue, considers them important intensifications of the satire (109–22).

11 Grojnowski, ed., "Notice," "Un Dilemme," *Nouvelles* 138n1.

12 Jérôme Solal, "Le Code qui tue: A propos d' 'Un Dilemme'," *Bulletin de la Sociéte J.-K. Huysmans* 97 (2004): 48, 50.

13 René de la Croix de Castries, *Monsieur Thiers* (Paris: Librarie Académique Perrin, 1983) 465.

14 Villiers, to Léon Bloy, 11 Feb. 1888, letter 106, *Correspondance à trois* 109.

15 Solal points out that *Mou-* is the first syllable of *mourir*, while *-veau* is the last of *nouveau(-né)* (49).

16 See Solal 44 for a partial list; for a more complete list, see below. The many names ascribed to her are generally negative if not openly insulting. A list of terms used to characterize Sophie include "certaine personne" (146), "cette creature" (146), "la coquine" (146), "la drôlesse" (147, 160), "cette fausse bonne" (147), "la donzelle" (147, 189), "une personne experte et dangereuse" (147), "la poulette" (147), "une gourgandine" (156), "la femme" (156, 165,

50 Huysmans and the Bifocal Dilemma

166), "une appétissante gaillarde" (159), "une superbe drôlesse" (160), "la femme de son petit-fils" (160), "Mlle Sophie Mouveau" (161), "une forme de femme" (162), "la mâtine" (163, 170), "un ennemi retranché" (163), "un souillon" (163), "cette femme" (164, 182), "ma chère enfant" (165), "la brave fille" (166), "la poupée à Jeanneton" (166), "Mademoiselle" (166), "cette fille" (170), "ce torchon-là" (170), "une mauvaise tête" (170), and "belle dame" (171). Almost without exception, the terms are, or are used, in a demeaning fashion. It is almost a relief to have her referred to as a simple "pécheur" ['sinner'] (199), when Le Ponsart and Lambois are disclaiming any ill will toward the girl, after she has passed away.

17 See Pierre Larousse, *Le Grand Dictionnaire universelle*, 24 vols. (1866–90; rpt. Paris: Nimeo, 1990) 8.851–52.

18 "Un Dilemme" 195. Robert Ziegler writes insightfully that Le Ponsart imagines becoming the "object of the same gossip he is accustomed to spreading"— *The Mirror of Divinity: The World and Creation in J.-K. Huysmans* (Newark: U of Delaware P, 2004) 186.

19 156. For other mentions of possible blackmail, see 146–47, 156, 189, 195, 196, 200.

4 Sequence Denied in Barbey's "Don Juan" and "Le Dessous de cartes"

In 1850, when Barbey d'Aurevilly published the first story of what was to become a major cycle of short stories, he titled it, "Les Ricochets de conversation, I, Le Dessous de cartes d'une partie de whist"[1] ['Conversational Ricochets, I, Beneath the Cards in a Game of Whist'].[1] As he told his friend Trebutien, he planned a volume that would have this same title. Some years later, the original "richochet" fell away to assume in 1866 or 1867 the general title that it bears today, *Les Diaboliques* [*She-Devils* 1874]. The change was a stroke of genius, sure to gain the volume publicity or notoriety. Indeed, it attracted those interests that eventually caused the public prosecutor to order its confiscation and charge Barbey with immorality, thus placing the little volume of stories in such select company as *Les Fleurs du mal* and *Madame Bovary*. The resulting publicity made it the author's best-known work. Barbey was terrified by the legal action, however, and of an age when people seldom welcome trouble (he was 66). Even after an acquittal, he did not republish the volume until years later in 1882.

The two titles have considerably more than historical importance. As Jacques Petit suggests, the first does indeed mark the importance of technique to the stories (2.1274). Barbey changed it, I believe, not because technique became less important, but rather because the title became inadequate. Ricochet is the generally forward, glancing motion that an object makes when it rebounds one or more times after hitting a surface, reminding readers of a game that plays one interest off against another. While the concept of such movement has the advantage of suggesting directed development in these stories toward a revelation, it leaves aside far too much of their sophisticated complexity. Other titles that he considered—"Conversational Sonatas" and "Four Hand Sonatas"[2]—are more evocative of the interchanges between the multifaceted texture of the narrations. Still, Barbey's final decision seems particularly apropos, given the seductive sexuality of the stories.

In the minds of many readers, the sequences of the stories considered here either lead to confusion rather than conclusion or else they are dominated by an image. As numerous scholars have revealed, even at the end of what could be considered a sequence, the tales' meanings

52 Sequence Denied in Barbey's Works

remain enigmatic, if not nonsensical. These difficulties and frustrations posed by Barbey d'Aurevilly's *Les Diaboliques* have been regularly mentioned in the secondary literature. Anne Giard points out, for example, that readers commonly feel irritation when reading the collection.[3] There are many explanations for this frustrated expectation. Perhaps most obviously, some of the stories do not apparently fit with the rest. If the volume is organized around rhythms of conversation and a hidden reality, as Jacques Petit suggests, then, "La Vengeance d'une femme" ['A Woman's Revenge'] is different from the others (2.1277). And if the stories should be insisting on the diabolical, then it is disturbing that the heroine of "Le Rideau cramoisi" ['The Crimson Curtain'], the teenager of "Le Plus Bel Amour de Don Juan" ['Don Juan's Most Beautiful Love'] and Rosalba "are not diabolical, but rather sick," as one scholar puts it.[4] Moreover, the adolescent of "Le Plus Bel Amour de Don Juan" is "very pure" (2.1279). Finally, Julien Gracq believes the collection title is scarcely appropriate for the six stories.[5] While we are left in the dark concerning the motivations of most of these devilish women, nothing could on the contrary be more explicit than the Duchess de Sierra-Leone's quest for vengeance. And, finally, Petit considers four of the six stories downright inconclusive.[6] Only when readers grasp that Barbey's presentation of *Les Diaboliques* poses the stories as revealing a world dominated by Satan do they make sense.

Without question, however, the justification for the inclusion of "Le Plus Bel Amour de Don Juan" in *Les Diaboliques* has been one of the most difficult to grasp. Philippe Berthier reminds us: "[P]eople have occasionally wondered what it was doing there."[7] In fact, as Petit says in his edition of Barbey d'Aurevilly's works, this is the story "which has bothered critics the most; the girl is not a diabolical person, much to the contrary" (2.1307). Gisle Corbière-Gille mentions that it is one of the most frequently translated because it is one of the "least shocking,"[8] a conclusion that I shall suggest is far from accurate. B. G. Rogers simply terms it "a lightweight piece,"[9] and Bornecque finds it "unpleasant [and,] lacking the [stylistic] embellishments, absolutely absurd."[10] In short, as Berthier put it, "Le Plus Bel Amour de Don Juan" is "decidedly the least understood of the six short stories."[11] To explain how these stories are intimately and viscerally related to each other under an exquisitely appropriate title, we have to go to the heart of Barbey's creation, paying relatively less attention to what the various characters do than to what they are. Why do so many readers remain puzzled about what happens in these tales? What, in fact, is the "hidden reality that the story teller unmasks?" (Petit 2.1277). Or, as Le Corbeiller wonders, "Where is the diabolical in all that?"[12] The answer comes on closely reading the details that coalesce in an image of sin made tangible.

Each story in *Les Diaboliques* opens by introducing a narratee-narrator, before presenting a narrator-witness, who is often a participant

Sequence Denied in Barbey's Works   53

as well. Each story then proceeds to the account of a sin or crime and the revelation of an always feminine *diabolique* and her impact. With the introduction of each character and, later, each revelation, the perspectives change, rather like a kaleidoscope taking the same fragments of glass to configure a different image. The discoveries open a new view of preceding events and change their implications radically, so that the reader finally understands how each *diabolique* has served Satan, how, as Barbey put it in his preface to the first edition, she serves as a "means." She then reveals Satan in that she exemplifies his "use of the simplest means" (2.1291).

In this collection of short stories, Barbey's world shows a vitally active devil. There are many textual indications. In one instance, he observes, "[I]n Paris, when God plants a pretty woman, the Devil in reply immediately plants a fool to support her" (2.233). Although this observation might well be considered the flippant remark of a worldly cynic, it joins so many others and so many references to hell and the diabolical that the devil's existence gains form and consistency for a reader who takes Barbey's expressions in good faith. As pointed out in Barbey's preface, the author "believes in the Devil and in his influences and does not laugh about it" (2.1290–91). *Les Diaboliques* leaves us with no doubt that each of the heroines has been responsible for knowingly or unknowingly, innocently or brazenly leading other people into the pit of hell.

"Le Plus Bel Amour de don Juan" reveals that even in his old age the legendary Don Juan still had sufficient charisma to excite a naïve adolescent. If this were meant to be a narration, it is too slight to satisfy informed readers. Determined participants may turn to the evocative interplay of themes and images. Some represent the legendary powers of Don Juan in the context of sacred literature, while others emphasize symbols and historical movements that emphasize the over-riding image of evil. Nonetheless, as the tableau of the adolescent girl fills in, the representation has little apparent connection with other *diaboliques*. Numerous scholars have admitted that everything about the tale seems inconsequential. The only act of any importance is telling the absurd story.

"Le Plus Bel Amour de Don Juan" provides a good point of entry to Barbey's cycle of stories. The factors that render it understandable are also those that integrate the others under the collective title, *Les Diaboliques*. The tale's introductory narrator seems the same as in the other stories. Though Barbey often begins his account as in "Le Rideau cramoisi" with a description of the setting where he himself might have heard the story, here he immediately starts by telling the story to someone else. The narrator is never named, but he has all the marks of a wealthy, urbane aristocrat, a worldly man about town who frequents brothels and cathedrals, as well as provincial and Parisian salons where the arts of conversation and story-telling are welcome and practiced. Let me call him the *auteur* to distinguish him from Barbey, the author. The

54 Sequence Denied in Barbey's Works

auteur is the fictional character who heard the various stories and who controls their retelling in the fashionable salons that grace *Les Diaboliques*. But the *auteur* is only the principal narrator, who, like the others, prepares the ground in which a subsequent story will be embedded. In all, "Le Plus Bel Amour de Don Juan" contains five embedded stories, each opening onto another. The *auteur* heard the story from the Count de Ravila de Ravilès, the recent reincarnation of Don Juan, who heard the story from one of his mistresses, who heard it from her daughter's confessor, before getting the details from the daughter herself. At each level, the revelations provide a perspective on the audience or on one of the characters and on the enigma posed by the story's title. We are going to learn of Don Juan's "most beautiful love."

The *auteur* begins his tale in the salon of the old, pious Marquise Guy de Ruy. As the celebrated *Carte du tendre* would indicate, since permitting the lover to utter endearments constitutes engaging in a love affair, when the religious marquise permits the *auteur* to tell of "this old scoundrel" (2.59), she allows herself to be contaminated to some degree. The audience for the story also highlights belief in the Catholic religion, which is essential to the story. Nonetheless, despite a few pro forma objections—"[P]lease spare me details of suppers with your strumpets" (2.60)—the aggressively bigoted hostess' curiosity is aroused, she begins to daydream of Don Juan (after all she is a woman, thus subject to Don Juan's charms), and the *auteur* is encouraged to continue. Twelve of Don Juan's former "victims" have offered him a dinner in the Countess de Chiffrevas' boudoir, "the theatre of his glory, there where memories blossom rather than orange trees" (2.60). The mention that oranges, which symbolize fecundity, have been replaced by memories raises the possibility that the celebration ("to celebrate... what? they didn't say"—2.61) may have been called to commemorate Don Juan's former powers and mark his current impotence. "Ordinarily it is joy, the thirst for amusement that causes suppers; but here it was memory, it was regret, it was almost despair" (2.62). The suspicion gains substance when the *auteur* tells us that this is "Don Juan in the fifth act," near the end, a fifty-year-old Alcibiades (2.63), that is, a great general past his prime. Despite the aging lover's pact with the devil, "the tiger's claws of life were beginning to draw lines across the divine forehead, [...] the first white hairs [...] announced the coming invasion of the Barbarians and the end of the Empire..." (2.62). Alluding to Molière's *Don Juan*, the auteur tells us that there is nothing left for Don Juan but the vengeful Commander of white marble and the "hell of old age, while waiting for the other one" (2.62). There is no doubt about the memorial significance of this festival when the text twice mentions Sardanapalus' death, and reminds readers of Delacroix's great painting, *La Mort de Sardanapale* [*The Death of Sardanapalus*], for this painting stands as one of the most explicit representations ever of impotence.[13]

Sequence Denied in Barbey's Works   55

With but a slight shift of perspective, the scene becomes a parody of the Last Supper, not in a dining room but in a boudoir, with Don Juan taking the place of Jesus in the center. At his right is the Duchess de ***, "like one of the righteous on the right of God" (2.66). As Berthier recognizes, the twelve, female disciples constitute the "Ladies of Perpetual Adoration" (2.60), and Don Juan modestly accepts their worship. He is "the god of this celebration" (2.66) whose "divine forehead [is] crowned with the roses of so many lips" (2.62). Seated at a round table, they feast their eyes on Don Juan across from them: "They drank him and ate him with their eyes" (2.67). He has become a satanic god, offering himself as wine and bread in a transubstantiated Black Mass. He will soon say explicitly that the woman with whom he was involved when he experienced his "most beautiful love" was rather like the object of practice masses that young priests say without the Eucharistic elements. Don Juan glances around at his charming hostesses "who breathed in this old serpent's words" (2.68) and offers himself as the real thing. "I was the one who was the true Mass, and he then said it sumptuously, like a cardinal, with the appropriate ceremonies" (2.69). As Berthier summarizes, "Ravila's [i.e., Don Juan's] body becomes an altar, on which the erotic service celebrates the mystery of an Incarnation that no longer has anything supernatural about it."[14]

Twelve worldly, cynical, overblown women drinking in Don Juan's story establish a contrast and set off the artless incomprehension of the Marquise, whose child the legendary lover remembers as his "most beautiful love." The Marquise did not understand very much about either her daughter or Don Juan—"She had [...] love; but she lacked the art of love" (2.70). When she had the "imprudence" (2.75) to tell him what had happened with her daughter, she clearly does not grasp the implications. As for Don Juan's audience, "the faces of Cherubs before the throne of God" (2.75), "[t]hey were thoughtful... Had they understood?" (2.79). Earlier when the duchess had insisted on a physical description of the Marquise, Don Juan provides a few details, but he says, "You don't see clearly enough!" At the end of the story, with all the details in hand, the Duchess muses, "If it weren't for that!..." and we know that she understands no better. The key to the enigma is close reading and grounding in the Catholic tradition.

Early in the adventure, the Marquise was not jealous of her daughter, and did not see her as competition. Her only fear was that the girl would make life difficult because Don Juan occupied her time and attentions. As she explained later to Don Juan, "Her instinct tells her that you are taking a portion of her mother's love" (2.73). Certainly the daughter gave every indication of detesting Don Juan, though we eventually learn that it was in fact proof of a young, awkwardly shy adolescent's adoration. At thirteen, the girl only knew that Don Juan could not be interested in her, especially next to her beautiful mother, for she doubtless

56 Sequence Denied in Barbey's Works

considered herself basically uninteresting, without a figure, with nothing to offer. Then came the day that she thought herself pregnant by Don Juan. When the last details were dragged from her, only the most naïve would have laughed, which is, of course, what her mother eventually did on telling the story.

The girl explains,

> Mother, it was in the evening. He was in the big armchair at the corner of the chimney, in front of the love seat. He stayed there for a long time, then got up, and I had the misfortune of going to sit down after him in the chair that he had left. Oh! Mommy!... It was as though I had fallen into the fire. I wanted to get up, I couldn't... my courage failed! and I felt... yes! Mommy... that what I had... it was a baby!.... (2.78)

Don Juan's audience believes that the mother was foolish to tell the story (though it is worth noting that she does not do so until after her daughter's death, when the girl can no longer be a rival), for such a powerful love might have tempted Don Juan to pursue the daughter further. After all, the story's epigraph has posed the situation clearly: "The devil's favorite treat is innocence" (2.59). As Michel Crouzet says, "[T]he 'little minx' ['petite masque'] whose piety and innocence is guaranteed by everything has shown herself the most capable of love, more, the most expert in pleasure."[15] Crouzet thus shares the Duchess' belief that Don Juan would have pursued and consummated her love.

In fact, however, the temptation posed by the girl is quite different from physical pleasure. It is spiritual, like the greatest of temptations and sins. Barbey's works are distinct from those of other writers like Pétrus Borel, Monk Lewis, or Hoffmann, who regale the reader with horrible events, focusing not on the characters' souls but rather on what they do. With Barbey, one should always seek the spiritual context, the hidden corners of their characters, and the mysterious, motivating reality that exists behind the deeds and persons of the stories. Barbey may have been interested in evil deeds, but he was far more interested in the indescribable quality and spell of evil. Only then do we break the sequence and enter the realm of the spirit. We are told early on that Don Juan is "a rugged spiritualist" (2.64); he feeds on the blood of souls (2.60). Despite his commitment to love, it is not primarily the physical sensations that draw him. He is looking rather for something more elemental, more central, something beyond the body, something spiritual, if satanic rather than divine. It is for this reason that Barbey maintained in the legal proceedings against his volume, "This short story is the most spiritual that I have done."[16]

Julia Przybos follows up on this claim and offers a capital insight into parallels between Barbey's adolescent and the Virgin Mary. The story

Sequence Denied in Barbey's Works   57

is heard every Christmas by anyone like Barbey who attended Mass regularly. The angel Gabriel was sent to Mary to explain what was about to happen:

> Fear not, Mary; for thou has found favor with God. And, behold, thou shalt conceive in thy womb, and bring forth a son, and shalt call his name Jesus [...]. Then said Mary unto the angel, How shall this be, seeing I know not a man? And the angel answered, and said unto her. The Holy Spirit shall come upon thee, and the power of the Highest shall overshadow thee; therefore also that holy thing which shall be born of thee shall be called the Son of God. (Luke 1.30–31, 34–35)

In addition, Przybos points out that Barbey's virgin is thirteen, as, according to tradition, was Mary (57). And Mary, a virgin, conceived and bore a son.[17]

Barbey's point of departure for *Les Diaboliques* was his militant Catholicism. In truth, as Jacques Petit says, "Outside of Christianity, ['A un dîner d'athées'] loses all sense" (2.1324). Petit is here discussing just one story, but it is true of each of *Les Diaboliques*. Don Juan is but one example of a collective truth. The notorious lover has sensed and has apparently succumbed to the ultimate temptation. When he hears that the girl thought herself impregnated merely by being near him, his sin is to see himself as though he were empowered like God Himself. As the Holy Spirit visited Mary spiritually, so Don Juan with the little girl. This, of course, was the sin that was responsible for Satan's expulsion from heaven: "Thou hast said in thine heart [...]. I will be like the most High" (Isaiah 14.15). Later, Herod falls into the same temptation. "Upon a set day Herod arrayed in royal apparel, sat upon his throne, and made an oration unto them. And the people gave a shout, 'It is the voice of a god, and not of a man.' And immediately the angel of the Lord smote him, because he gave not God the glory: and he was eaten of worms, and gave up the ghost" (Acts 12.21–23). Where God is a creator, in the Manichean world that Barbey mentions in the preface (2.1291), the devil is his negative—"[H]ell is heaven reversed," one of the narrators observes (2.155). It is consequently not surprising that Don Juan's powerful but inadvertent seduction produces no fruit. Instead of accepting the adulation of his twelve female disciples, instead of reveling in the spiritual high from his imitation of an act of God, by rendering a maid pregnant without physical intercourse (or so the little girl imagined), Don Juan should have refused the ego-driven comparison to God, the Father. He did not, however, turn away, and he is condemned, not like Herod to serve as a feast of worms, but to continue living into an impotent old age remorseful over lost virility. In fact, Don Juan has had the traditional roles reversed. Although he may have unknowingly seduced the girl, it

58   Sequence Denied in Barbey's Works

is far more important to recognize that through her perception of his powers she has seduced him, for he entertains the temptation to godhead she represents. Another, similar episode occurs in "La Vengeance d'une femme." The Duchess de Sierra-Leone was also adored "like a Madonna in her golden niche" (2.250), when she allows Esteban to be "at my feet, before me, as though he were before the Virgin Mary" (2.251), and the love of her life will shortly be murdered, his heart eaten by dogs, and the duchess committed to vengeance through prostitution and adultery, thus, mortal sin.

It is important to examine the substance of each story in *Les Diaboliques* carefully. Only then will the whole tableau become clear. In fact, following Barbey's hints and clues, one can occasionally push beyond earlier critics and propose answers and solutions to the author's enigmas. "Le Dessous de cartes d'une partie de whist," the second of Barbey's stories considered here, explicitly answers a few questions.[18] The Chevalier de Tharsis tells us, for example, that the Countess du Tremblay de Stasseville was Marmor's mistress. It all takes place in a story the narrator recounts about a mysterious Scottish whist champion, Marmor de Karkoël, who arrives in a small provincial town, and of the tragedy that mysteriously befalls the mother (La Comtesse du Tremblay de Stasseville) and daughter (Herminie) who, we eventually learn, both love him. According to Barbey, the tale describes "the horror that the countess de Stasseville's subterranean passion inspires, revealed by this appalling conclusion and revealed by *that alone*" (2.1289). In truth, the author has over-simplified. Although the *fact* of a crime is revealed by the discovery of the "the body of an infant that was born alive!" and buried in a parlor planter (2.169), the crime can only be unraveled by considering a number of clues: a diamond ring, Herminie's racking cough, Marmor's departure, the deaths, the trump card, the queen of diamonds, and the reseda plant, also known as mignonette and love herb (*l'herbe d'amour*). Although the Chevalier de Tharsis says the story is "very obscure" (2.167) and adds that the child's parentage "will always be a mystery" (2.169), such discouraging pronouncements serve as challenges. A little thought will resolve most of the mysteriousness. The conviction (solution) may be based on circumstantial evidence (Vassilev and others maintain it remains a mystery),[19] but readers have far more proof than is common in many cases brought before a jury.

The narrator who hesitantly and, in the end, inconclusively conducts the investigation, as narratee and witness, is never named, though he resembles all the worldly narrators of *Les Diaboliques*. Nor does he identify the town where the murders happen. Still, like Valognes, where Barbey was raised, it is dying. Given the importance of the nobles living there, it signals the death of the aristocracy. "[T]his burrow inhabited by nobles" (2.148) is "the most profoundly and ferociously aristocratic in France" (2.134). Those who have settled there are notable for their

Sequence Denied in Barbey's Works   59

adamant stance against misalliances. As a result, of course, the noble young women who were impoverished by the Revolution lack fortune and dowry and will never marry, but rather will grow into a proud but virginal old age. Their youthful beauty is useless (2.134). That the town is too small for a theatre and that the cafés are vile are but further indications that the aristocracy stands on the brink of the grave. The nobles stay behind their walls, and many live in poverty seemingly relieved only by sporadic conversation and the mutual pleasures of cards, where each person is played off against others. The underlying pattern of sex and murder cannot be hidden, however. Minor signs float on the surface, while vanity and boredom foment a nice little scandal in this "nest of nobles" that no court of justice will ever hear (2.134). It will be secreted behind the facades of their fortresses, but only for a while. Silence and mask-like, indecipherable countenances characterize the town's preeminent citizens and elicit an understanding of why murder is possible.

Like the town's walled compounds, the characters of Marmor de Karkoël and Madame de Stasseville are difficult to penetrate. "Their attitudes and faces corresponded to each other, so that what I had dared think was [apparently] impossible!" (2.163). Marmor is around twenty-eight years old, with facial features that form a fixed, inscrutable mask and make him appear to be thirty-five. There is something sinister about him, as though he wants to set aside remorse, but no one ever knows, since he never talks of his past (2.140). He is tanned, however, for he has traveled well beyond foggy Scotland to India. Short but extraordinarily vigorous and athletic, his fashionable attire makes him appear to be a "tiger in a velvet skin" (141). Some will remember the adage that "un tigre de change pas de rayures" ['a tiger does not change its stripes']. By equating him with "a silent Cleveland" (2.150), Barbey alludes to Walter Scott's buccaneer in *The Pirate* of 1821, who had good reason to hide his early history and who was fully capable of the most desperate acts. Marmor, the "god of *slam*" (2.167), is a master at cards and, like Cleveland, of life. "Slam" is, of course, the English word for the French "chelem," or "win." The anglophile locals use the more fashionable English version.

The aristocratic residents of this provincial town are especially dedicated to playing whist, a card game of enormous popularity in nineteenth-century France. Barbey's choice of this game is thus not a randomly chosen detail but rather an integral part of the society and of the complex that reveals hidden images behind the masks. It was known as a game that attracted players of considerable intelligence, who had great powers of concentration and analysis.[20] Although there are a number of variations, the most common rules for whist involve the numbers of tricks taken by four players, split into two partnerships. Thirteen cards are dealt to each player. When the dealer receives his final card and turns it up, it indicates the trump suit. Barbey's players have adopted the

60   Sequence Denied in Barbey's Works

game because it is dignified, silent, and contained, rather like their own existence and that of their town. They use it to fill "their empty lives" (2.138).

The primary clues to the mysterious but sordid reality at the heart of the story occur during a game of whist. Madame de Stasseville gives every indication of gloating when she flings (*jeta*) down a ring, so that her companions might inspect the stone. The narrator had previously seen Marmor fill the ring's secret compartment with poison. The latter had likewise flung (*jeta*) this ring in a drawer when the narrator caught him filling it (2.163). The repetition of the verb *jeter* emphasizes the connection between the events and, in both cases, the characters give the impression of a certain insouciance, as though wishing to hide its importance from the narrator. Marmor nonetheless describes its slow but mortal effect:

> You won't lose anything in waiting; its efficacy is as sure as it is hidden. It attacks life at its roots slowly, almost languorously, but unfailingly, by penetrating and developing in the depths of the organs which it affects, like these illnesses known to everyone, whose symptoms are familiar to science, thus diverting suspicion and providing an answer should there be an accusation of poisoning. (2.161–62)

The narrator is reminded of the poison while considering "Herminie's suffering face, her pallor, this cough that seems to come from sponge-like, soft lungs that were already being poisoned by deep lesions that medicine calls [...] *cavitations*" (2.163). By some inexplicable coincidence the flash of the ring's diamond attracts attention as the girl coughs, and Madame de Stasseville explains, "It is my diamond and my daughter" (2.159). In passing, readers might wonder how it becomes "her" diamond, since it seemed to be Marmor's ring when the narrator previously saw it. The narrator subsequently highlights the link by noting that the Marquis de Saint-Albans is more concerned "with the human diamond than with the mineral diamond" (2.160). Madame de Stasseville shows no evidence of sharing his solicitude. Indeed, it will later be revealed that she has inexplicably come to hate her daughter (2.167).

Years later the narrator learned that Madame de Stasseville and Marmor were lovers. Given the woman's ways with him—"she fired the kinds of words that whistle and pierce"—readers are forced to ask with the author, "Why, if she loved Karkoël and if she was loved, why did she hide it under the ridicule that she threw at him from time to time in the form of apostate, renegade, impious pleasantries that degrade the adored idol... the greatest sacrileges in love?" (2.153). Such blatant attacks rendered it difficult to believe that she loved Marmor, and what we know of the Scotsman makes it unlikely that he could be reduced to abject servility, subject to her demeaning barbs. Her neighbors' belief

Sequence Denied in Barbey's Works   61

that she never entertained him at her chateau and only "very publicly" in her town house (2.153) had long been considered an indication of her disinterest. The narrator explains that any widow who is also the mother of a charming girl would be very careful about inviting a bachelor home since gossip could be very damaging (2.153), and the possibility of surprising accidents, like Herminie's pregnancy, can also not be denied.

The final outcome, according to the Chevalier de Tharsis, was a planter of reseda in which was discovered an infant's dead body that was not stillborn but "had lived" (2.169). "[T]he god of *slam* had *slammed* the entire family" (2.167), he says. The Chevalier tells us that Madame de Stasseville was Marmor's mistress (2.166); yet the phrase, "that he had *slammed* the entire family" ('toute la famille'), opens the possibility that he was involved in the murders of Herminie and the baby as well. Should one surmise from this statement that while pursuing an affair with Madame de Stasseville, the Scot had seduced Herminie, killed the resultant baby, poisoned Herminie (2.167), and subsequently had done away with the mother, as well?

Many critics have weighed in on assigning guilt and motive with varying opinions. Petit offers two other explanations in his *Essais de lectures des* Diaboliques: first, Madame de Stasseville sought vengeance by murdering both the child and the daughter, thus eliminating her rival, Marmor's complicity being unimportant. Or, second, there was no revenge involved, but rather an unwelcome pregnancy on the part of Madame de Stasseville, the baby's mother. Le Corbeiller also claims that Madame de Stasseville killed the infant, though Berthier calls this "[a]n absolutely gratuitous affirmation" (*Imagination* 295). B. G. Rogers explains Madame de Stasseville's death as a suicide. He later decides, however, that her death is shrouded in mystery like the others (227, 267). Several scholars have suggested that Herminie murdered her own baby at the behest of her mother and, thus, have covered up the pre-marital affair. None of these explanations consider all aspects of the story's deadly game, as will be clear from what follows. The new, maternal enmity makes it very likely that the baby is Herminie's, as Jacques Petit declares without supporting his conclusion (*Essais* 58). Berthier arrives at the same finding by different means. After considering this story in conjunction with "Le Plus Bel Amour de don Juan" and *Une Histoire sans nom* [*A Story without a Name*], he concludes that the example of other of Barbey's creations, plus an interrogating mother and tears indicate a pregnant daughter (*Imagination* 295). With considerable hesitation, Michèle Raclot likewise agrees that the child is Herminie's. Furthermore, she correctly points out that the cadaver "imposes the idea of an assassination."[21] Michel H. Philip joins in by pronouncing without textual support that Madame de Stasseville interred her own love child in the love-herb planter.[22] Pierre Tranouez says, however, that we do not know the infant corpse's mother.[23] Finally, there is no evidence that

62 Sequence Denied in Barbey's Works

Madame de Stasseville committed suicide, as Petit suggests (*Essais* 60, 111). To the contrary, what the narrator tells us of her willfully assertive, domineering character makes suicide seem improbable.

Close reading of the text brings much more comprehension. Madame de Stasseville and Marmor's public demeanor with each other was, for the most part, cold but polite. For some four years, her caution and his habitually taciturn reserve allowed them to veil their affair with mendacious hypocrisy, while enjoying intense but secret sensual pleasures "which go as far as the supernatural" (2.155). Her "fascinating scales and triple, serpentine tongue" were accompanied by extreme prudence (2.153). "When, after having fired one of these pleasantries, one of these sparkling barbs as fine as poisoned fish bones, [...] she passed the tip of her viperous tongue over her sibilant lips" (2.154). The repeated references to Madame de Stasseville's serpentine tongue leave no doubt of her relationship to the Edenic snake. Nonetheless, when the young narrator subsequently returns to the town, the little society seems to accept that Marmor and Madame de Stasseville have had a torrid affair, though one wonders why she treats him so poorly. The pair's impenetrable masks finally hinted at their true relationship played out "beneath the cards," though the parentage of the child still remained a mystery.

Barbey points out that Herminie's mother was in this period fond of tuberoses, known to be fatal for women giving birth (2.168). We do not know for certain whether Barbey chose to reveal the Countess de Stasseville's age because he accepted the common misconception that women could not become pregnant when they were over forty (2.144). (Napoléon doubtless shared this belief and waited until the childless Joséphine had passed that age before divorcing her.) If Barbey did not believe in quadragenarian infertility, he certainly knew that contraception was widely used among the upper classes, whether *coitus interruptus* or condoms fashioned from the small intestines of sheep, and was expected of sexually active, mature people of the eighteenth and nineteenth centuries.[24] If the infant were the countess's child, there would be no reason for her to be so jealous and to hate Herminie so vehemently (2.167). Clearly, the girl has become a rival, a rivalry unmasked for the mother by the girl's pregnancy.

Given Herminie's "silent" love, the mother's hatred, and the daughter's extreme pallor and tears, the latter's pregnancy is the most likely cause. When the girl's condition becomes evident within the Stasseville mansion, it would only be reasonable for the daughter to insist on marrying the countess's errant lover and, moreover, to be importunate in her demands. After all, at twenty-eight years of age, Marmor would make a far more suitable mate for the daughter than he would for her forty-some-year-old mother. Furthermore, the girl clearly loves Marmor (2.167–68). Thanks to the maids, we learn of the hours-long sessions from which mother and daughter "came out each paler than the other,

Sequence Denied in Barbey's Works 63

but the daughter always the more red-eyed and tearful" (2.167). One can only imagine what mother and daughter said during these confrontations. Did Herminie threaten to reveal the *ménage à trois*? Given what later happens to her, she may have become so strident that it was necessary to do away with her. She was in a desperate situation.

Although late eighteenth- and early nineteenth-century novels are replete with upper-class girls who marry despite previous affairs and illegitimate children, such marriages would have been very difficult to arrange in the real world. Unquestionably, some of the numerous infants left in foundling homes can be explained by a desire to dispose of embarrassing evidence. Herminie's possibility of marriage to anyone other than Karkoël would be highly unlikely. The Chevalier de Tharsis does not know how appropriately he speaks when he notes, "[T]he mother [...] had begun to hate her daughter, which contributed more than a little to her death" (2.167). Although Mme de Stasseville's feelings about her daughter are obvious, there is no textual evidence that Herminie died by her mother's hand. The readily available and much simpler solution proposed below remains.

For Herminie to marry Marmor was especially impossible because the mother would have refused to relinquish her hold over him, as the story points out unequivocally: "The mocking countess du Tremblay was far too proud to sacrifice a single one of her caprices to public opinion" (2.147). How much less will she bow to the desires of a daughter she hates. Furthermore, given that Madame de Stasseville has an "all powerful will" (156) and now is in competition with her daughter, the girl has no hope of benefitting from a future fortune capable of preserving her from the fate of other young, dowerless women of the town. Because the legal code and religious rule give Madame de Stasseville close to absolute control over the daughter, she has no reason to kill the girl, who can be sidelined in other ways. Most easily, a small dowry to a local convent would have put the underage girl out of sight and mind. Forcing her complicitus silence in the meantime is quite another affair. Madame de Stasseville's animosity over the contested Karkoël might have encouraged her to leave her sizeable fortune uniquely to her son, mentioned in passing, thus disinheriting the daughter and making her an undesirable mate for Marmor. Although at the time such a will would have been illegal, prejudicial primogeniture inheritance could be effected in many different ways, as Balzac made clear in *La Rabouilleuse* (1842) and Zola in *Fécondité* (1899).

Primogeniture was a subject of considerable discussion in the 1820s when the story was set, and Barbey pertinently brings up the issue (2.165–66). Although Jean-Baptiste Villèle, president of the Counsel, had attempted to establish the right of the eldest to inherit the family fortune, he failed in the midst of considerable controversy, and was forced to resign in 1828. Marmor, obliged to live on the half-pay of a retired

64 *Sequence Denied in Barbey's Works*

infantry officer, supplemented by his winnings at whist (2.156), cannot have failed to have had a very clear understanding that the widow was in control of her fortune. His need to supplement his military emolument with winnings from whist makes it virtually inconceivable that he would have considered marrying a disinherited daughter, however attractive. If, as seems likely, Herminie was pressing her claims on the impecunious and thus unwilling Marmor, it would have become even more important to silence her. The baby was easily and quickly disposable shortly after birth, and marrying the girl would condemn him to poverty.

When the narrator catches him in the act of filling the ring with a powerful poison he had brought back from India, the Scotsman explains its unfailing power (2.161–62). Because the death it causes so resembles a common illness (2.162), probably tuberculosis, no one would bring the accusation of poisoning (2.162), but if we recollect the details of Herminie's illness and death, it is likely that she has been poisoned by the means Marmor describes. In short, she is a "victim of a languorous illness" (2.165). As Marmor informs the narrator, the poison constitutes "a resource against everything" (2.161). It provides the means for a desperate act by a man able to "brush aside remorse" (2.140), and he appears to be capable of doing whatever is necessary to protect his relationship and potential marriage with Madame de Stasseville or, very simply, to protect himself. The poison-filled ring's repeated appearance signals it as a crucial element in the story. The mother clearly knows of the baby's death. She appropriates the glittering diamond as proof of Karkoël's perfidious affair with her daughter and his murderous guilt in the death of both infant and, given the ring's role in the daughter's slow-motion murder, Herminie.

Several scholars have suggested that Herminie murdered her own baby, yet this is unlikely, regardless of how much her mother might have wished her to cover up the pre-marital affair. The baby is Herminie's one weapon to force marriage to Marmor, and it is consequently doubtful that she killed the child. If the infant had been allowed to live without the daughter's marriage, however, it would have represented a continuing danger to Marmor and of embarrassment for Madame de Stasseville. This is an offspring that would have rendered Herminie's marriage to someone other than Marmor difficult, if not impossible, whatever her fortune and beauty. Furthermore, it would have been a continuing interference in Madame's pleasures. The baby would also have revealed the sordid story of mother and daughter sharing the same lover, as it did later, when the corpse was discovered.

During this period in France, before abortion became easily available, infanticide was by no means unheard of. As Barbey commented in *Une Histoire sans nom*, "[T]he crime, this crime of abortion and infanticide [...] has become so abominably frequent in the current state of our contemptible behavior, [...] that it could be called: *The crime of the nineteenth century*" (emphasis in text, 2.325). While it is not certain that the baby was murdered, since infantile mortality was very high,[25] the possibility of infanticide is textually raised when the narrator mentions exposing children on the Yellow (or Blue) river in China (2.147). The countess's emerald green eyes are moreover so cold that they remind the narrator of the bejeweled ring belonging to Polycrates (2.145), who took power over Samos with the aid of his two brothers, after which he killed one and exiled the other. The mythological ring also hints at the power of Madame de Stasseville's "subterranean passion" (2.1289) and signifies that something very wrong is taking place behind the doors of her home. Her indomitable will and self-control have already been mentioned, implying that Madame de Stasseville is capable of any action necessary to serve her self-interest (145).

The concatenation of images during the "*diamond hand*," the focal point of the game of whist (2.166), has considerable importance. In addition to the "homicidal stone" (2.163) and Herminie's "dreadful cough" (160), there is also the reseda that Mme de Stasseville "seized with her thin, colorless lips [...] and ground with her teeth accompanied by a wild, idolatrous expression as she looked wide-eyed at Karkoël" (164). The narrator takes "these chewed flowers devoured in silence" as a sign of their wordless, lascivious complicity, though he is ashamed of his thoughts on watching "the countess's expression of crystalline calm, melting momentarily in the sensation of the resedas that she breathed in and ground up with an almost voluptuous expression" (2.164–65). Her lips have already been compared to hydrangeas, which in the "language of flowers" have long represented "boastfulness and frigidity."[26]

Readers are encouraged to suspect that she especially emanates menace. Not only does the countess hold the ring, the weapon that served to kill her daughter, but she knows of the infant's body buried in the reseda planter. We understand that she never felt sufficient remorse or repentance to confess to the priest, since he would have removed the baby from its resting place to give it burial in holy ground. And, more important, in verbally lacerating Marmor with insults and ridicule as a means of subjecting him to her control, thus unquestionably degrading their love, she leaves no doubt that she has the upper hand (2.153). Her fierce mastication of the love herb growing above her daughter's love child may have signaled both Madame de Stasseville's passionate, vengeful love and her hatred arising from full comprehension of his self-serving, murderous deeds, which, she thought, gave her the upper hand and control. She knew the baby's resting place and had acquired the ring. Too proud to submit to her domination, he decided to eliminate his former mistress. The game was over, as Marmor recognized. He nonetheless had one last card to play. He held the trump card, and he had the poison.

The final clue lies in front of Karkoël at the card table. Used to dominating (2.152), he now appears unable to quell the power of the

66 Sequence Denied in Barbey's Works

ruthless woman who does not hesitate to mark her authority with cutting, demeaning banter that is mentioned on two occasions (2.144, 168). For good reason, she is called *"madame de Givre"* ['Madam Frost'] (2.156). "Nothing, then, altered the ferocious brilliance and use of her apostate, renegade, impious pleasantries that degrade the adored idol... the greatest sacrileges in love" (2.153). She, after all, has been betrayed by both Marmor and her daughter. As the implacable Madame de Stasseville tosses the diamond to the chevalier, her lover looks vaguely at the trump card, the queen of diamonds (2.160). Moments pass while the text dwells on the ring, Herminie's cough, and the anthropophagic countess chewing the reseda she has taken from her funereal planter. She begins to smell the resedas with "sensuality you would certainly not have expected with a woman like her" (164). While she might have murdered the baby, it seems improbable, since at any point an anonymous trip to a foundling home would have without danger disposed of the child. The ruthless Marmor likely took care of the issue as soon after the birth as possible, perhaps while the mother was involved in the daughter's childbearing and before the servants noticed the activity. Madame de Stasseville's knowledge, nonetheless, marks her as also culpable.

The narrator remembers, "I have never forgotten the wild and almost amorously cruel way she breathed and ate the flowers of her bouquet during this game of whist" (2.168), and he notes that something changes in Marmor. "He continued to look at the queen of diamonds as though it represented the last, definitive love of his entire life" (2.165). Marmor apparently has a sudden, penetrating understanding of his mistress, for the next time the narrator describes him, he has become "as black and tenebrous as the night" (2.165). The queen of diamonds trump card that he displays on the table before him represents the powerful, beringed whister across the table. Her knowledge of his guilty role seems to hand him into her power. She owns him. Revolting against the wealthy Madame de Stasseville's domination, however, he abandons all thought of marriage, and decides instead to murder her. Fully aware of the poison's potential, Marmor exploits what he earlier called "the marked cards with which you are certain to win the last hand against destiny" (2.161). The countess believes she holds absolute authority over Marmor, authority symbolized by her possession of the murder weapon, by the knowledge of the burial place of his child, and by the queen of diamonds, indicating the trump suit. She believes she is the queen of diamonds. Unfortunately for her, however, both ring and trump card belong to her lover. It is *his* ring and *his* "queen of diamonds" (2.160). Soon Marmor will leave, and she will die as does her daughter "of a pulmonary illness [...] one month after the departure of the devil of a Marmor de Karkoël" (2.166). Though both Marmor and Mme de Stasseville are immoral, it is the girl, a *diabolique*, who has brought Marmor to the "grand slam" of killing the baby, her, and Madam de Stasseville.

Sequence Denied in Barbey's Works   67

Barbey implicitly expects the reader to become a sleuth, but no one clue is capable of bringing unequivocal conviction in this case. To fathom the secret story the author tells, one must plumb each bit of evidence in the context of the entire short story, whether trump card, or cough, or diamond, or reseda, or the poison itself, or the change in the mother-daughter relationship, or the menacing change in Marmor's demeanor. Once this has taken place, it seems clear that no other solution can explain all of the salient details, and no other pattern will satisfactorily include every aspect of the story and reveal what Barbey would call a wicked, indeed diabolical reality. As the baroness de Mascranny broke "off a very innocent rose's flower" (2.171), so Herminie, the *"Rose of Stasseville"* (160), and her baby die. The heinous nature of the relationships that the narrator perceives percolating beneath the surface explains the horror that causes him to repress his suspicions and leave his questions unasked (2.165, 167). By his silence, like that of Dr. Torty of "Le Bonheur dans le crime" ['Happiness in Crime'], he becomes an accomplice and thus shares the guilt of the murderers. Just as in "Le Plus Bel Amour de Don Juan," where a thirteen-year-old girl seduces Don Juan and brings him to irremediable condemnation, "Le Dessous de cartes d'une partie de whist" ends with three people, Madame the Countess du Tremblay de Stasseville, her daughter, the *diabolique* Herminie, and Marmor de Karkoël involved a series of murders. For all her innocence, Herminie has become the means bringing both her mother and her lover to damnation.

Only the image of the *diabolique* as a satanic tool provides a satisfying focus for this and for each of the other stories. When readers pay close attention to the clues that indicate the devil's work, they easily perceive other elements that strengthen the analogical structuring which provides cohesion to the volume. In the process, they join with Barbey in the story's creation. Patterns of themes and images change position and emphasis in various stories, but as they are repeated, they strengthen the whole. A narrator's breezy worldliness remains a constant in every story, and each of the stories turns on a triangular relationship between lover, *diabolique*, and victim(s). Sex is essential to each. If one sees Barbey's pervasive underpinning and orientation toward his church and his faith, most of the otherwise intractable problems with *Les Diaboliques* fall away. However profound our understanding of Barbey's characters, only this religious context explains their evil. Only a very real and active demonic power undermining and directing the play happening "beneath the cards" can explain such actions. As though through frosted glass, the reader observes the unchained Satan manipulating Herminie, Madame de Stasseville, and Marmor under the surface until they commit murder, just as he pulled the strings of the other main characters in *Les Diaboliques*, and we are left with a magnificently unified cycle of stories.

68 *Sequence Denied in Barbey's Works*

There are several lessons to be learned from "Le Dessous de cartes d'une partie de whist." The first is a response to the legions of critics that have claimed with apparent impatience that the daughter is not diabolical, to the contrary innocent and pure, and that furthermore nothing happens. I would say rather that Barbey portrays her as a *diabolique* because she serves however unintentionally as a means, a device, and a tool for Satan to drag others into the pit. Particularly in regard to the two stories considered here, the sequences are unimportant, for they are subsumed by the diabolical morass beneath the apparently calm surface of the town's nobility. Not only did Barbey render them difficult to decipher with the multiple narrators, it is only after having understood the depths of evil that it becomes possible to untangle the chronology. Just as images can have subordinate importance in sequential structures, so the series of murders in "Le Dessous de cartes" seem inconsequential in the light of what Barbey called "the horror that this subterranean passion inspired" (2.1289). When Satan's evil activities are brought from behind the obscure glass and displayed in the glare of clear light, it is the essence of the iniquity that has importance, rather than the process of its taking place. What matters is the osmotic pattern of evil that underlays Don Juan, on the one hand, and the little, unnamed town where so many murders occurred, on the other. The evil even reaches the narrator, because he becomes an accomplice on covering up what facts he knows. The diabolical heroines of all the stories in *Les Diaboliques* act in the same way. Just as the thirteen-year-old girl seduces Don Juan into perdition, so Alberte tempts Brassard into cowardice and the betrayal of hospitality, and Hauteclaire de Stassin subjugates Serlon. Not only is she diabolically superior in the male sport of fencing, she poisons Mme de Savigny, thus encouraging Serlon, the countess, and Dr. Torty to keep silent and act as accessories to murder. All three are then guilty both before the law of capital crimes and before God for breaking one of the Ten Commandments.

We do not know in every case exposed in *Les Diaboliques* what punishment was meted out to those ensnared by the *diaboliques*, although it is clear that like many of Pirandello's characters, they change. Brassard is reduced to being nothing but an ineffective pretty boy, for all his courage in battle. Tressignies, who was once delightfully joyous, became "somber" (2.261). "From somber he became sick. His complexion turned leaden" (2.261). The impotent Don Juan is kept alive by order of God himself, perhaps as punishment for his many sins now that he is reduced to a permanent sense of regret and loss, recalling former conquests with no prospect of engaging in new ones. Elsewhere Barbey quotes Saint Theresa: "I die from not being able to die!" (2.250). Ménilgrand loses his zest for life, and like Brassard relinquishes his military career. We have no knowledge about the ultimate disposition of Hauteclaire, Serlon, or Torty, in "Le Bonheur dans le crime," or about

Sequence Denied in Barbey's Works   69

Marmor de Karkoël. Nor do we know the fate of two other *diaboliques*, Hauteclaire and La Pudica. Clearly, the culminating destiny of these personages is not central to the meaning of *Les Diaboliques*. What matters is the damning means and motives.

At some point, readers of good will accept the author at his word and finally grasp the essential fact that *Les Diaboliques* advances: every single *diabolique* serves Satan. Whether or not she is aware of her function, because of her innocence, as Barbey put it in his preface to the first edition, she is a "means." She then reveals the Devil himself in that she exemplifies his "use of the simplest means." There are many clues to this mysterious, satanic force, which is vitally active in the background and which, for Barbey, provides the only possible explanation of pure evil. Despite the principal female characters' lack of worldly experience in *Les Diaboliques*, they lead others into crime and sin, indeed inescapably into hell itself. Eugène Grelé charges that Barbey's devil is but a facile method of avoiding psychological depth, "*Satanas ex machine.*"[27] To the contrary, both psychology and diabolism are important for Barbey, though I suspect the author hoped his reader would perceive Satan only after conceding that probing psychological analysis cannot account for unmitigated evil. The devil rises to the surface of the reader's perceptions only after psychology reveals its inadequacy before such wickedness.

Of the images that reorder themselves in the reader's mind, only that of a *diabolique* as a means or tool produces a satisfying focus that occurs in all of the stories and ties them together in a thematic whole. It joins with a narrator's lively worldliness, the triangular, sexual relationship between lover, *diabolique*, and victim(s), and Barbey's pervasive commitment to his church and its traditions. With that in mind, it becomes a simple matter to point to other elements that strengthen the analogical structuring that gives the volume such cohesion. They twist like a kaleidoscope with a dominant color, each of the stories arranging the same and related pieces of "color" into differing configurations. Sequences of themes and images shift in position and emphasis throughout the various stories, but, by their repetition, strengthen the entire *Les Diaboliques* and the evil, "subterranean" world that exists beneath easily perceptible reality.

The stories are at best vague until the reader partners with the author and adds the additional level of analogy. Prior to that moment, the deaths have little direction, hidden motivation, and freedom from condemnation. Like most popular authors, Barbey tells a good story, though the frustration of so many critics and scholars with the enigmatic tales comes from the suspicion that there is something elusive and intractable taking place. In general, they are bothered by the fact that the stories apparently lack motivation and do not seem to fit together. In effect, Barbey helps faltering readers by revealing the unifying theme in the early preface: he wants to warn readers of a controlling, spiritual force hidden from view that dominates and destroys men. And this

70 *Sequence Denied in Barbey's Works*

force is Satan. Barbey's analogical images rising above each of his stories seem to say that the satanic reality in his tales is similar to the Devil's concealed, powerful, and evil work in our world. Until the reader takes an active role, forcing his mind to perceive the analogical level of the various devilish revelations of sin made tangible, he will remain ignorant and frustrated. Only as the reader reads closely and discovers the spiritual similarities will Satan take form and consistency. Barbey depicts a powerful devil everywhere, whether his means are obvious or not, indeed whether the feminine tools he exploits are aware that he is pulling their strings. The very real danger confronting spiritual evil is that it can evolve into degradation, destruction, and damnation. For Barbey, no one is safe.

Notes

1 Jacques Petit, ed. *Œuvres romanesques complètes*, by Barbey d'Aurevilly, 2 vols., Bibliothèque de la Pléiade, (Paris: Gallimard, 1964, 1966) 2.1275. All references to *Les Diaboliques*, to Barbey's preface to the 1874 edition, and to Petit's "Notice" are to volume 2 of this edition.

2 Jacques-Henry Bornecque, *Les Diaboliques*, by Barbey d'Aurevilly (Paris: Garnier, 1963) xcvii.

3 Anne Giard, "Le Récit lacunaire dans *les Diaboliques*," *Poétique* 41 (1980): 39.

4 Jacques Petit, "Note sur la structure des *Diaboliques*," *Revue des Lettres Modernes* 199–202 (1969): 88.

5 Julien Gracq, "Préface," *Les Diaboliques*, by Barbey d'Aurevilly (Paris: Livre de Poche, 1960) 3.

6 Jacques Petit, *Essais de lectures des* Diaboliques *de Barbey d'Aurevilly* (Paris: Lettres Modernes Minard, 1974) 33.

7 Philippe Berthier, "L'Ensorcelée," Les Diaboliques *de Barbey d'Aurevilly* (Paris: Champion, 1987) 102.

8 Gisle Corbière-Gille, "*Les Diaboliques* dans le domaine anglo-saxon," *Revue des Lettres Modernes* 403–08 (1974): 114.

9 B. G. Rogers, *The Novels and Stories of Barbey d'Aurevilly* (Geneva: Droz, 1967) 112.

10 Bornecque, *Les Diaboliques* c.

11 Philippe Berthier, "*Les Diaboliques* et la critique française," *Revue des Lettres Modernes* 403–08 (1974): 92. For Jean-Paul Bonnes, it is "doubtless the least interesting of these stories and [...] the least diabolical"— *Le Bonheur du masque: Petite Introduction aux romans de Barbey d'Aurevilly* (Tournai: Casterman, 1947) 99.

12 Armand Le Corbeiller, Les Diaboliques *de Barbey d'Aurevilly* (Paris: Malfère, 1939) 93. Philippe Berthier is just as blunt: "Where is the devil?"—"L'Ensorcelée," *Les Diaboliques de Barbey d'Aurevilly: Une Ecriture du désir* (Paris: Champion, 1987) 117. His more accurate response concerns the entire collection: "[T]he devil is nowhere because you breathe him everywhere, infused in the beings that furiously listen together to the sirens from the bottom or down there" (119).

13 For echoes of Delacroix, see Bornecque 79n1; Petit, *Œuvres romanesques* 2.1305n2. For Petit, the image of Sardanapalus' pyre is simply the "triumphant image of destruction" (*Essais* 111), but as Patrick Brady has

Sequence Denied in Barbey's Works   71

pointed out in detail, the painting turns around impotence: *Interdisciplinary Interpretation of Art and Literature: The Principle of Convergence* (Knoxville: New Paradigm Press, 1996) ch. 2.

14 In respect to this erotic mass, I have followed the arguments of Marie-Claire Ropars-Wuilleumier, "'Le Plus Bel Amour de Don Juan': Narration et signification," *Littérature* 9 (1973): 118–19; Jean-Pierre Boucher, *Les Diaboliques de Barbey d'Aurevilly: Une Esthétique de la dissimulation et de la provocation* (Montréal: P de l'U du Québec, 1976) 52; Philippe Berthier, "Les Diaboliques: table," *Barbey d'Aurevilly: L'Ensorcelée et les Diaboliques: La Chose sans nom*, Actes du Colloque du 16 janvier 1988 (Paris: SEDES, 1988) 134–35.

15 Michel Crouzet, "Barbey d'Aurevilly et l'oxymore: ou La Rhétorique du diable," *La Chose sans nom* 88.

16 Jules Barbey d'Aurevilly "Le 'Procès' des Diaboliques," ed. André Hirschi, *Revue des Lettres Modernes* 403–08 (1974): 19.

17 Julia Przybos, "'Le Plus Bel Amour de Don Juan' or a Child's Phantom Pregnancy," *Notebook in Cultural Analysis* 2 (1985): 56–57.

18 The story was first published in *La Mode* in 1850 and eventually made its way into *Les Diaboliques* (1874).

19 Kris Vassilev, "Histoire et fiction dans 'Le Dessous de cartes d'une partie de whist' de Barbey," *Neophilologus* 93.4 (2009): 599. Thomas M. Kavanagh claims the story proposes an "impenetrable mystery"—"Whist, or the Aristocracy of Mystery: Barbey d'Aurevilly's 'Beneath the Cards in a Game of Whist'," *Dice, Cards, Wheels: A Different History of French Culture* (Philadelphia: U of Pennsylvania P, 2005) 164. The Larousse *Grand Dictionnaire universel du XIXe siècle*, 17 vols. (Paris: Larousse et Boyer, 1866–90) has also been helpful.

20 Philippe Berthier, *Barbey d'Aurevilly et l'imagination* (Geneva: Droz, 1978) 276n120.

21 Michèle Raclot, "L'Enfant mort," *Travaux de Littérature* 5 (1992): 251–52.

22 Michel H. Philip, "Le Satanisme des *Diaboliques*," *Etudes françaises* 4 (1968): 73.

23 Pierre Tranouez, *Fascination et narration dans l'œuvre de Barbey d'Aurevilly: la scène capitale* (Paris: Lettres Modernes Minard, 1987) 44.

24 Jacqueline Hecht, "Forum: From 'Be Fruitful and Multiply' to Family Planning: The Enlightenment Transition," *Eighteenth-Century Studies* 22.4 (1999): 536–51; Christine Théré, "Women and Birth Control in Eighteenth-Century France," *Eighteenth-Century Studies* 22.4 (1999): 552–64; François Lebrun, "Les Débuts de la contraception," *L'Histoire* 63 (1984): 28–31; Etienne van de Walle, *Motivations and Technology in the Decline of French Fertility* (Philadelphia: U of Pennsylvania P, 1980): 135–78.

25 The subject of infanticide regularly comes up in Barbey's work. See, Raclot (249–65) and Petit, "L'Enfant mort et la naissance du héros," *Revue des Lettres Modernes*, 600–604 (1981): 67–83). Still, in the mid-nineteenth century the death rate among infants during the first year was very high, though statistics are unreliable. See Jacques Dupâquier, *Histoire de la population française* II (Paris: P.U.F., 1988) 221–23.

26 Ernst and Johanna Lehner, *Folklore and Symbolism of Flowers, Plants and Trees* (New York: Tudor, 1960) 118.

27 Eugène Grelé, *Jules Barbey d'Aurevilly: sa vie et son œuvre d'après sa correspondance inédite et autres documents nouveaux*, 2 vols. (Paris: Champion, 1904) 2.123. Grelé does admit that Barbey's belief in Satan is an integral part of his religion and that his work would have been impossible without his intense Catholicism (pp. 121–23).

5 Sequence Framed in Mérimée's "Carmen"

Of late, considerable importance has been attributed to the structure of the "modern short story," which is taken to depend on "paroxysm," "focus," "reduced spatial field," "enclosed space," "economy," "fragment," or "epiphany." These and other related terms appear with surprising frequency, as theorists devote themselves to describing this variety of recent brief fictions.[1] Although critics are by no means unanimous about when the short story became "modern," or, even, how to define its nature, it is generally said to have come into being early in the twentieth century. Theophil Spoerri thinks, however, that Mérimée should be recognized as "the creator of the modern French short story," since he put "Carmen" (1845, 1847) in a framework and gave it a "general meaning."[2] Mary Ann Caws suggests that a modernist story is one where the frame, other than explaining the inner core, becomes the *raison d'être* of the whole.[3] While this emphasis on the outer rather than the inner does seem more common these days (like the "unreliable narrator"), it is crucial to remember the importance of Marguerite de Navarre's much earlier frame for the *Heptaméron* (1558). Slowly, as her *devisants* tell their stories we gain an increasingly clear understanding of their psychological profiles and a vision of Marguerite's conception of her society. Whether the frame becomes the focus of the cycle can be debated, though there can be no doubt about its significance.

As Torgovnick points out, a frame is common in narratives.[4] It recalls the physical structure surrounding paintings or photographs and consists of the terminal repetition of something that occurred liminally, and often elsewhere as well. There are several kinds of frames. I am less concerned here by the distinction between those that are implicit and internal (for example, the philosophic opposition between "exile" and "kingdom" in Albert Camus' cycle)[5] than by those that are an explicit part of the text (adducing what might be considered a different story, whether in parallel or in opposition, or simply deviating). Often the frame story enclosing the embedded tale introduces an account that may alter the emphasis from what has seemed central. As a pertinent example, Bizet extracted and adapted the core tale about the gypsy girl from Mérimée's short story "Carmen" for his famous opera of the same name.

Sequence Framed in Mérimée's *"Carmen"*   73

When Mérimée's definitive 1847 version is, however, considered as a single unit, with the ethnographer/narrator's introduction and conclusion, we get a very different cast. Suddenly, the gypsy Carmen becomes not so much the object of attention, but the representation of Bohemia and the focus of the bourgeois ethnographer's timorous, dangerous obsession. David R. Ellison maintains that the central opposition occurs in the Greek epigraph from Palladas: "Each woman is a poison who has only two good hours, one in bed [*thalamos*, the bridal chamber or bed], the other in death [*thanatos*]." The quotation lays the ground between the *thalamos* and *thanatos*. From the beginning, as Ellison explicates the quotation, bed and sex can slide into death.[6]

Occasionally, critics advance evocative images to illustrate the modernist short story. I think, for example, of Christian Congiu's version of the quotation on the novel that Stendhal attributed to San Réal: "The short story is a mirror that is taken for a walk along a path, but this mirror is broken. The writer of short stories proceeds to play with the splinters, the smears, without trying to mold them into a single tale, without claiming harmony."[7] Though this kind of story based on fragmentation seems to have predominance today, it occurs in the best writers of most periods, without for all that casting aspersions on tales that are oriented by plot or sequence. The potential power of anacoluton on the small and large scale was known to classical authors, as Lesage's *Gil Blas* and Rabelais' works demonstrate.

The following pages consider one of Mérimée's masterful stories, "Carmen," in the hope of better understanding this work, this kind of frame story, and the short-story genre. Although Mérimée was a master of plot, he made use of extremely powerful devices and techniques that exploit the potential of an encompassing image, which I call "image structure." This type of organization has been a focus in earlier chapters. Although it has many iterations, it is especially powerful when it exploits more than one story in the span of a single text.

As said before, the two basic structures of literature have been labeled variously. I prefer to use those terms that recall the psychological categories into which the human mind processes information: sequence, which in the normal brain is handled by the left hemisphere, and shape or image, which is processed by the right cerebral hemisphere. Paul Ricoeur proposes "episodic" and "configurational" dimensions for these widely sensed ways of organizing information.[8] René Godenne refers to a *nouvelle-histoire* [short story-narration] and a *nouvelle-instant* [short story-instant].[9] And Jakobson's "syntagm" and "paradigm," like Joseph Frank's "temporal" as opposed to "spatial" structures, have had considerable currency.[10] Temporal is often equated with metonymic and sequential, though in fact the latter is the more inclusive term. It would include any number of sequences that depend not only on time or causality, but also on those organized around a discrete system like

74 Sequence Framed in Mérimée's "Carmen"

the alphabet, exemplified by Butor's *Mobile*, or, perhaps, the classical elements (fire, air, earth, water) placed carefully along the alchemical path to *aurum philosophicum*. Many sequences exist, and works of art are not limited to the concepts of time and causality. Nor are chronology and causality necessarily the dominant traits in those works of art that use them. In many cases, sequential plot is subordinated to description, image, or metaphor.

Mérimée's "Carmen" (1845, 1847), a case in point, poses a number of problems. It pushes the limits of brevity for our concept of the "short story" and, consequently, has occasionally been termed a novella or even a novel.[11] Certainly, at some 21,000 words, it is beginning to challenge any attempt to read it at one sitting, and one can wonder whether or not it communicates the single impression that Poe and others have felt essential for the short story. Not only does it have three principal characters, each of whose point of view differs significantly, but it also gives the essential features of three different lives: that of Carmen, the wild gypsy who only appears peripherally,[12] that of Don José Lizarrabengoa, the criminal known as José Navarro, and that of the frame-narrator, a foreigner or *payllo* (non-gypsy), who has an important part as a young man ripe for adventure in the exotic clime of Spain. We meet him in the first paragraph, in his guise as an aging archeologist who pedantically claims to have solved "the geographical problem that holds the whole of scholarly Europe in suspense" (345), that is, the location of one of Caesar's battles. It had surely occurred to Mérimée that few if any of his readers would share the narrator's misplaced enthusiasm about his inconsequential obsession. The scholar/critic, David R. Ellison, also points out that the thesis is not original, having been previously proposed by Miguel Cortes (73). While waiting for publication and, he assumes, acclaim, the narrator decides to tell a "little story" (345) from his youth. He reappears in part two of his subsequent tale as a much younger man when he meets José and listens to the latter's story. In part four of Mérimée's 1847 version, he comes back as an ethnographer, confidently parading his limited knowledge about gypsies and their language.

Bizet and his two librettists, Henri Meilhac and Ludovic Halévy, chose to elide the narrator of Mérimée's definitive version from the opera, content to rely on the music to invest the themes of youth and passion with beauty. They consequently simplify Mérimée's definitive story substantially by leaving out the narrator, who is remarkable for his ignorance, his mediocre scholarship, his diffident lust, and his continuing fascination with the Bohemia that he will one day prissily keep at arm's length. In the end, he will remain on the outskirts, apprehensive about getting too close now after the threatening lessons of his youth, preferring to savor it vicariously. Mérimée uses this narrator / character as an exemplar of bourgeois deficiencies and an object of mockery. Cropper

Sequence Framed in Mérimée's "Carmen" 75

goes further, calling him "a wink and a nudge" that Mérimée is in fact making fun of both the narrator and the July Monarchy.[13] Mérimée's antipathy toward his government and its middle-class supporters is well known, as Cropper makes very clear. *Carmen* provides a thoughtful critique of the French bourgeoisie, in contrast to the superficial lessons of Bizet's opera.[14]

Most of Mérimée's story focuses on Don José, who narrates chapter three and blames Carmen for leading him into a life of crime. "[Y]ou know, you are the one who ruined me" (401), he tells her. Near the end, he begs her to stay with him and offers to remain a brigand "to please her" (401). He is proud of being Basque and old-line Christian, despite his callused workman's hands and his inability to play a nascent form of tennis with aristocratic insouciance (after all, it was nothing but a game). The genuineness of his nobility may even raise doubts, especially since he does not go into detail, however true that it may have been recorded on parchment (366). Though his parents destined him for the church, he refused to study, spending his time playing tennis. About a fight with another tennis player, whom he had just beaten at the game, he explains, "Once again, I had the advantage, but that obliged me to leave the country" (366). The paucity of information is surprising, and one is left to assume from the necessity of flight that his opponent died. The reader is then obliged early on to wonder whether the unmentioned death indicates that the juvenile fight was only important because of the results it had on Don José's life: although he won, he had no choice but expatriation. It is a signal that one must not take this character at face value. His selective recounting and the over-riding irony are by no means accidental. At best, he is an unreliable narrator, and his "nobility" has lost its luster.

The tragic death of another human being has no significance for José Navarro, and he takes no responsibility: "I loved playing tennis too much; that was the ruin of me" (366). Later, following his enrolling in the cavalry, he falls under the spell of Carmen's allures, and, after her arrest, he allows her to escape. He has then broken the law and been derelict in his performance. Still, he tells us, he cannot help himself. Despite being punished for his clear infraction of the law and neglect of his duty, he takes the first opportunity to spend a day with her. "[F]rom that day [...], I could no longer think about anything else" (379). Because of his "weakness" (380), he allows Carmen and her five smugglers / companions to slip by his post. Later, when he finds her with one of his superiors, he is again drawn into a fight. The lieutenant tells him to get out and roughly shakes him. Don José does not remember what he said in response, though they drew their swords. Running after José, the officer struck him. Only then does José touch the officer with the point of his blade. The outlaw assures us that the lieutenant "thrust himself" on his sword (382).

76   *Sequence Framed in Mérimée's "Carmen"*

As P. W. M. Cogman argues in an excellent article, Don José's passivity and self-exculpation are striking. He indicates repeatedly that he could not help himself, so consequently he remains blameless.[15] He tells the narrator at one point, "Sir, one becomes a rascal without being aware of it. A pretty girl makes you lose your head [... then] you have to live in the mountains, and from smuggler, you become a thief without thinking" (388). Don José's narration is singularly imprecise in three of the instances where he is doubtless guilty of murder. It is almost certain that he killed his tennis opponent in his youth, then his lieutenant just a few years later while he was in the cavalry, and, similarly, the Englishman that Carmen led into an ambush. He views himself as a victim of circumstances rather than a causative agent. Speaking Basque with José and brazenly revealing that she has had sex with her English companion, she tells the officer that *maquila* means orange rather than club, thus laughingly continuing the alliterative Monda / Munda / Marbella / Montilla of the introduction with *maquila / minchorrò / madone* (392), a minus device that the French reader is left to complete with the phonetic *maquereau* or procurer,[16] a word that aptly characterizes José's apparent role in this episode.

Given Don José's repeated demand for Carmen's faithfulness in their affair, her gaiety and incongruously luxurious dress leave little doubt of what she has been doing with the English officer. Whether justified or not, she makes José feel as though he is indeed the pimp who will profit from her prostitution. His anger and jealousy would be perfectly understandable for Mérimée's middle-class reader, whose women are expected to remain faithful, though Carmen insists that her *rom* Garcia would not object to her infidelities (391). While José's actions and reactions in this regard are predictable, the paltry excuses for his crimes become increasingly disproportionate and unconvincing. The Dominican provides a good summary: "[H]e committed several murders, every one more horrible than the others" (364). Each episode turns around a graphical representation of the next step down in his degradation. Finally, after killing his mistress's *rom*, he murders her.

José Navarro is worth looking at carefully. Though minor aristocracy and Basque, he joins the Spanish military to make his fortune and rise in society. His initial rank is low, but it has potential, and he regrets that his lapses due to helping Carmen will surely slow if not reverse his military advancement. Whatever minor nobility he might have enjoyed back home does not suffice to assure professional rank in Spain. Promoted to corporal, he nonetheless fully expects to receive another promotion soon. Then he meets Carmen. From being a Basque, noble, Christian, and filled with middle-class ambition, his orientation changes. His life turns increasingly around a passion for the gypsy girl. In fact, his background is in opposition to hers, and the antitheses continue. He is "old Christian"; she is committed to the dark arts (597, 400). He is guided

Sequence Framed in Mérimée's "Carmen" 77

by tradition and traditional goals; she wants only to be free. He wants her to be a faithful wife; she will not compromise her liberty. By the social rules for French marriage in the eighteenth and early nineteenth centuries, they are not *sortable* (suitable for each other), and it seems likely that the same would be true in Spain. His passion leads him into thievery and smuggling, but he will not, perhaps cannot, compromise his expectations of her faithfulness. First, he does in his lieutenant, whom he finds consorting with a band of gypsies that includes Carmen, then the Englishman, followed by her former *rom* or husband, before finally claiming that he is "tired of killing all [her] lovers" (399). Fortunately, the bull gores the girl's toreador, but José's anger is unabated. And as though she were imitating one of the bulls she has seen, she defiantly stamps her foot at him.[17] He grabs the knife of her now-dead *rom*, one-eye Garcia [Garcia le Borgne], and, like a bullfighter, drives it into her twice. Caught between his rather lusterless aristocratic heredity, on the one hand, and the untamed gypsy mentality, on the other, he buries her with both a cross and the magic ring.

Don José so occupies this text that we are perhaps justified in wondering why Mérimée did not call his story "Don José." Lilian Furst points out that "so many works of this [Romantic] period bear as their title simply the name of the main character [...who] holds the centre of works whose primary purpose is the presentation of his character."[18] While entitling Bizet's simplified operetta "Don José" might have been appropriate, Mérimée's definitive version of 1847 is far too complex for such a revision. In Mérimée's "Carmen," José becomes less a character than the portrayal of overwhelming desire, dominated and stoked by Carmen's intense sexuality incarnating Bohemia. The emphasis is displaced as Mérimée completes the frame focused on the ethnographer / narrator. Carmen remains the central figure, but her significance shifts away from mere sensuousness to configure Bohemia. She becomes less the temptress than the symbol of the attraction the narrator feels for the bohemian world, an ungoverned and ungovernable society, where exotic inhabitants exemplify not just liberty, but license, a lack of restraint that is impossible in bourgeois France. In short, by completing the frame, Carmen becomes less a character than an imago. Likewise, the pedantic narrator who in the story clumsily introduces the bandit's tale and then appends his own "study" to the end, thus, circumscribes the story and casts it in a larger context. He is a bourgeois comically yearning for the freedom of Bohemia that he is afraid to live.

Cogman's most important contribution to our understanding of "Carmen" has been to direct our attention back to the narrator. In other criticism of Mérimée's definitive story, a long list of scholars have frequently ignored the storyteller; most feel that his patronizing and tiresome display of erroneous knowledge serves as a serious detraction to the work (Cogman 1–2). They point especially to the self-satisfied

78   Sequence Framed in Mérimée's "Carmen"

introduction, but the chatty quasi-erudition of the conclusion appended in 1847 to the original publication seems even worse. With pompous, punctilious self-disparagement, the narrator tells us that he "puts his meager understanding of the Romany language on display..." (409). This narrator's "little story" about Carmen looks back fifteen years to his young adulthood. It is perhaps appropriate for us to understand that in the intervening time, he has more fully appreciated the danger of the life that attracts him. His self-satisfied condescension and false modesty about what looks to be his own self-described "meager" knowledge gives him the air of a pretentious bore. His footnotes, liberally sprinkled with Greek, Spanish, and Romany, add the bizarre air of a fragmented tourist guide to the tale, and seem particularly adept in elucidating the inconsequential, the insignificant, or the false. After complacently stating, "I was well enough acquainted with the way Spanish people are to be very certain that I had nothing to fear from a man who had eaten and smoked with me" (349–50), he discovers "a certain charm in finding myself next to a dangerous person" (350), and spends the night with the bandit, Don José. We know that Carmen would have happily killed the *payllo* for his ring and money, and there is little doubt that the murderous Garcia would have done the same. The French narrator comes from another culture; he does not understand, and he does not belong. At first he tentatively experienced Bohemia, and was lucky to survive, while by the end he is unquestionably a wary outsider, a *payllo*.

Some time after making the acquaintance of Don José, the young narrator of parts one and two meets and follows Carmen to a café, where they apparently share some ice cream. He invites her to take him to her home, explaining that it would have been ridiculous for her to tell his fortune in a café (361). Carmen and the reader know perfectly well that he has sex on his mind. Few would be surprised that she leads him to a place where her prostitution was prevented only by the arrival of José, whom she then urges to slit her prospective client's throat. The narrator / *payllo*'s hesitant dabbling in the exotic encourages other questions. What gave him the right to watch the female cigarmakers' evening ablutions, for example? And, if ringing the Angelus a little early would expose the nude bathers to bright daylight, how does he know the time-keeping bell ringer is incorruptible? In addition, could his decision not to report the theft of his watch to the *corregidor* be explained by his qualms about explaining why he was with Carmen at all? To the narrator's interest in sex and bandits, he adds a fascination with illegality and the occult. "[S]everal times I had tried to conjure up the spirit of darkness" (359), he says. Although he tells us he was no longer interested in the black arts, it is surely significant that he continues to wear what Carmen recognizes as a magic ring that she would like to possess (397). As is clear in the text of the story, from the time that the *payllo* meets Carmen, his attention is directed either in person or through Don José to the gypsy.

Sequence Framed in Mérimée's "Carmen" 79

Today's readers who come to Mérimée's story with the enriched background of Georges Bizet's dazzling opera probably have no trouble envisioning Carmen as the central figure. And on considering the story attentively, there is little question that, however brief and sporadic her actual presence may be, she is indeed a primary focus. Because of her impact on Don José, she is so striking that she could never be ignored. Though often poorly dressed, she is extraordinarily sensual and, particularly beautiful for a Spanish gypsy—so, at least, the narrator informs us: "She was a strange, wild beauty, with a face that astonished at first, but that you could not forget. Her eyes especially had an expression that was both voluptuous and ferocious. [...] Gypsy's eye, wolf's eye" (360). Ready at any time to tell a fortune, her talents are more than a sham—"she was a full blown witch" (361). She seems to have long known that her affair with Don José would end fatally. She tells him, "You have met the devil, yes, the devil" (379). Eventually, he agrees: "'You are the devil,' I said to her.—'Yes,' she responded" (387).

The fact that Carmen brazenly addresses the *payllo* with whom she is unacquainted as he strolls beside the Guadalquivir River proves her lack of virtue, and we quickly learn that prostitution may be the least of her misdeeds. She sets up most of her gang's crimes, whether smuggling or highway robbery. Given that she refuses allegiance to the laws of Spain and the church, she is unquestionably an outlaw. Seducing the English officer and leading him into a trap where he will be killed and robbed is merely one instance of a series of crimes. She urges José to slit the narrator / *payllo*'s throat, after she has led the latter into a quiet place. While she says she accepts gypsy law, her submission has peculiar exceptions. She tells Don José, for example, that as her *rom*, he has the right to kill her (401), but she does not hesitate to attempt to betray her former *rom*, one-eye Garcia, so that he would be killed in an armed robbery. After José murders Garcia and becomes Carmen's *rom*, she soon tires of his jealousy and loses patience with him: "Be careful not to push me too far. If I get sick of you, I'll find some nice boy who will do as you did to [Garcia]" (395).

It is Carmen that attracts and employs men like José in the activities of her friends' banditry. When her smuggling compatriots need to get past the city guards, she uses her seductive powers on the still reasonably law-abiding José, so that he will let them slip by unchallenged. For herself personally, freedom is the one value she holds above all others: "What I want is to be free, and to do as I wish" (395). Finally, as Gillian Horrocks explains, the name Mérimée chose for her is strikingly suitable for her and for the story. In Latin, it means either (1) a tune or a song, (2) a poem, whether epic or lyric, (3) a prophecy, or (4) a religious or legal formula. In addition, there is the homonymous *carmin* suggesting sensuality, passion, and blood, and we remember that she likes to wear red, which evokes all three.[19] With all this, however, Carmen makes

80 Sequence Framed in Mérimée's "Carmen"

surprisingly few appearances in the actual text. She is present almost always by indirection, through the accounts of others. Even so, when she is mentioned, it is primarily to explain either a cause or an excuse for her egregious actions.

There is nonetheless no ignoring the alluring Carmen, for the gypsy is the principle point of José's entire story. Only in the first episode where the narrator and Don José become acquainted is she not mentioned. The scene very clearly functions to introduce the narrator as he was fifteen years before, that is, both incredibly naïve and ignorant of the significant danger he runs in associating with brigands and, as well, dabbling in lawlessness and the occult. On seeing the ferocious air of Don José, the young *payllo* brushes aside any anxiety, since, he says, he does not believe in thieves, never having met any. As it turns out, his behavior is appropriate for this particular bandit, though almost accidently so. By treating Don José as an equal, happy to share cigars and food, he encourages him to respond with camaraderie. A minute's thought about what would have happened if the young man had encountered not Don José but Garcia leaves no doubt about the Frenchman's foolhardiness and good fortune. The *payllo* / narrator is fascinated by criminals, and though he expresses some doubt about the correctness of warning the bandit about the coming lancers, he does not hesitate to do so. Shortly, he will use his evening with Don José as an excuse for taking another step down the paths of danger: "I ate supper with a highwayman; let us now go have ice cream with one of the devil's handmaidens" (359). He accompanies Carmen, he says, because he wants her to tell his fortune and because he retains from his youth "curiosity about all superstitions" (360). The narrator's experience of watching Carmen's little hand flutter back and forth beneath her throat as she urges Don José to dispose of him (very different from what he expected of Spanish hospitality) apparently frightens him sufficiently to make him leave crime, criminals, and the occult alone. From this point on, his research will be from a safe distance.

Starting from the moment when the protagonist makes Carmen's acquaintance, though rarely depicted, the gypsy is the cause, the center, or the goal of every episode through the end of part three. She lures the *payllo* off to a lonely room, where his life is spared only because of a shallow friendship with the murderous highwayman. She seduces José, encourages his dereliction, puts him in touch with a band of lawbreakers, arranges his smuggling jobs, encourages the murder of her husband, and sets up the robbery that ends in murder. Although she maintains that she obeys the laws of Bohemia, for the nineteenth century this was no law at all, and she comes to represent absolute unruliness, lawlessness, and anarchy as opposed to civilization. She frightens the older narrator / ethnographer into henceforth haunting only the edges of her world, but she lures José deeper and deeper into crime. Although Carmen is

Sequence Framed in Mérimée's "Carmen" 81

seldom allowed to speak, and we are only infrequently allowed to see her, as José describes the context of the events of his life, Carmen gains consistency and substance. She stands for freedom, the narrator explains repeatedly: "For people of her race, liberty is everything" (373). This liberty is defined in opposition to those who obey the laws of church and state and who are not gypsies (362). When José tries to convince her to accompany him to the New World, she rises as a female Cain, a hunter: "We are not made for planting cabbages," she said, "our destiny is to live at the expense of *payllos*" (396).

The young narrator's search to learn more of bandits, gypsies, and the occult opens him to danger. Despite his voyeurism in watching the local women bathe and his willingness to consort with a prostitute like Carmen, he attracts a certain sympathy due to his lack of sophistication and his hunger for experience, as well as because of the shame he obviously feels at being fleeced by the gypsy. When he meets Don José for the first time and considers the possibility that he might be robbed, we discover that he even has a sense of humor. He wonders what a bandit would do with his shirts and Elzevir's *Commentaires*? And there is a certain boyish charm in the enjoyment he gets from showing off his chiming watch. The Dominicans' affection for him can doubtless be explained by such traits. The gold watch, of course, is an amusing toy and may represent social distinction, perhaps even civilized order, on one hand, and wealth, on the other. It is easy to understand why Carmen would steal it, for it has value. Readers may also sense that time is a dominant factor behind the behavior of society. To own a time-piece is to control time, one of the most important forces of the modern world. Curiously, unlike Moktir's treatment of the scissors in Gide's *L'Immoraliste*, the gilded watch returns undamaged.[20]

Fifteen years later, the narrator / ethnographer has matured into a significantly different person, though still very much a foreigner. When readers confront the pretentiousness of his anecdotal considerations, it is difficult to understand why he continues to be interested in what he condescendingly calls the "little story" that he has just told. After the passage of time, while he seems to feel that his youthful adventures have little importance, he has not followed José in embracing Bohemia. Now, maintaining his distance, he values his trivial erudition far more than whatever might be learned from his experiences with Carmen, and the last six pages of the text show little sympathy and no empathy whatsoever for the gypsies. To the contrary he makes *ad hominem* judgments that call the scholarly value of his remarks into question: "You can only compare their eyes to those of wild animals. Audacity and timidity were simultaneously depicted there, and in this regard their eyes revealed rather well the character of the nation: sly, daring, but like Panurge fearing a beating [...]" (403). Throughout this concluding segment, he views the gypsies ironically, carefully positioned at a safe distance from Bohemia.

82 Sequence Framed in Mérimée's "Carmen"

When the older *payllo* / narrator returns, he completes the frame in a late addition to the story. His self-satisfied humility in referring to the "display of my meager understanding" of the Romany language (409) encourages us to question his competence. Certainly, his complacent pretentiousness is annoying and seems distasteful. The very few samples of similar lexical items in different languages that he believes reveal borrowings, the questionable conclusion that speakers of Romany in Germany and Spain could not comprehend one another but would quickly recognize that they speak different dialects of the same language, the paucity of evidence for his claims about Romany and other languages, and finally the culmination of his linguistic comments in what Parturier claims to be an inaccurate derivation of *frimousse*, or "little face."[21] All this obliges readers to recognize that the evidence he adduces for his conclusions is both limited in accuracy and shallow in significance. Still, careful consideration and reconsideration of the last section highlights the contrast with other major characters.[22] The *payllo* / narrator says that his terminal remarks are "enough to give to readers of *Carmen* an advantageous idea of [his] study of Romany" (409). (Peter J. Rabinowitz points out appositely that for Mérimée a lack of linguistic fluency constitutes a very negative trait.)[23] The narrator then brings his "study" and the frame story to an end with a proverb—"Flies don't go in a closed mouth" (409)—an adage that aptly expresses the sensible credo the narrator has learned from the close calls of his youth. Even though the thrills of a vicarious Barbary continue to entice him, by refusing nonetheless to give open access to the foreign, noxious influences of the gypsies, he avoids distasteful and ultimately fatal consequences. He will keep his distance, and his mouth "closed," believing he can then remain protected from its dangers.

The oppositions that form tensions from the beginning of *Carmen* must be taken into account. Mérimée has emphasized a number of a "gypsy's" negative connotations, leaving aside those of a positive nature, to insist on the tempting allure and danger this unusually beautiful embodiment of Bohemia itself holds for bourgeois Frenchmen. Carmen as a gypsy, a witch, a prostitute, a thief, a spy, and a kind of business manager for a band of smugglers and robbers, is in every sense of the word an outlaw. Even Don José, who cannot control her, and who nonetheless makes the narrator think of Milton's Satan (352), seems considerably less forceful, if not bereft of her force. Described as "a handmaiden of the devil" (359), "Satan's godchild" (369), and, indeed, as the devil himself (379), she serves as a mesmerizing temptation for any man within the ranks of the *payllos*. She has no respect for property, enjoys wasting, damaging, and destroying what comes her way, and she disdains the law. The fact that she preserved the watch indicates her cultural confusion, for it indicates her attraction to civilization. Although she claims to accept gypsy law, she does not hesitate to arrange for her husband's assassination, only to have José prefer to kill him face to face without ambush or subterfuge. Though lacking physical strength, her manipulative sexuality makes the

Sequence Framed in Mérimée's "Carmen" 83

English soldier an object of mockery, she effectively emasculates Don José, and she makes the *payllo* / narrator look the fool. As the assertive representative of Bohemia, capable of seducing anyone she wishes to attract, she has enormous power. Civilization has few competing attractions, and those represented by the susceptible narrator are unimpressive. The rigid expectations and unexciting regularity imposed by society may even encourage readers who themselves feel Carmen's compelling attraction to begin to yearn for the exhilaration of existence on the other side, a life of excitement and passion. Carmen becomes the image of a life without constraint, without law, a life of unfettered freedom. As should be clear, however, the Bohemia inhabited by Mérimée's Carmen is not that of the indulgently unrestrained artists and writers of Parisian Romanticism; it is rather Barbary. The one sign of the narrator's good sense is his withdrawal so as not to follow Don José's decision to join the gypsies.

Both the *payllo* and José serve as foils to elucidate and set Carmen off. Indeed, the other main characters exist only to highlight Carmen, the representation of Bohemia. She herself serves her own ends and her own destiny. Committed to liberty, desirous only to do as she wishes, she rises as a female Vautrin, a Satan, a sensual child of nature who highlights civilization's controlling restraints. In visual terms, Mérimée's short story presents a classic background / foreground study. The supporting characters function to highlight Carmen, the relatively absent center, defining and silhouetting her. José's and the narrator's activity in the foreground can be distracting, but a slight shift of reader's point of view snaps the shadowy image of Carmen into focus. Although Aristotle is unequivocal in his insistence that "action is brought about by agents" and that it is the actions and choices that define the characters' natures (*Poetics* ch. 6), Carmen exists through relationship, as the purpose, goal, and object of other characters' attentions. She is the main character because she is the fulcrum of almost every episode and the focus of every character. She has a purpose which she herself does not suspect: she stands for the temptation of absolute, self-serving liberty and the opposition to a vapid civilization, whose insipid lack of passion is illuminated by the *payllo* / narrator's egregiously empty and erroneous scholarship. She solicits our attention, not like José because of what he does, but because of what she is. She exists because José and the narrator resemble each other, because each of them is oriented like flowers facing the sun toward Carmen. Their actions make sense only because of her presence, and while they inevitably have impact on her, we finally understand that the conflict of their colliding worlds functions to lure José and herself toward their predestined ends. The cowardly narrator runs away, appropriately and wisely raising walls of scholarly objectivity between himself and the dangerous freedom of Bohemia.

"Carmen" has two explicit tales in the stories of both Don José and the young protagonist / narrator and a third implicit narration in the development of the narrator during the fifteen years since he made the

84   Sequence Framed in Mérimée's "Carmen"

acquaintance of Carmen and Don José. Don José's story is essentially about the events and circumstances that changed him, as is that of the *payllo* / narrator. In both cases, Carmen is the cause of a complete reorientation, though that of the narrator seems of less moment, given that it leads to his survival rather than dramatic thrills (and death?). The mere fact of the formative experiences with her keep the emphasis on Carmen. The series of episodes in the bandit's life show us the intensification of his passion for Carmen, and, because of the bohemian forces she embodies, a further step in his own degeneracy. Looked at from the point of view of function, each of the episodes differs from each of the others in that it more clearly shows Carmen's power. As with all short stories where repetition is a factor, the importance of the repetition is not in the similarity of the elements repeated, but rather in the emphases, the differences, and progressions that each episode indicates. The third narration is focused particularly on the frame and exists only to the degree that we can infer it, for we only see the beginning and the end. The young *payllo* / protagonist who was anxious to come to grips with raw life is shown finally committed in entirety to dead scholarship. Readers are invited to compare Carmen and her vitality with the negligible importance of the location of one of long-dead Caesar's battles and the *payllo* / narrator's detached bewitchment by generic Bohemia. Unquestionably, Carmen stands out brilliantly against the lackluster anemia of the *payllo*'s pathetic scholarship. The frame reflects Carmen as a temptation of lawless freedom for the narrator, for the bandit, and perhaps even for the reader. Consequently, the story, "Carmen," has impressive economy and univocal focus.[24]

Not all short stories have such extensive narrations. Many recent examples of the genre center on an epiphany, or image, or character with little or no story. But when a plot is central to the structure, that plot is often, at some point, either subsumed to a core image or theme or situation, or the plot leads to some sort of epigrammatic point that may dramatically enhance the whole. It may also reveal and explain whatever mysteries remain at the core, or resolve the complications, or encourage the reader to reconsider the story in the light of the new material that dramatically changes its meaning. Both Don José and the scholar / *payllo* are narrators that take an active part in the recounted adventures. Each tells his story after the actual events, and for the most part years afterwards, but the *payllo* has particular importance, not just for what he has done, but especially because of the frame that reveals what he becomes, thus by opposition making Carmen seem even more dangerous and enticing. Because of this development, another light is thrown on the attraction and power of Barbary. Although one has the sense of a rich description of Spain when reading the pages of "Carmen," on rereading, the actual dearth of detail is particularly striking. Mérimée uses a few Spanish words and terms—*Dom, corrégidor, piastre, venta*—a few

Sequence Framed in Mérimée's "Carmen"   85

gypsy words—*payllos, lillipendi, rom, romi*[25]—and very few descriptive details—the holes in Carmen's stockings, the red of her shoes, the hole in a roof serving as a chimney, highly spiced food—to give the flavor of the land and its people. Any need to gain more than a very vague idea of Spain in the 1830s would oblige one to go outside the story. Mérimée devotes his text to the characters and actions that throw light on what is important, that is, on Carmen. The brief introduction and the slightly longer concluding, fourth part function to represent what in essence is not Carmen but her opposite, the bourgeoisie. Thus by antithesis they emphasize the high motivation of every detail, every element, every episode, every character, every part of the story to portray the dangerous enticement of Bohemia for the middle class. They frame and modify the significance of the story of the gypsy Carmen. She is no longer a simple portrait, in a period when readers loved the generalized types of the *physiologies*. The frame rather enlarges her sensual unruliness, magnifying her significance as a major factor capable of eradicating civilization. However, amusing the obvious trepidation of the aging narrator may be, his fear highlights the destructive illegitimacy characterizing a Barbary that the bourgeoisie must eschew.

Mérimée's "Carmen" is not so much a short story because it is under so many words, say 40,000 words (to pick the outside limit chosen by the now defunct *Studies in Short Fiction*), although indeed it is and could thus be read at one sitting. Nor is "Carmen" a short story because of its subject, for its subject could easily permit more length, easily be fleshed out into a much longer novel. Its impact would, however, have diminished drastically. The considerable power that Carmen has as a sultry temptress, as an outlaw, and as an exemplar of unrestrained liberty would have been reduced, if not lost, for much of her attraction comes from the constant, consistent intensity of the reiterated scrutiny of the dangers of Bohemia. With part four, the reader is abruptly confronted by the flaccid bourgeois "scholar" and "scholarship," the very opposite of what Carmen heralds

Short stories are by definition brief, and great short stories are particularly adept at exploiting the quality. They heighten and exploit its impact. Writers are correct in suggesting that short stories exploit concision, ellipsis, symbols, in short, lexical overload, where the vocabulary bears more than its normal significance, and readers are more prone than with the novel to universalize. Because repetition is not needed to remind readers of crucial elements, the multiplication in "Carmen" is used not as a reminder, but as a way to mirror the contrasts and parallels that emphasize the feared dangers of unrestrained freedom. For readers who are trained by the short-story genre to seek the full implication of all details, Carmen then represents the bourgeois temptation to Bohemia, or, perhaps better, the degree to which the bohemian life is undermining the moral character of society. The meaning has changed from

86 *Sequence Framed in Mérimée's "Carmen"*

a minor though intense portrait of a gypsy to the description of a major factor in the coming fall of the July Monarchy.

In fact, of course, only exceptionally fine short stories are capable of making brevity work in interesting ways, just as only the best novels give luster to length. But in great short stories, the brevity works to provide force and brilliance to the texts, while functioning within their narrations to provide the particular intensity that characterizes the most exceptional of them. Charles May would call shortness a dominant.[26] It then seems perfectly reasonable to say that neither Kate Chopin's *The Awakening* nor André Gide's *L'Immoraliste* are short stories for in neither case is brevity exploited. "Carmen" most definitely takes advantage of its potential. It further seems to me that some works of 40,000 words will be novels and some will be short stories (and a few, perhaps, hybrid creations). The distinction is not worth making in the case of mediocre works, but, in outstanding creations, the difference lies in whether brevity is used for aesthetic purposes and whether the reader will be sensitive to it.

The attraction, not of Carmen, but of the story "Carmen" resides on at least three levels. We may stop with the imago of the gypsy girl, remaining *à la* Bizet content with the color and excitement of Don José and Carmen's passionate love. One cannot, however, ignore Mérimée's 1847 version, where the frame / narrator completes the frame and forces us to wonder why the author included the passages. The narration of the frame resists meaning, as Armine Mortimer would say,[27] and although we readers may laugh at the narrator's limitations, we are forced to question the aesthetic function of this character tantalized by Bohemia but unable or unwilling to become a part of that world. Indeed, on reflection, one recognizes that Mérimée's irony spares no one, not even himself, for the portrait of the narrator uncomfortably resembles an abbreviated version of the author Mérimée's life. Both dabble in languages and their dialects, both "study" the gypsy culture, without getting deeply involved. A satirical view of such brief biographies might not be accurate, but it is the way of irony to generalize a limited number of traits. Such a vision could easily be interpreted negatively. The author and the narrator remain seated on the sidelines, frustrated by the failings of civilization, and enticed by the treacherous promises of unlimited liberty. In effect, Mérimée has caricatured himself,[28] perhaps even more brilliantly than he did in *La Vénus d'Ille*. Whether others see him in the same way or not, his self-mockery presents an amateur linguist and ethnologist, if not an archeologist, who watches from the sidelines as the July monarchy implodes. Too aware of the dangers to become deeply involved but too attracted to move away from the fire, he is, in short, at significant risk. In the case of "Carmen," the power of the gypsy's portrayal of lawlessness is turned on its head when the frame story closes and the reader is compelled to recognize that despite the narrator's ridiculousness, he has

Sequence Framed in Mérimée's "Carmen"   87

almost made the right choice. The satire insists not on his tremulous temptation, but on his inability to wholeheartedly choose civilization over barbarous savagery.

Notes

1 Though these terms can be found in a number of analyses of recent short fiction, I quote almost at random from Florence Goyet, *La Nouvelle 1870–1925: Description d'un genre à son apogée* (Paris: P.U.F., 1993) 16; Johnnie Gratton and Brigitte le Juez, eds. "Introduction," *Modern French Short Fiction* (Manchester: Manchester UP, 1994) 16–17; and John Wain, "Remarks on the Short Story," *Les Cahiers de la Nouvelle: Journal of the Short Story in English* 2 (1984): 66. For an excellent introduction to the "modern" or "impressionist" or "lyric" short story, see the essays by Charles E. May, "Introduction: A Survey of Short Story Criticism in America," *Short Story Theories*, ed. Charles E. May (Athens: Ohio UP, 1976) 3–12; Suzanne C. Ferguson, "Defining the Short Story: Impressionism and Form," ed. May 218–30; and Eileen Baldeshwiler, "The Lyric Short Story: The Sketch of a History," ed. May 202–13.

2 Theophil Spoerri, "Mérimée and the Short Story," *Yale French Studies* 4 (1949): 4.

3 Mary Ann Caws, *Reading Frames in Modern Fiction* (Princeton, NJ: Princeton UP, 1985) 137–38, 263.

4 Marianna Torgovnick, *Closure in the Novel* (Princeton, NJ: Princeton UP, 1981) 13. Ian Reid breaks the technique into four different manifestations, though there are many more (some of which have been covered in previous chapters)—"Destabilizing Frames for Story," *Short Story Theory at a Crossroads*, eds. Susan Lohafer and Jo Ellyn Clarey (Baton Rouge: Louisiana State UP, 1989) 300–01. Mia Gerhardt's definition is pertinent: "A frame-story may be defined as a narrative whole composed of two distinct but connected parts: a story or stories, told by a character or several characters in another story of lesser dimensions and subordinate interest, which thus encloses the former as a frame encloses a picture"—quoted from: Parvin Loloi, "The *One Thousand and One Nights* and Its Influence on English Short Fiction: Some Examples," *Tale, Novella, Short Story: Currents in Short Fiction*, eds. Wolfgang Görtschacher and Holger Klein (Tübingen: Stazuffenburg Verlag, 2004) 7.

5 See, my study of *L'Exil et le royaume* in, *Inner Workings of the Novel: Studying a Genre* (New York: Palgrave Macmillan, 2010) 35–50.

6 All references to Mérimée's *Carmen* are to Maurice Parturier's edition, *Romans et nouvelles*, Vol. 2 (Paris: Garnier, 1967), and all translations are my own. This passage comes from 402. Ellison discusses the antipathy separating bourgeois and gypsy—"The Place of *Carmen*," *Geographies: Mapping the Imagination in French and Francophone Literature and Film*, eds. Freeman G. Henry and Jeanne Garane (Amsterdam: Rodopi, 2003) 79. Such oppositions are common in *Carmen*. Elsewhere Ellison states that *Carmen* is a "conflict of cultures" (83). Jerrold Seigle agrees, further suggesting that in defining itself, the bourgeoisie is likewise conflicted, though it hides its bohemian yearning to break rules and live in absolute freedom—*Bohemian Paris: Culture, Politics, and the Boundaries of Bourgeois Life, 1830–1930* (New York: Viking, 1986) 9–10. I might add that *Carmen* makes this bohemian desire all the more obvious in the frame / narrator. As Evlyn Gould argues "the story has two narrators, two moral imperatives, two sets

88   *Sequence Framed in Mérimée's "Carmen"*

of rules for readers to follow. The result is [...] an oppositional world"— *The Fate of* Carmen (Baltimore, MD: Johns Hopkins UP, 1996) 60. The oppositions begin at the beginning of *Carmen*: Munda vs. Monda, past vs. present, Barbary vs. civilization, gypsy vs. bourgeois, passion vs. marriage, dog vs. wolf (379), or, in other terms, disobedience, thievery, murder, and anarchy vs. obedience, law, government, and middle-class respectability, if not rigidity.

7 Quoted from Blin 122. Charpentier suggests that as a short story writer he "chooses to fracture his writing [*écriture*]." He is "deliberately fragmentary" (36). François Géal focuses on the fundamental fragmentation of *Carmen*'s part four—"Mérimée et les gitans: Quelques réflexions sur le dernier chapitre de *Carmen*," *Mérimée et le bon usage du savoir: La Création à l'épreuve de la connaissance*, ed. Pierre Glaudes (Toulouse: PU du Mirail, 2008) 236.

8 Paul Ricœur, "Narrative Time," *Critical Inquiry* 7 (1980): 178.

9 René Godenne, *La Nouvelle française* (Paris: P.U.F., 1974) 125.

10 Roman Jakobson, *Essais de linguistique générale*, trans. Nicolas Ruwet (Paris: Éditions de Minuit, 1963) 209–48; and Joseph Frank, *The Widening Gyre: Crisis and Mastery in Modern Literature* (1945; rpt. New Brunswick, NJ: Rutgers UP, 1963).

11 See, for example, the title page indication: "adapted from the novel by Prosper Mérimée," in Bizet.

12 Tilby argues that just as *Carmen* is "the embodiment of a lie, [...] creating herself as a fiction" (260), Carmen is an "emptiness" in the text. We in fact have but scant details of her appearance and personality. Still, like the two narrators, we accept her as a *femme fatale* (260–63).

13 Corry L. Cropper, *Playing at Monarchy: Sport as Metaphor in Nineteenth-Century France.* (Lincoln: U of Nebraska P, 2008) 34–35. See also: below, n14.

14 See Corry L. Cropper, "Haunting the Nouveau Riches: Bohemia in Mérimée's 'La Vénus d'Ille' and *Carmen*," *Nineteenth-Century French Studies* 38.3 & 4 (2010): 188–95; Cropper's *Playing at Monarchy* 34–43; Elizabeth Wilson, *Bohemians: The Glamorous Outcasts* (New Brunswick, NJ: Rutgers UP, 2000); Anthony Glinoer, *La Bohème: Une Figure de l'imaginaire social* (Montreal: PU de Montréal, 2018).

15 Cogman, "The Narrators of Mérimée's *Carmen*," *Nottingham French Studies* 27.2 (November 1988): 4–6.

16 François Géal, "Le Polyglottisme, instrument de mystification et vecteur d'étrangeté, l'exemple emblématique de *Carmen*," *L'Etrangeté des langues*, eds. Yves Clavaron, Jérôme Dutel, and Clément Lévy (Saint-Etienne: PU de Saint-Etienne, 2011) 113. Géal goes on to say that for Borrow, *minchorro* means a prostitute's "bully," though Mérimée inserts a note with the translation of Borrow's English as "lover, or my caprice" (391, note a). According to the OED, a "bully" may be a "lover" or "one who lives by protecting prostitutes."

17 I repeat Cropper's insight that links the image of a bullfight to José murdering Carmen (*Playing* 35).

18 Lilian R. Furst, *The Contours of European Romanticism* (London: Macmillan, 1979) 42–43.

19 367. See also Gillian Horrocks, "A Semiotic Study of *Carmen*," *Nottingham French Studies* 25.2 (October 1986): 60–72.

20 See my consideration of lawlessness and civilization in "Subversive Structure in Gide's *L'Immoraliste*," *Novel Configurations: A Study of French Fiction*, 2nd ed. (Birmingham, AL: Summa Publ., 1987) 99–122.

Sequence Framed in Mérimée's "Carmen"   89

21 Parturier, n. to p. 409 (676), to which the Pléiade editors, Jean Mallion and Pierre Salomon, subscribe—*Théâtre de Clara Gazul, Romans et nouvelles* (Paris: Gallimard, 1978) 1587n6. The position is however nuanced by François Géal, "Mérimée et les gitans" 229–30 and n130.
22 Parturier refers to part four in his "Notice" to *Carmen* in the Garnier edition: "The purpose of this dissertation, which escapes me, has appeared in general inopportune. A desire to affirm his philological knowledge, or more simply to enlarge a volume that is in reality a little thin? we do not know" (342).
23 Peter J. Rabinowitz, "Singing for Myself: *Carmen* and the Rhetoric of Musical Resistance," *Audible Traces: Gender, Identity, and Music*, eds. Elaine Barkin and Lydia Hamesley (Zürich and Los Angeles: Carciofoli Verlagshaus, 1999) 136.
24 Sergio Sacchi says, Carmen is "triumphant disorder, a free, primitive Eros menacing civilized order"—"Carmen et le toréador," *Sport, lingua, letteratura francese*, ed. Mariagrazia Margarito (Alessandria: Dell' Orso, 1991) 93.
25 François Géal says there are just shy of forty such examples—"Mérimée et les gitans" 204.
26 Charles E. May, "Prolegomenon to a Generic Study of the Short Story," *Studies in Short Fiction* 33 (1996): 463.
27 Armine Mortimer, "Secrets of Literature, Resistance to Meaning," *Confrontations: Politics and Aesthetics in Nineteenth-Century France*, ed. Kathryn M. Grossman (Amsterdam: Rodopi, 2001) 55–66.
28 Michel Cégretin, ed., *Carmen*, by Mérimée (Paris: Bordas, 1980) 39.

6 Reforming Society and Genre in Hugo's "Claude Gueux"

Victor Hugo's desire to reform both society and art marks all of his work, as one would expect of the leader of the Romantics. Determined to create a militant, utilitarian work that was also aesthetic, he reformulated the fable as a helpful tool in his appeal to reform society. Like most writers who used the short-story form in a quest for literary art, he was surely aware of the disrespect in which it was held. For those who were satisfied with the few francs they earned in providing short-story filler for the newspapers, there was little impetus to reformulate the genre. Two columns worth in francs more or less would pay for a night or two on the town, even if the author were not invited to a late dinner with the actress or dancer who had caught his eye. Balzac uses his character Lousteau to illustrate this business at some length in *Illusions perdues* [*Lost Illusions*]. A few authors like Hugo were dissatisfied with the scant regard in which short stories were held. He and other innovative writers considered in these pages were determined to expand the genre into a vehicle that was both worthy and able to deal with important subjects. They may have modeled their aspirations on those of the classical dramatist Racine and his seemingly effortless ease in overcoming the restrictions imposed by the *Académie française*. For him, at least, the "three unities" were certainly no more restrictive than the brevity that defined and defines the short story.

Numerous ways to expand the scope of a story beyond the physical limitations of brevity and to emphasize its possibilities have been employed. Denon's method was to invent a story so complicated that the reader would be enticed into the creative heart of the story in the attempt to resolve the puzzle posed by his "Point de lendemain." Others, like Huysmans and Balzac, would leave conclusions open, as though the characters lived on to complete their actions. Here again, these overtures function only when readers engage their creative will and energy as they empower the stories into the future. Barbey would suggest a background tapestry of Church tradition that would envelope the characters in eternal condemnation. He was attempting to bring cultural knowledge to his text that would almost certainly be shared in that day by most of his readers. Hugo followed another route to enhance his short story.

Reforming Society and Genre in "Claude Gueux" 91

He adopted a familiar, age-old genre that had no requirements of either verse or length, and which would allow him explicitly and pointedly to address the social ills of the French prison system. In the process he gives the impression of considerable scope and is able to insist on the "ulcers" he perceives in his world. His "Claude Gueux" tells a pathetic tale that reveals the inadequacies of education and the penal system's profound injustice. Much as he explicitly liberated the *drame* [drama] of certain requirements, including verse, he opened the fable to a "shadow" tragedy taking place in his contemporary world.

Victor Hugo seldom waits for the conclusion of his works before offering readers the moral of the story. When he explicitly explains the meaning or lesson of his creation, it may be particularly hard for modern sensitivities to bear, for it frustrates sophisticated readers accustomed to the subtleties of nineteenth-century literature and the pleasures of arriving at their own understandings.[1] This, after all, is the century when such writers as Balzac, Flaubert, Huysmans, Zola, and indeed Hugo brought prose fiction to maturity. In "Claude Gueux" (1834), well before Hugo saw himself as having particularly profound insights into metaphysics, the narrator promises different fare: "I tell it like it is, letting the reader pick up the morals as the facts sow them on their way."[2] If readers are expected to grasp the lesson taught by the "facts" of the story, one can justifiably ask why the narrator proceeds to raise a stentorian voice and a clerically pointed finger as he instructs in acceptable standards of right and wrong, of virtue and vice? Is there an additional, hidden lesson? Hugo suggested that the true joys of some literature are in the details.[3] Certainly, his work rewards close reading, however enmeshed he becomes in his potentially conflicting desires to teach, on the one hand, and to create art, on the other.

Hugo's dramatic reiteration of a moral that is already clear within the work often drowns whatever pleasure a reader may have received from the poetic qualities of his lyrical verse or prose or in the moral victory or defeat of his characters. The use of this didactic repetition in "Claude Gueux" may however be a special, justifiable case. Not only was the author anxious for society to recognize that poverty breeds crime, that capital punishment cannot be justified, and that universal education is essential to a healthy society, he was under considerable pressure from friends and acquaintances to create "militant literature" devoted to the betterment of society and to distance himself from those poets who were uniquely engaged in art. When he came across the newspaper article on the murderer, Claude Gueux, probably in mid-March of 1832, the account's appropriateness as an example for several of his major concerns could hardly be missed. As is clear in a number of prefaces and essays, the question for the author was how he could deal with the vital lessons suggested by the criminal's life, without compromising his commitment to creating art. "Claude Gueux," the result of these varied impulsions,

92   Reforming Society and Genre in "Claude Gueux"

was far more than a "tract."[4] It is a fine work of art that significantly engages his reading audience. It deserves critical attention.

As "Claude Gueux" was germinating, Hugo was in the midst of constant personal and professional turmoil.[5] Especially in the prefaces to the plays *Cromwell* and *Lucrèce Borgia,* and to the *Odes et ballades,* but most insistently in the collection of essays originally written from 1819 until 1830 and gathered together in *Littérature et philosophie mêlées* of 1834, Hugo was meditating profoundly on art and its role in the nineteenth century. This collection represents Hugo's attempt at what Bernard Leuilliot calls a "recapitulation" (LP 5) and provides an excellent window into the mind and heart of the writer during the period of the creation of "Claude Gueux." The included, revised fragments and essays written from 1819 through to 1834 were chosen and arranged by the author for publication in 1834. All testify to his growing social consciousness, increasing politicization, and critical pressure as a leading figure of Romanticism. Sainte-Beuve and Pierre Leroux, among others, had pointed to his regrettable "dilettantism" and obeisance to "art for art."[6] If nothing else, he felt obligated to ask himself a number of probing questions about the function of literature in regard to beauty and to the social good. While variations on the discussions recur regularly in these and other essays, his work indicates increasing sympathy for didactic literature. "To the [author's] eyes, there are many social questions in literary questions, and every work is an act."[7] Certainly, even before Hugo fell profoundly under the temptation of messianism, he wished to have a lasting impact on society, and he felt his obligation to humankind deeply. It is understandable that, surrounded by social activists like the Saint-Simonians (whom he mentions repeatedly), he would likewise concentrate on bringing his social observations and remedies into a harmonic whole with art and artistry.

The various essays in *Littérature et philosophie mêlées* demonstrate that Hugo thought it possible to have his art serve larger social issues, thus contenting his contemporaries like the aborning sociologist Saint-Simon, and, at the same time, satisfying aesthetically oriented friends like Gautier. The technically interesting *Le Dernier Jour d'un condamné* (1829), an "anonymous" work that was published as though it were the dead man's veritable confession, was Hugo's early attempt to turn public opinion against the guillotine. Still, the work had met widespread criticism and was manifestly unsuccessful: after all, there was little pause in the use of Dr. Guillotin's invention.

Hugo also began to consider the validity of traditional genres. His ruminations on the structures of literature leave no doubt that he wished not only to rework, but indeed, to reform the concepts defining theatre and other genres, as well.[8] He was, of course, not the first to seek such change. Generic reformulation was particularly important for Romantics, and was a consistent effort through the rest of the century. From the

Reforming Society and Genre in "Claude Gueux" 93

early 1820s in essays on Voltaire, Sir Walter Scott, and Chénier, republished in *Littérature et philosophie mêlées*, Hugo displayed his interest in generic literary models. The most revealing passages turn on theatre, for he was also deeply involved in the genre, but he also refers to other forms of literature. His essays reiterate that well-established literary traditions (LP 41) regarding odes (LP 34, 177), novels (LP 76, 128–34), elegies (LP 81), or drama[9] must not be violated, though they may be reconfigured. In some cases, a particular genre might be subdivided, as, for example, between the "bourgeois *drame*" and the "royal *drame*," each with its own rules.[10] Not only does theatre teach and civilize, Hugo felt it had become what the church was in the Middle Ages, "a central and attractive place," and the function of the dramatist, "a sacred calling" (LP 37). Modern theatre could maintain the grandeur that it enjoyed under Louis XIV, though it must adapt in accordance with this new period after the Revolution. I suggest that for Hugo the generic rules of classical tragedy served as a sort of shadow genre for his *drames*, rather like a shadow cabinet can exert occult but significant influence on a government. Numerous studies of Hugo's theatre emphasize the important influence of the great dramatic works of the French classical age on his *drames*. With *Hernani*, Hugo proved that in one work he could follow most of the rules of traditional tragedy, while simultaneously in five acts and lyrical alexandrines satirize recent practitioners and the dreary, tumescent plays dominating the *Comédie française*. *Hernani*, however, was a work of circumstance, designed to push the classicists out of the way and off the stage. More important was the effort to adjust art to modern sensitivities. The sublime and the grotesque, lyric and drama, comic and tragic, high and low could all indeed be integrated aesthetically into one work, as he insisted in the preface to *Cromwell*. In general, "[A]rt must be serious, candid, moral, and religious" (LP 41). Hugo regarded the nineteenth-century French *drame* as in the same tradition as seventeenth-century tragedy, and it should in no way sacrifice excellence (LP 40).

Victor Hugo believed that the mission of theatre had not changed either; it continued to be basically educative. Nonetheless, "[D]rama, an oeuvre looking forward to a long life, can but lose everything in turning itself into a preacher with three or four momentarily fitting truths" (LP 38), and it must never veer from its goal of art: "Art [...] must be its own end" (LP 39). The preferred, modern "form" was no longer tragedy but "drama" and certainly not "mundane shop and sitting room tragedy, [that is,] rambling, ugly, mannered, epileptic, sentimental, and whimpering" (LP 40–41). He wrote that this relatively new theatrical genre of the *drame* could once again bring theatre to greatness, but only if it continued the basic structure of the traditional tragedy, though amended with modern language and style that could speak to the masses (the sense of "popular" in the period). "Basically moral. Formally literary. Basically and formally for ordinary people" (LP 41).

94 *Reforming Society and Genre in "Claude Gueux"*

Contemporary drama spoke directly to the people (LP 40), and commitment to verse was no longer necessary. In his *Discours sur la poésie* of 1709, the aggressively "modern" Antoine Houdar de La Motte had long before brought versification into question (Pascal 79). Verse, after all, could compromise clear thought. Hugo, however, recognized that discarding verse did not release theatre from all rules. Indeed, effective theatre carried with it, as an aura or a shadow, the requirements and traditions of its past. Audiences could be expected to be sensitive to this powerful shadow-context, whether it was explicit or not.

Prose as well had its traditions and expectations that were established by predecessors. As Hugo said,

> [T]hose who study [prose] know that it has a thousand of its own laws, a thousand secrets, a thousand properties, a thousand resources born as much from its own substance as from that of the three languages that preceded it and that it multiplies by each other. It also has its particular prosody and all sorts of little internal rules known only to those who practice it, and without which prose would no more exist than verse. (LP 34; see, also 44)

Whether in prose or verse, ancient creators wrote in accordance with their traditions (LP 44). Though Hugo's theatrical works had often before used verse, as a result of this thought, his next play, *Lucrèce Borgia* (1833), turned from verse to prose. He did not feel that he had violated the tradition of the dramatic genre, and, in fact, Hugo insisted that Romanticism had the task of renovating prose, as it had renewed the alexandrine.[11] Hugo's desire to free art from the stultifying chains of tradition is too well known and understood to devote more space to acknowledging its importance here. His primary argument is in reference to the *drame*, but his inventiveness marks all of his work, whether he mentions a genre specifically or not. He made so many changes to most poetic forms that they could best be perceived together as lyric rather than as odes or ballades.

We do not know assuredly what propelled Victor Hugo to turn to the short story and the fable when he composed "Claude Gueux," but we can be certain that it was not an accident. We know that he considered himself a master of those contemporary genres that had importance. In the introduction to *Littérature et philosophie mêlées*, he discusses such traditional genres as they are tied to the artist's genius.

> An idea never has more than one form that is appropriate, that is its excellent form, its complete form, its rigorous form, its essential form, its form preferred by it, and which always rushes with it as a whole into the mind of a genius [...]. So it is that all art [...] must begin by posing formal, linguistic, stylistic questions of itself. (LP 30)

Reforming Society and Genre in "Claude Gueux" 95

At the time when Hugo came across the newspaper account of Claude Gueux, an analysis of his concurrent essays and prefaces indicates his inclination to make prose a possible if not preferred mode of expression. Georges Piroué's related comment, "Behind the anecdote he looks for an edifying example, and to the rational analysis of a case, he prefers the powers of a fable" ("Présentation," CG 228), deserves further development. We may infer in the essays from this period that what Hugo explicitly did for the *drame*, he wished to repeat for other literary forms, as well. By making use of the tradition infusing the modern fable, Hugo seems to have turned to a short account in prose allowing him to exploit many touching details, nobility of character, and a reiterated moral that would give the story the emphasis to highlight the reforms France needed and make them unquestionable.

The fable was extremely popular among the reading public. Jean-Noël Pascal refers to its voluminous production during the period between 1770 and 1815 as "the rage for fables" (121–24). Examples are "*innumérable[s]*" (229). The genre had furthermore been the subject of considerable controversy. Although fables were generally in verse, Abbé Le Monnier ridiculed practitioners who insisted on rhyme and meter. Most fables submitted to the best-known models, however loose the standards became, and the genre attracted many of the period's notable authors, including Dorat, Florian, and Madame de Genlis (Pascal 139–213). Rather than highly regarded social commentary and entertainment like that of La Fontaine, late eighteenth-century fables emphasized the norm of pedagogy, philosophy, and politics. The fable seemed to be moving toward something more simplified, a short work unified around its lesson, written aesthetically but in the language of the day, and developing an allegorical story about human concerns, without, however, bothering with rhyme, while continuing to express its normally explicit moral.

Prepared by his early experience with boulevard theatre and consideration of the classical tragedy that was being recast in modern form, the fable must have seemed a promising genre to Hugo. Many fabulists were, like Antoine-Vincent Arnault (1766–1834), also dramatists. Both genres permitted a lesson or apologue; but in the case of fables, it was expected. Furthermore, the best fables offered practical impetus and a kind of lingering image (Pascal 20) that Hugo cultivated in his poetry and elsewhere.[12] While much ink had been dispensed on whether a fable's moral should be at the beginning or end, the genre's unity was the most important factor for most practitioners. The definitions that established the fable insisted on the action, the unity, and the lesson (Pascal 35–37). Although most scholarly evaluations then and now consider fables versified stories of animals personifying human situations, seventeenth-, eighteenth-, and early nineteenth-century thinkers permitted both animals and people without prescribing a basic

96 Reforming Society and Genre in "Claude Gueux"

pattern. Eighteenth-century fabulists occasionally ignored the demand for brevity (Pascal 27), and as Lessing had recently, and successfully, demonstrated in theory and practice, whether the fable was in verse or in prose, it focused increasingly on the present. Lessing's over-riding position was clear: "Truth requires the graceful aid of fable, but needs fable the ornament of rhyme? [......] Enough, that the invention of fable belongs to the poet, but the delivery of it that of the historian, its moral that of the philosopher."[13] Hugo seemingly decided to go beyond such masters as Aesop, Hyginus, La Fontaine, Florian, or others in developing a modern version of the fable or moral tale, for which Lessing's definition seems appropriate: "A fable is the account of a series of changes which together form a whole. The unity of the fable consists in all the parts leading up to an end, the end for which the fable was invented being the moral precept."[14] Utilizing prose allowed Hugo more freedom to emphasize the thesis.

Prior to Hugo, prose fables were not standard fare, though subsequently in Tolstoy, Bierce, and Thurber, for example, they increased in frequency. Using prose and human characters would give Hugo freedom to illustrate concepts that might be foreign to the social consciousness of the war-weary population that had been immersed in the fractious turmoil of post-revolutionary transformation. The ideas driving Hugo were neither general psychological truths about pride, envy, and persistence, nor about universal values like justice, honor, and truth that most fables defend. A reformer, he preferred rather opinions that were not widely supported, if only because they favored social reform in a society already exhausted by change. His positions on capital punishment and universal education required effective argument. He had tried the internal monologue of a banal personage in *Le Dernier Jour d'un condamné* (1829). This time, in "Claude Gueux," he would turn to a very sympathetic character in a work echoing the fable, though in a short prose narrative with human characters. The story was fleshed out around the covert armature of the fable, which allowed him to develop a terminal thesis that brought the illustrative story to a point.

Hugo's very modern approach to employing the fable genre but substituting prose instead of verse and contemporary, real human beings instead of stereotypical personages or animals makes it much more direct and immediate. Such a way of working might have elicited a skeptical, raised eyebrow from the readers of his day, since it went beyond journalistic reporting and elevated the result to socially conscious art, but as Sainte-Beuve pointed out, "The Fable is a genre in nature, a form of invention that is inherent in the mind of human beings, and it is found in all places and in all countries. [...] The Fable is everywhere, and people would reinvent it every century, if it were forgotten." Indeed, as Sainte-Beuve went on to point out, despite La Fontaine's mastery, he had many excellent successors.[15] Given that the fable was a rather short form that

Reforming Society and Genre in "Claude Gueux" 97

was always organized around an illustrative example and often included a moral lesson explicitly expressing its main point, the basic structure of the fable was perfect for Hugo's needs. He could exploit the traditional irony, the subtleties of implication, or explicit emphasis, the tight unity, as well as the philosophical grounding. He could lengthen it by a few pages and reformulate the concluding apothegm to serve as a means of reforming an evil in society, all without betraying the elastic form of the generic fable. While La Fontaine's explicative morals generally support widely espoused wisdom that would find few in disagreement, "Claude Gueux" illustrates what might be seen as a literary form of social activism or, more explicitly, a shadow-fable proposing an ideal rejected by many but, if implemented as reforms in the penal and educational systems, it could raise society to a new, enlightened level.

As the text of "Claude Gueux" demonstrates, Hugo's resuscitated and reformulated fable genre takes advantage of its long tradition where, unquestionably, "[w]hen you dig into art, at the first blow of the pickax, you cut into literary questions, with the second into social questions" (LP 28). In truth, "[t]he art of today must not limit itself to the search for beauty, but even more what is good" (LP 38). "Claude Gueux" poses the problem of acceptable didacticism well. More readable than the fiction of Eugène Sue or much of the edifying literature of the 1830s and 1840s designed to lead young ladies aright, Hugo's remarkable talent and his creative power are evident as he spins out his story and the concluding aphorism in rhythms approaching verse that attract and hold a reader's attention. He turns an ancient genre meant for instruction in the guise of entertainment into a weapon capable of changing society. The aphoristic conclusion exhorts attentiveness to the worthy needs of people, no matter their class, social position, or circumstance.

Baudelaire would one day dream of "the miracle of poetic prose, musical without rhythm and without rhyme, sufficiently supple and sufficiently halting to adapt to the lyrical movements of the soul, to the undulations of reverie, to the convulsions of conscience."[16] Hugo had already approached this ideal in "Claude Gueux" by inventing a system of intertwining repetitions that perfume the story with the scent of legendry. As he himself said in a review of Théophile Gautier's *Mademoiselle de Maupin*, "Poetry no more makes the poet uncomfortable when he writes in prose than wings make birds uncomfortable."[17] Hugo's lyricism acclimates readers to a world of symbols and archetypes and to the realm of modern fables and moral tales bearing arguments of transformative importance.

Hugo's narrator in "Claude Gueux" does not hesitate to use the first-person pronoun and is thus able to enter into the story as a champion who attacks two of the day's injustices. His story stigmatizes contemporary justice, as well as bourgeois society's disregard for the lower classes moldering in illiteracy, malnutrition, and disease. Hugo

98 *Reforming Society and Genre in "Claude Gueux"*

wanted profound social reform, so that ignorance and utter destitution, which grew from the bourgeoisie's selective blindness to the needs of the laboring classes, would no longer engender thieves and assassins among men and prostitutes among women. He was firmly convinced that prisons served as schools where crime was propagated and promoted, where young people with minor offenses devolved into hardened criminals. Men and women who were born free and full of potential were being perverted into monsters of nightmare scenarios by incarceration. Claude Gueux, the main character of this story, for example, has been transformed by the justice system. "[H]onest worker, not long ago; thief, from now on" (CG 236). Hugo would say that the prison workshop director has the task of reforming a thief into a socially useful worker. Unfortunately, rehabilitation was a little understood concept, and the prison official, "Monsieur D." (CG 245), is not up to the task. His major quality is "stubbornness without intelligence, it is foolishness welded to the end of stupidity" (CG 236). Of course, the director has no self-awareness. He is one of "these stubborn, little accidents of fate who think they are providential" (CG 237).

Rather than a preface or an epigraph, Hugo's story begins with a letter supposedly written to the *Revue de Paris*' director, asking that a copy of the text of "Claude Gueux" be sent to each of France's deputies in the National Assembly. Scholars know that the story's title was indeed the name of a real person, however different he was from Hugo's serendipitous incarnation based on the name's linguistic meaning ("Claude" derives from an etymon meaning "crippled,"[18] and "Gueux" is good French for "rogue" or "beggar"). The author's clever renewal of the eponymous character may have been replaced by invention when it came to the introductory letter, asking that copies of the story be sent to every legislator. It is signed by "Charles Carlier" (CG 235), both names deriving from the same etymological root for "man" or "humankind" (Dauzat 112; Yonge xli, 385–86). Such repeated onomastic good fortune is most likely too good to be true. Still, while an authentic letter-document has not surfaced for scholarly scrutiny, the printed version serves very well as a literary preamble for the story. It sets the tone and signals the importance of what follows. Whatever the truth of the initial letter, Hugo is doing everything possible to use his reformulated fable as a means of rectifying illiteracy and capital punishment. While the tale has some historical antecedents,[19] every element reveals the story's design, structured to stimulate sympathy and raise the moral outrage of his audience.

If the historical background of Claude Gueux is important, the scholar Savey-Casard has elucidated it with admirable clarity. Certainly Victor Hugo did not fail to wring every ounce of pathos from the events that had appeared in the newspapers. Nonetheless, during his entire career, the author seldom took his eyes off the legacy that he and his

Reforming Society and Genre in "Claude Gueux" 99

works would offer to future generations, and there seems little doubt that he was considerably less interested in writing history than in creating "useful art." Jean Massin's edition resurrects a fragmentary draft that he dates in the spring of 1832, when Hugo was writing the new preface for *Le Dernier Jour d'un condamné*, as well as contemplating the possibility of composing and, even, perhaps, beginning a draft of "Claude Gueux."[20] In fact, we do not know which work he had in mind during the fragment's creation, though it does offer good insight into his point of view on the relationship of historical reality and moral truth and usefulness. As Hugo said, "To those who ask us whether this story *happened*, as they say, we would answer that it matters little. [...] It will always be real enough, if it has some usefulness. The important thing is not that a story be veritable, but that it be true" ("Portefeuille romanesque," Massin 4.896).

Hugo's character, Claude Gueux, is an impoverished worker from Paris. Like many lower-class people of the period, though he has both a mistress and a child, he is not married, for marriage was expensive. While physically large and healthy and a good worker, he has no education, "not knowing how to read and knowing how to think" (CG 235). When he lacked employment one winter, his family went hungry and suffered from the cold. Claude stole and was caught. Although the proceeds of the theft only resulted in three days' worth of bread and heat, he was condemned to five years of prison. He lost both his child, who disappeared, and his mistress, who became a prostitute. For Claude the sentence was devastating. More than ninety percent of infants in the foundling homes died, and prostitution was widely thought to be the first step to syphilis, disfigurement, madness, and death.[21] In respect to the story, the themes of suffering and judgment are established with this episode. An irrevocable change has taken place in Claude. He has been judged and is now incarcerated in Clairvaux. Not only has he been declared a thief, he is a convict.

There is no question about the criminal's suffering. Claude feels the distress of imprisonment, the loss of his family, insufficient food, the cruel comments of the workshop director, Monsieur D., and finally the pain of being separated from Albin, the young friend who shares his ration of bread and makes Claude's life possible. "He had [...] suffered a great deal" (CG 236). Albin's name derives from "white," a color that often symbolizes both "purity" and "potential."[22] When Monsieur D. removes Albin to another workshop, not only does Claude lose the extra food he needs, he loses a caring, supportive friendship. And his large frame once again feels the pangs of hunger.

The story is built on oppositions. The prison where Claude is incarcerated exemplifies the device. Once an abbey that ministered to the spirit, it has become a prison that punishes the body and brutalizes the spirit. As the narrator says, a pillory was made from an altar (CG

100 Reforming Society and Genre in "Claude Gueux"

235). Claude rapidly gains near absolute authority over his workshop in the prison. He is large, with a serious and dignified demeanor. His high, wrinkled forehead is set above a young face below black hair showing a little grey. He has a handsome, imposing head that does not suggest a criminal, though it will soon be separated from his body. Something imperious about him imposes obedience on others, though he makes few gestures and speaks little (CG 236).

The director contrasts with Claude. He is "a curt, tyrannical man, obeying his own ideas, always keeping his authority on a tight rein; moreover, on occasion, a good companion, generous, jovial even, gracefully bantering; hard rather than firm, which is duty rather than virtue; in a word, not evil, [rather] bad" (CG 236). Moved neither by ideas nor sentiment, his anger is icy, making fire without heat. His most salient trait, according to the narrator, is that he holds tenaciously to whatever he has decided, however absurd the decision may be. His variety of virtue finds needling the prisoner about the loss of his wife and child perfectly acceptable (CG 237). Certainly, this representative of society's law and order is jealous of the high regard in which the other prisoners hold Claude. One can understand how a man like Monsieur D. would hate Claude Gueux. The historical director's name was in fact Delacelle (Savey-Casard, *Edition critique* 51). That Hugo terms him Monsieur D. may be another example of Hugo's serendipity, for in some traditions the letter "D" bears the connotations of hostility.[23] The narrator finds it natural that "loved by the prisoners, [Claude] was detested by the jailers" (CG, p. 237). As the friendship between Claude and Albin grows, so Monsieur D.'s jealousy and hatred of Claude strengthens. Albin nourishes Claude with food and companionship; by removing Albin, Monsieur D. withholds food, respect, and friendship, leaving the prisoner hungry and alone. It is only right that Claude refuse the generous offers of nourishment from other prisoners, for Albin's gift of food was coupled with the close friendship binding Claude to Albin. Clearly, it is not merely food that is in question, and Claude's loyalty attests to their profound bond.

The narration shows that we are not restricted to mundane comparisons. In fact, the struggle between Monsieur D. and Claude constitutes a battle between spiritual and physical reality, between good and evil. The director "had a secret, envious, implacable hatred for Claude in the depths of his heart, the hatred of the legal sovereign for the real lord, of temporal power for spiritual power" (CG 239). The oppositions become more marked. Claude is respectful; Monsieur D. is not. Claude speaks to him as an adult, while the director uses the familiar form with the prisoner, as with a child or inferior or, as the narrator adds, with a dog (CG 245). When Claude asks, "Why are you separating me from Albin?" the director also uses the answer that has been favored by numberless parents wearied by repeated challenges of their decisions:

Reforming Society and Genre in "Claude Gueux" 101

"Because" (CG 240, 245, 246). He never explains, though his reasons rooted in jealousy and vanity are clear.

Hugo's allusion to the account of the "Lion and the Dog" is pivotal, for it strengthens the pathos resulting from Claude's utter devastation when he loses Albin. When the director rebuffs him for the first time, "Claude dropped his head and did not answer. Poor lion in a cage from whom they have taken his dog!" (CG 240). Hugo is probably alluding to a well-known, true story of a pet lion, Woira, sent as a gift from the director of the Compagnie d'Afrique in Senegal to Versailles in 1788 and accompanied by his close, canine friend and constant companion. Following the dog's death of mange, the lion also passed on, whether from despair or tainted meat depends on the version. The relationship between Woira and the dog attracted considerable popular attention.[24] After the first etching and text published in 1794, the story was re-published numerous times with various meanings through the course of the century, until Tolstoy wrote his famous fable adaptation of 1872. The archetypal story that was reinterpreted repeatedly suggested that the lion's friendship with the little dog was like the king's relationship to his people, or an image of the Revolutionary Terror's dispensation of capricious "justice," or, indeed, in Bernardin de Saint-Pierre and others, like the benevolence, virtue, and fidelity of nature, where the lion's death becomes a "moral crime against nature" (Lee 33). Eventually, after the king and his family were hauled from Versailles to Paris, the lion and the dog followed. There was even some discussion in the Revolutionary Convention about the possibility that the aristocratic lion should also be executed (Lee 32–33).

The story in whatever version made a deep impression on Hugo, for, as Kathryn Grossman pointed out to me, he alludes to it again in *Les Misérables* (1862). Considering this later allusion sheds light on its meaning as an important aspect of the earlier allusion in "Claude Gueux." Jean Valjean has just discovered that Cosette loves Marius. "Then he heard his soul roar dully in the darkness, having once again become terrible. Go ahead and see what happens when you take the dog that the lion has in his cage!"[25] The various reconfigurations of the tale of the lion and the dog seem to have been less well known in the second half of the century, since Hugo felt the need to continue and explain what was unnecessary in his earlier 1834 version: "Jean Valjean's love of Cosette is like that of a father or mother or sister. [T]his [familial] sentiment […] was mixed with others that were vague, ignorant, pure with the purity of blindness, unconscious, celestial, angelic, divine; less like a sentiment than like instinct, less like instinct than like an imperceptible and invis-ible but real attraction; and the love, properly put, was in his enormous tenderness for Cosette like the gold thread in the tenebrous and virgin mountain" (*Misérables* 9.810). Hugo continues for several pages in the attempt to make his readers grasp why even the possibility of losing

102   *Reforming Society and Genre in "Claude Gueux"*

Cosette, the object of Jean Valjean's unmitigated love, could bring his soul to the point of weakening, how even with all the wisdom and generosity that had long directed his path, he could look deep within himself and find the specter of hatred for Marius, who is taking a person he loves away. The feelings that Jean Valjean has for Cosette echo those of Claude Gueux for Albin and those the lion feels for the little dog. For the author of "Claude Gueux," the lion and dog story represents something far deeper than friendship. It was a love that was all-encompassing and that would make life without Albin impossible. In Hugo's mind, the lion unquestionably died of despair when his little canine friend passed on. The allusion then not only builds sentiment, it prepares Claude's death.

As Monsieur D. represents the arm of the law, so Claude has quickly become "the soul, the law and order of the workshop" (CG 237). When queried about Albin's displacement, the theme of judgment returns in binary form. The director has made a *décision* (CG 241; emphasis in original), from which there is no appeal. After the murder of Monsieur D. and Claude's new judicial condemnation, the convict will appeal the jury's decision without success. His careful consideration of Monsieur D.'s guilt makes a striking contrast with the official court conviction for murder. That Claude follows the biblical model of Matthew 18.15, which advises to "go and tell him his fault between thee and him alone," makes the prisoner seem all the more reasonable. Claude addresses the director directly. He leaves ample time for the director to rectify his injustice. Only after having given repeated warnings does he bring the matter to the entire workshop. Unlike Monsieur D., who settles repeatedly for the uncommunicative "Because," Claude justifies his judgment and the reasons for it clearly and without passion. We remember the narrator's early conclusion: Monsieur D. is "not evil, [rather] bad" (CG 236). The narrator subsequently makes a lexical shift and chooses the stronger term: Monsieur D. is "evil" (CG 243). Claude Gueux has consequently judged him (CG 243), a condemnation that his fellow prisoners shortly validate. In so doing, he takes on the role of an examining magistrate in a society of unfortunates. "Once this strange court of appeals had, so to speak, ratified the sentence that he had reached" (CG 244), Claude moves to the execution stage. Even at this point, he pays attention to the cautionary recommendation from a fellow inmate that he ask Monsieur D. once more for the merciful return of Albin. Only thereafter does he execute his judgment, reached thoughtfully and with deliberation, while his own, later official conviction is so rapid that it betrays the injudiciousness of the bourgeois jury. Claude is tranquil once he has been condemned. He returns to his work, much the way "Jacques Clément went back to prayer" (CG 244). Although Clément is remembered as a fanatical assassin, he and other members of the Catholic League thought he was doing God's will when he murdered Henri III (indeed, canonization was even discussed). Likewise, Hugo's hero is at peace with

Reforming Society and Genre in "Claude Gueux"   103

his decision and with what will follow. "[H]e found it good to give his life for a just cause" (CG 243). Hugo understood that such radical solutions as murder flow inevitably from poverty and illiteracy.

The tools of the jailhouse execution reflect two stages of the history of humankind. In order to exact his vengeance, Claude will kill the director with a hatchet, "man's first arm-tool" (Chevalier 397). While the more civilized mechanism of execution is, of course, unavailable to him, though he will himself eventually be guillotined, Claude turns to an even more refined blade for his own suicide. He takes the scissors that had belonged to "his woman" (CG 246) and stabs himself repeatedly in a failed attempt to commit suicide, for he accepts the talion and knows that "he could not take the director's life without giving up his own" (CG 243). Appropriately, scissors were the tool with which the Erinyes cut the thread of life, thus punishing criminals.[26] Claudie Bernard, in an excellent study of the story, sees, as well, that on the one hand the ax which serves as a carpentry tool is turned to evil and becomes an arm for murder, so a seamstress's scissors become a tool for suicide and a prefiguration of the guillotine.[27] While mistress and child stand in Claude's mind for love, the jailer's relentless needling uses references to them as weapons to express his hatred.

The lesson comes through with dazzling clarity. Hugo wishes to bring this society before the bar, for the lower, working class's abject poverty and illiteracy has made it into a festering underclass that will inevitably damage, if not destroy, the whole of civilization. The illiterate Claude's tattered belongings, which include an incomplete copy of Rousseau's *Émile*, are coupled with his later counsel to a sixteen-year-old inmate to learn to read, and further highlights the theme of education. The scissors remind readers of the importance of the hero's intimate life in his family. Ill-prepared for the industrializing world of the late eighteenth and early nineteenth centuries, Claude's status as an unskilled worker will simply not permit him to feed both a wife and child during one of the many periods of economic turmoil. Nor was the seamstress work of his woman sufficient to satisfy the needs of a family.[28] Prostitution that remained for well over a century at nearly four to five percent of the population in Paris and the larger French cities was a result.[29] The companion of poverty, illiteracy, and prostitution was, inevitably, crime.

Recent readers might well ask why the story does not conclude some five pages before the end. The narrator's attitude is decidedly in favor of Claude Gueux, though authorities arranged the trial prejudicially to cast a negative light on the accused. The hero enters the courtroom in the dull, grey clothing of those incarcerated at Clairvaux. Furthermore, the room was full of the arrondissement's soldiers. Should the jury not understand what caused this crowd of militia, the prosecutor explains that it is to control all the criminals who were to testify (CG 247). In fact, these prisoners are Claude's friends and under his direction, and

104   *Reforming Society and Genre in "Claude Gueux"*

they refuse to testify until he orders them to speak. Claude corrects any of their mistakes. The royal prosecutor's discourse is, however, reduced in the account to two cliché-ridden lines characterizing Claude as a very guilty person, after which the narration dismisses the attorney's remaining words with an "etc." (CG 247). Although readers are given little of the hero's speech, because we project with considerable assurance from our understanding of his character what the eloquent but uneducated hero would have said, we accept the narrator's judgment that his presentation would have favorably disposed "an intelligent person who [...] came back struck with astonishment" (CG 247). He is, we are told, "rather an orator than an assassin. [...] He says things simply, seriously without adding or subtracting. [...] [H]e had moments of true eloquence" (CG 247). The narrator summarizes as he steps in with a clarion call for social justice.

Only when the prosecutor claims that Claude acted without justification does the accused react angrily (CG 248). At this point, readers are left to envisage "a whole theory of moral provocation forgotten by the law" (CG 248). It is no doubt true that Claude Gueux has committed a number of crimes detailed in the Code: he has lived in adultery with a woman, who is now, indeed, a prostitute, and he has fathered an illegitimate child. He has stolen. And he has killed. All true. Still, Claude asks pertinent questions: "But why did I steal? Why did I kill? Ask yourself these two questions, gentlemen of the jury" (CG 249). The conviction is not long in coming. Condemned to death, he repeats: "There are two questions that they don't answer" (CG 249). On the morning of his execution, his head falls before the last bell rings eight o'clock, a number that signifies resurrection and regeneration (Chevalier 412). The ultimate meaning of Claude Gueux's life and death will not go away.

Nature has fashioned Claude admirably. "This man, certainly, was well born, well organized, well gifted. [...] Well made mind, well made heart" (CG 250). Society on the other hand has not met its concomitant responsibility. It has put Claude "in a society so badly made that he ended by stealing; society put him in a prison so badly made that he ended by killing" (CG 251). How then could Claude Gueux be guilty? Society has not done its duty, for it has not provided an education, and he has been crippled by societal strictures and neglect. Deprived of these civilizing benefits, he then acts according to natural law rather than the Civil Code. The reader has consequently read the exemplum and is now prepared for the concluding pages long apothegm that serves not just to explain, for there is little left vague, but to emphasize in the manner of a fable. "The head of this man of the people: cultivate it, prepare it, water it, fertilize it, enlighten it, teach it, use it; you will never need cut it off" (CG 254). Victor Hugo argues cogently through these concluding pages that Claude Gueux's life and death serve as the narrator's determined pleading against society before the bar of civilization. As Claude

Reforming Society and Genre in "Claude Gueux" 105

is judged, first for theft, then for murder, as Monsieur D. is judged for cruelty, so the narrator rises to demand of governors and legislators that society be judged. "Who is really culpable? Is it he? Is it us?" (CG 251) Claude's is just one of a number of heads that have recently fallen (CG 252). With such weighty matters to consider, it is time to stop worrying about futilities like the number of white or yellow buttons on National Guard uniforms. "The people are hungry, the people are cold. Poverty pushes it to crime or vice, depending on the sex. Have pity on the people" (CG 252). Stop concentrating on the convicts and prostitutes. Ask yourself about the malady that produces these "ulcers." Society has done away with branding. It should do likewise with ball and chain and executions.[30] The narrator demands that economy be practiced in a way that makes a real difference. Stop killing criminals; get rid of executioners. Turn rather to schools and education. Teach the French, all the French, to read.

Savey-Casard cites the *Moniteur* of 29 April 1834 in claiming that three-fifths of the French of less than twenty years of age did not know how to read, and, according to an official report of 1833, thirty-one percent of boys did not even go to school (*Edition critique* 125n128). Having focused on the sickness and the symptoms, on incarceration and capital punishment as ineffective cures, Hugo asks that society turn to promising restorations, not just teaching to read but education that will help the poor to look up and find "the belief in a better world made for him" (CG 254). Reminding readers of "a more philosophic book than *le Compère Mathieu*," which caustically satirized the church and society in 1766, he raises the issue of belief in "a better world" (CG 254). Then metaphorically turning to an archetypal figure that will be exploited in future literary works, from the executions of Julien Sorel to Meursault surrounded by similarly unruly crowds, he points to the person of Jesus (CG 254), thus suggesting that Claude is a messianic figure who willingly sacrifices himself for the betterment of the "people." He brings his peroration to a close by insisting that, before it became necessary to separate heads from their bodies with the guillotine, it would be better to cultivate them.

Hugo's earnest, terminal moral lesson was sincere, if sincerity can be judged by a lifetime of consistently similar pleas. Although not explicitly referring to "Claude Gueux" as a fable, or indeed as a short story, his attempt to call his society to justice and renewal plays on the ancient fable genre that exists in the background and undoubtedly affected readers of Hugo's day. The example offered by Claude Gueux provides a clear, meaningful example, and by bringing all the story's strands into an uncluttered conclusion, the narrator is able to emphasize his message effectively. As classical tragedy was a "shadow" genre for the *drame*, so the fable was a "shadow" genre for Hugo's short story. The case that he paints of an arguably innocent hero allows him explicitly to discuss the

106　*Reforming Society and Genre in "Claude Gueux"*

waste of a good man and the need to prevent further depredations among the poor and helpless. More important, he begs that society prepare the miserably uneducated to become productive citizens. Hugo's exploitation of prose in this fable skillfully uses stylistic devices, rhythms, and symbols, which were well known among his friends and acquaintances, and allows him to paint the pathetic representation of a potentially fine human being with no future, destroyed by society's lack of interest, but who points the way to a better world. Even before Monsieur D.'s assassination, Claude's incarceration solved nothing, for, on leaving prison with the indelible label of felon, he would have had even fewer possibilities than before the theft. As Claude Gueux symbolizes the working class, so Monsieur D. represents society. By small, seemingly unimportant acts of neglect and degradation, the bourgeoisie enhances the damage and rot endemic in the underclass that is in desperate need of a cure. Not only does the bourgeoisie lock away men and women who could be salvaged and redirected, it tortures its victims by denigrating what was good about them: Claude Gueux says, "I had a wife, for whom I stole, he tortures me with this woman; I had a child, for whom I stole, he tortures me with this child" (CG 248). As Hugo reaches the end, he pleads for his audience to give the right judgment that will declare *le réellement coupable*. He suggests that the all too common treatment of a man like Claude Gueux can in the future be reversed, so that the working classes will benefit themselves and civilization itself.

Using the meaning invested in a short story that exploits a reformulated fable, Hugo stands in front of the ultimate judge for the prosecution of society and for the defense of the abused. It permits Hugo in a renewed kind of concluding apologue to argue for justice as a literary prosecuting attorney. Now, he rests his case. The charge is important, of that there is no doubt. Perhaps only Victor Hugo could have taken the little short story and turned it into a powerfully reverberating call for reform that condemns society for the way it relegates the poor to hopelessness.

Notes

1 The import of critical interpretation by readers of fables was established well before Hugo. Antoine Hudar de La Motte, for example, was drawn to the textual position of a moral thesis, arguing that when it was placed at the beginning of a work, "I am unable to penetrate the meaning, and I am annoyed that you did not believe me capable to do so"—"Discours sur la fable," quoted from Jean-Noël Pascal, *Les Successeurs de La Fontaine au siècle des lumières (1715–1815)* (New York: Peter Lang, 1995) 24.

2 Victor Hugo, "Claude Gueux," *Œuvres complètes*, ed. Jean Massin, 18 vols. (Paris: Club Français du Livre, 1967–70) 5.235. Further references to this work will be to the Massin edition and preceded by CG.

3 In this case, Hugo is discussing La Fontaine's fables—*Littérature et philosophie mêlées*, ed. Massin, 5.35. Further references to this work will be to the Massin edition and preceded by LP.

Reforming Society and Genre in "Claude Gueux" 107

4 Victor Brombert's otherwise splendid consideration of Hugo's work relegates "Claude Gueux" to an endnote: *Victor Hugo and the Visionary Novel* (Cambridge, MA: Harvard UP, 1984) 249n8.

5 For a more adequate account of this period, see, Jean-Marc Hovasse, *Victor Hugo*, vol. 1 (Paris: Fayard, 2001) 270–626, and Graham Robb, *Victor Hugo* (New York: Norton, 1998) 158–211.

6 See, Hugo, "But de cette publication," LP 23, and Bernard Leuilliot, "Présentation," ed. Massin, LP 5–10.

7 Hugo, "Préface," *Lucrèce Borgia*, ed. Massin 4.655.

8 Most important is the preface to *Cromwell*. Still, as I document below, generic considerations were a major consideration of *Littérature et philosophie mêlées*.

9 LP 23–221 *passim*, "Préface" to *Cromwell*.

10 "Préface," *Angelo, tyran de Padoue* (1835), ed. Massim 4.268–69.

11 Maxime Du Camp, *Souvenirs littéraires*, 2 vols. (1882; Paris: Hachette, 1906) 2.317.

12 Victor Brombert (supra n4) and Kathryn Grossman argue convincingly that Hugo rises above the oppositions which have drawn legions of critics in a kind of transfiguration of sequence and image or grotesque and sublime—Grossman, *The Early Novels of Victor Hugo: Towards a Poetics of Harmony* (Geneva: Droz, 1986); *Figuring Transcendence in* Les Misérables: *Hugo's Romantic Sublime* (Carbondale: Southern Illinois UP, 1994); and *The Later Novels of Victor Hugo: Variations on the Politics and Poetics of Transcendence* (Oxford: Oxford UP, 2012).

13 Gotthold Ephraim Lessing, "The Vision," *Fables and Epigrams*, book 1 (London: J. & H.L. Hunt, 1825) 1–2. A volume of Lessing's fables was published in 1759. Pierre Thomas Antelmy's translations into French appeared in 1764 and 1799.

14 Quoted from the "Introduction," *Lessing's Fables*, trans. F. Storr, 2nd ed. (London: Rivingtons, 1832) xiii.

15 C.-A. Sainte Beuve, "Florian (Fables illustrées)," *Causeries du lundi*, Vol. 3 (Paris: Garnier, 1852) 242–43.

16 Charles Baudelaire, dedication "À Arsène Houssaye (Texte de 1869)," *Œuvres complètes*, éd. Claude Pichois, 2 vols, Bibliothèque de la Pléiade (Paris: Gallimard, 1975–76) 2.275–76.

17 Hugo, *Le Vert-Vert* (15 décembre 1835), ed. Massin 5.222–23.

18 Albert Dauzat, *Dictionnaire étymologique des noms de famille et prénoms de France* (Paris: Larousse, 1951) 134; Charlotte Yonge, *History of Christian Names* (1884; rpt. Detroit: Gale, 1966) xlii, 145–46.

19 Claude Gueux was in reality an illiterate prisoner who killed one of his jailers. A recidivist who began his career at fourteen with petty crime, he was condemned to prison on four occasions before becoming a murderer. He was physically imposing, without sharing the good character of Hugo's fictional personage. For a much more complete study, giving both a careful comparison of Hugo's version and the historical context, see: Paul Savey-Casard, *Le Crime et la peine dans l'œuvre de Victor Hugo* (Paris: P. U. F., 1956), and his "Introduction," *Victor Hugo*, "Claude Gueux": *Edition critique* (Paris: P. U. F., 1956) 9–83.

20 Savey-Casard dates the first draft of "Claude Gueux" as September 1832—*Edition critique* 61–62.

21 Allan H. Pasco, *Sick Heroes: French Society and Literature in the Romantic Age, 1750–1850* (Exeter: U of Exeter P, 1997) 31–52; Suzanne Desan, *The Family on Trial in Revolutionary France* (Berkeley: U of California P, 2004) 196–97 and n52; Erica-Marie Benabou, *La Prostitution et la police des mœurs au XVIIIe siècle* (Paris: Perrin, 1989) 495–96.

108 Reforming Society and Genre in "Claude Gueux"

22 Carl G. Jung, *Mysterium Coniunctionis: An Inquiry into the Separation and Synthesis of Psychic Opposites in Alchemy*, trans. R. F. C. Hull, vol. 14 (London: Routledge, 1963) 132, 229–30, 287. Whether the symbolism comes from the painterly tradition where white pigment is the absence of colour or from optics where it is the combination of all colours, white stands at the point where experience will eventually give it an appropriate colour. While Hugo and other contemporary writers like Gautier, Nodier, and Baudelaire had considerable knowledge of traditional symbolism, the possible sources are legion and occasionally ambiguous. They and recent, documented sources must be used with discretion, for the text of the author under consideration is of crucial importance to understanding.

23 Jean Chevalier and Alain Gheerbrant, *Dictionnaire des symbols* (Paris: R. Laffont, 1969) 278.

24 Paula Lee, "Death of a King," *Raritan* 24.1 (2005): 31–50. In the tradition of Erwin Panofsky's "*Et in Arcadia* ego: Poussin and the Elegiac Tradition," Lee's fascinating account uses the story as an illustration of cultural drift in meaning because of social context. Hugo's allusion dates from 1834. Tolstoy's more elaborate version of the fable in 1872 was published in French translation in 1888. Although the versions considered by Lee are Hugo's most likely sources, D. L. Ashliman tells me in e-mails of 21 and 22 November 2013 that English sources give an account of a spaniel tossed into a lion's den in 1604 that lived there peacefully for several years—http://books.google.com/books?id=nGVZAAAAYAAJ&pg=PA70 - v=onepage&q&f=false and http://books.google.com/books?id=jQ4HAAAAQAAJ&pg=PA14 - v=onepage&q&f=false. In neither of these accounts does the lion show sadness at the dog's death. Professor Ashliman also located a Swedish report (1756) of a lion that accidently killed a dog with which he was living peacefully and sharing food. The lion shortly died of remorse—http://books.google.com/books?id=02hQAAAAcAAJ&pg=PA162 - v=onepage&q&f=false.

25 Victor Hugo, *Les Misérables*, ed. Massin 9.809.

26 Pierre Grimal, *Dictionnaire de la mythologie grecque et romaine*. (Paris: P. U. F, 1969) 146.

27 Claudie Bernard, "Rhétorique de la question dans *Claude Gueux* de Victor Hugo," *Romanic Review* 78.1 (1987): 59. The study is particularly useful in its analysis of the scales balancing various antitheses including a positive rhetoric of clarity and completion with understatement, litotes, and silence, resolved only in the answer to the question, "Who is truly culpable?" (CG 326).

28 Albert Soboul, *La Civilisation et la Révolution française* (Paris: Arthaud, 1970–83) 1.389, 425–35; Benabou 312. Although these sources refer primarily to the late eighteenth century, there was little change by the early 1830's. Indeed, "France stagnated" until the late nineteenth and early twentieth centuries, when universal education and democracy began to have positive results—Karl Gunnar Persson, *An Economic History of Europe: Knowledge, Institutions and Growth, 600 to the Present* (New York: Cambridge UP, 2010) 66, 211, and *passim*. Recent estimates put economic growth in 1780–1830 at "only slightly higher than in the pre-industrial period" (Persson 95). See, also, Paul T. Comeau who traces the history of Hugo's opposition to capital punishment and cites studies of the Restoration economy proper—"La Rhétorique du poète engagé du 'Dernier Jour d'un condamné' à 'Claude Gueux'," *Nineteenth-Century French Studies* 16.1 & 2 (1987–88): 60–63. As Balzac's Doctor Poulain puts it, "I pass my life looking at people who die [...] from that great and incurable wound, the lack

Reforming Society and Genre in "Claude Gueux" 109

of money"— *Le Cousin Pons* (1847), *La Comédie humaine*, Vol. 5 (Paris: Seuil, 1966) 200.

29 Pasco estimates that there were 30,000 prostitutes in the Paris of the 1830s with some 900,000 inhabitants—*Sick heroes* 62 and n16. See, also, Benabou 326–29, 445–46.

30 Hugo describes a "shackling day" in *Le Dernier Jour d'un condamné* 3.670–74. The cruelty of chains is highlighted by an anonymous article, "Départ de la chaîne des forçats," first published in the *Gazette des tribunaux* (4 October 1826), and republished in, Charles Simond, éd., *Le Consulat—Le Premier Empire, La Restauration, La Vie parisienne au XIXe siècle: Paris de 1800 à 1900*, Vol. 1 (Paris: Plon, 1900) 1.564–66.

7 Flaubert's Talking Heads in the Cyclical *Trois Contes*

Not only did Gustave Flaubert elevate the novel genre to a level potentially capable of expressing the highest form of art with the universally acclaimed *Madame Bovary*, he did similarly for the short story. Compared to tragedy, or lyric, or the epic poem, neither novels nor short stories had previously been taken very seriously, though a few artists like Balzac, Mérimée, and Hugo advanced them well beyond expectations. The novel was generally viewed as respectable popular entertainment, and the short story served merely as newspaper filler.[1] Flaubert's short story went further and laid down an implicit challenge for other authors to work more seriously and artistically. As one might expect from such an extraordinary artist, with *Trois Contes*, he wrote not just a random collection of tales, but rather a cycle. In his hands, a cycle was organized both as an image, as was the case with Barbey's *Les Diaboliques*, and as a sequence, imitating standard patterns of human thought. While each of Flaubert's stories retains its individual importance, the three tales are organized together to project a highly integrated image of sainthood, as though they were neither separate nor sequential but a comprehensive whole. Moreover, he implicitly encouraged readers to follow the texts in sequence as they were published in the volume. This sequential reading leads to an understanding of Flaubert's archaeological research into the past of saints' tales and may offer the most exciting of his visionary accomplishments.

I

Despite the fact that there is no explicit, overriding frame, or metanarrative, uniting Flaubert's tales with, for example, the use of common narrators, as in Marguerite de Navarre's *Heptaméron*, or an explanation of why all the stories were told, as in Balzac's *Histoire des treize,* frequent comments throughout the secondary literature demonstrate that informed readers appreciate the three tales individually, but sense their similar attributes as a group.[2] Justification for this claim of unity has, however, not been sufficiently elucidated. Still, it cannot be doubted that there are obvious themes like sainthood recurring across

Flaubert's Talking Heads in Trois Contes   111

the entire cycle, bringing a modicum of consistency by their very re-
appearance. In addition, unlike all other cycles of which I am aware,
Trois Contes successfully combines two differing, fundamental structures, which could be termed sequential and imagistic, or, in other terms
used in recent criticism, metonymic and metaphoric or diachronic and
synchronic, and which Flaubert exploited in a complimentary fashion to
unify *Trois Contes.* Numerous readers have discovered the intricacies of
the work as a complex synchronic image, while a few others have with
some success explored the sequence joining the three stories. In short,
just as each of the tales can stand independently of the others, so each is
enhanced when the three are read as one finely executed triptych.

Flaubert was certainly aware of other aspects of short stories, as
discussed in previous chapters. In addition, glorying in the concision
and necessary compaction imposed by brevity, the best exemplars of the
genre always seem to strive to go beyond their limits as *an artistically
designed, short prose fiction.* The most accomplished authors apparently
attempt consciously to force the reader to take the incomplete, suggestive
allusive items or movements and join the author in creating a larger conception of the masterpiece. P. W. M. Cogman terms these incompletions
"gaps" that "prompt even the critical and attentive reader to invent, 'see'
and recall what is not there."[3] Armine Mortimer views such "secrets"
as "resistances to meaning," and goes on to explicate their function:
they invite our collaboration with the text, drawing "us into its points
of resistance."[4] It is clear that such unanswered questions invite daring
readers to link the two or more images of the textual metaphors mentally, thus joining them in an amalgam of images.

All of the tales in *Trois Contes* begin in fragmentation,[5] followed
by gradually evolving equilibrium, if not resolution, and they end with
decomposition or deliquescence and sanctified death. The first, Félicité's
story, can be quickly told. An orphan girl, she lacks formal education,
and has little choice but to take what work she can get and accept the
misery and insecurity that accompanied agricultural labor in Flaubert's
day. Meeting Théodore gives her something to dream about until their
relationship expires like everything else in her life. She is abandoned so
that he can marry Mme Lehoussais and thus assure himself of wealth
and immunity from military conscription. Seemingly without the basic things that people find essential—family, food, shelter—Félicité
wraps her few possessions in a handkerchief and leaves for the village
of Pont-l'Evêque, where she seeks employment. Her subsequent life as
a low-paid domestic servant is delineated by her serial commitments to
Mme Aubain, to the latter's children, Paul and Virginie, to her nephew
Victor, to the Polish refugees, to Old Colmiche, and to her parrot Loulou. Each is taken from her, most through death. Michael Issacharoff
summarizes, "Félicité's existence is a series of contractions, a reduction
to zero, [...] as much on the spatial plane as on human and psychological

112 *Flaubert's Talking Heads in* Trois Contes

planes."[6] By the end of her life, she is deaf and almost blind, and, due to her infirmity, confined to her room on the second story of a leaking, tumbledown house.

Félicité's service to Mme Aubain is exemplary and stimulates the envy of the other bourgeois ladies of Pont-l'Evêque. In addition, not only does she risk her life to save the little family from a raging bull, like her namesake Saint Félicité,[7] in her subsequent attempt to save Loulou's remains, she suffers scourging near the roadside shrine commemorating the passion of Christ. Furthermore, as Lund points out, "After Easter, she spit up blood, it was as though the Passion was being repeated with her."[8] Much earlier, her simple faith is gradually stimulated by the visual images in the stained-glass windows of the local church. The priest's explanations of Scripture make her cry: "She thought she saw paradise, the flood, the tower of Babel, overturned idols; and this dizzying vision left her with respect for Almighty God and a fear of His anger. Then she cried in listening to the account of the Passion" (*3c* 601). Her strong visual sensitivities make it easy for her to envision the Holy Spirit as a bird. After all, the presence of the Holy Spirit, as described in Scripture, appeared in different guises: "[H]e was not just a bird, but also a fire, and other times a breath of wind. Perhaps it is his light that flutters around the edges of swamps at night" (*3c* 618). Furthermore, not only are the Holy Spirit's prophecies limited to what He has already heard from the Father (John 16.13), Félicité's parrot Loulou likewise says nothing but what he has heard.

The stained-glass window in the apse of the church illustrates the dove-like Holy Spirit anointing the Virgin as the mother of Jesus (*3c* 601), and perhaps explains Félicité's particular devotion to Mary, reflected in Loulou's mimicked phrase, "Hail, Mary" (*3c* 613). Hers is the uncomplicated, unquestioning faith of a peasant, like Bernardin de Saint Pierre's related character, and "[A]s a simple heart cannot be tricked, so it never tricks."[9] Félicité would find nothing amiss in her praise and worship with substituting Mary, the mother of Jesus, for Jesus, the Son. Flaubert's friend, Alfred Maury, explains this religious orientation by pointing out that, "Beginning with the eleventh century, Mary became truly a fourth person of the Trinity, a female divinity as Jesus was a male divinity."[10] She would have liked to join "the Children of the Virgin, but Mme Aubain talked her out of it" (*3c* 618). Loulou is Félicité's greatest comfort as her years of service go by, and she declines both physically and mentally. In order to preserve the parrot after his death, she has him stuffed and keeps his remains in her room. She has virtually no relationship with anyone outside her home, and except for her love of the stuffed, but spiritualized parrot, she lives in the torpid state of a sleepwalker (*3c* 617). She is a simple heart.

Flaubert went to some trouble to show that despite her uncomplicated, artless nature, Félicité is rather insightful. Her ability to expose the

Flaubert's Talking Heads in Trois Contes   113

tenant farmers' tricks and, indeed, her reasoning that the parrot is more suitable than a dove as the Holy Spirit provide excellent testimony. For Félicité, Loulou comes to resemble the Holy Spirit portrayed in a flashy Epinal print, which seems to be a portrait of Loulou (*3c* 617). While many have felt that with this representation Flaubert is mocking either the Church or Christianity, they do so with little corroborative evidence, though Alfred Maury would explain that faith had declined through the ages "until reason is [...] the only criterion of truth" (Maury xvi). Indeed, everything we read in this story highlight not the ecclesiastical coldhearted indifference of the cleric in *Madame Bovary*, but rather the compassionate faith of both the nun at Virginie's death and the priest in opening the street altar to Félicité's treasured parrot. The absence of irony in the following stories of Julien and Iaokanann merely emphasize the straightforward sympathy also demanded of Félicité and her story.

From the standpoint of "Un Cœur simple," however, it is far more important that the textual account of the biblical beatitudes be identified with the life of Flaubert's Félicité,[11] though one can go outside the story for authorial commentary and quote Flaubert's corroborative letter to Mme Roger des Genettes to support the claim that the novelist was in no way mocking his "simple heart" (*Corr* 5.56–57). The story radiates compassion from first to last. Careful reading attests to her goodness, and it justifies the etymological meaning of her name as "blessed." As Beck emphasizes, in both the Old and New Testaments "blessed" and "happy" are used as variant readings of the same Greek word, which denoted the highest stage of happiness and well-being like what the gods enjoy.[12] Nonetheless, though Félicité's existence is systematically reduced through the course of her life, when the Holy Spirit finally comes for her in the guise of Loulou, we understand that she is being taken away to eternal felicitousness. Those who see this as satire have ignored the contrary, quite explicit indications of the maid's saintliness. As Raymonde Debray-Genette says, "The ultimate symbol [of the parrot / Holy Spirit] remains completely motivated, and by that very fact, completely realistic."[13]

Like "Un Cœur simple," the second tale of *Trois Contes*, "La Légende de Saint Julien l'Hospitalier," is fragmented at the outset. Shoshana Felman explains that the saint is "torn from before his birth between two narcissistic programs, caught between two laws, between two unconscious minds, between two projects for his future."[14] Two prophecies accompany his infancy when he resembles "a little Jesus" (*3c* 626). In the first, an old man, resembling a hermit, comes to the mother and says, "Rejoice, Mother! your son will be a saint!" (*3c* 625). Shortly thereafter, a gypsy beggar rises before the father and, as though inspired, stammers, "Oh! Oh! your son!... The ellipses are in the text. Please leave ... a lot of blood!...... A lot of glory!...... forever happy! the family of an emperor" (*3c* 625). Neither parent reveals the prophecies to the other, though each

114   *Flaubert's Talking Heads in* Trois Contes

tries to bring the child along in the prophesied path, on the one hand, of saintliness, and, on the other, of the warrior. Flaubert has reduced Julien's father to his warlike and hunting propensities and his mother to her piety, so that the parents exist only insofar as they impinge on Julien's fate (Raitt 45).

The location of the family chateau with four towers (four being the symbolic number of this world) is bizarre, for it is unrealistic, especially after being trained by the realism of the preceding story, "Un Cœur simple." Placed on the slope rather than at the top of a hill where a chateau should be and where a legendary hero should live, the site seems wrong, if not merely in-between and incomplete. One wonders whether Flaubert was playing with the concept of *in medias res*. It is furthermore difficult to justify in the terms of legendry. Still, the boy's childhood seems uneventful, though he is unconsciously torn between the teachings of his pious mother and of his militant father. When he comes across the gigantic, black stag during his second hunt, the animal gives a triadic prophecy that structurally echoes the three phrases of the parrot Loulou's repertory ("Charming boy! Your servant, Sir! Hail Mary!"—*3c* 613), and moreover, proffers a third divine prediction to the two that his parents received at his birth: "Damned! damned! damned! One day, cruel heart, you will assassinate your father and mother" (*3c* 632).

In the medieval period a deer frequently symbolized Christ (Maury 257–61), thus preparing the conclusion. The imprecision of Félicité's previous *crut voir* "believed she saw" (*3c* 622) as the gigantic parrot soared above her, prior to taking her away, and that has generated so much ink, was perhaps required in the realistic "Un Cœur simple." A similar "vision" occurs between "dream and reality" during the prophesies of "La Légende de saint Julien," when the prophet "looking like a hermit," delivers the prophecy to Julien's mother, and then, "gliding along a moonbeam, he rose gently in the air, then disappeared" (*3c* 625). The second divine emissary likewise faded away, and Julien's father is left to wonder whether it was an hallucination (*3c* 625), whereas the talking deer's curse is presented as indisputable, though only in a world that accepts the supernatural could any of these events take place.

While there have been several indications that Julien has a conscience (so that no one will know about his savagery, for example, the boy quietly throws the mouse he killed away and cleans up the blood), the stag's prophecy raises his first significant crisis, for he is determined not to kill his parents. He is nonetheless tormented by another thought: "But what if I wanted to?" (*3c* 632). Julien has been like Nimrod, a mighty hunter, as though he were in the biblical account of a post-flood world: "And the fear of you and the dread of you shall be upon every beast of the earth, and upon every fowl of the air [...] into your hand are they delivered" (Genesis 9.2). And in Julien's ceaseless hunt for ferocious animals, "[h]e became like them" (*3c* 629). As Lasine puts it, "This

Flaubert's Talking Heads in *Trois Contes* 115

inverted Adam kills all the animals instead of naming them."[15] Soon, the events lead to the deceptive situations where he almost kills his father and his mother because both of them resemble the animals that their son had savagely pursued. The father always wears an overcoat of fox fur, and Julien confounds his mother's white headdress with the wings of a stork (*3c* 633). He flees the chateau rather than running further risk of accidentally assassinating his parents.

After nearly killing his mother and father, the fugitive slowly builds an army. Despite the difficult life of a wandering knight, he becomes sufficiently hard and strong to establish a company of soldiers. While escaping death in his campaigns "[t]hanks to divine favor" (*3c* 634) and protecting church people, orphans, widows, and especially the elderly, he succeeds in killing many infidels. His fame and his army grow. In his epic career, he kills both fabulous and real monsters, moving from one heroic event to another until, on slaughtering legions of Muslims and beheading the Caliph, he is rewarded with the emperor of Occitania's daughter and a castle. Still, images of hunting haunt him:

> [In a dream,] he saw himself like our father Adam, in the middle of Paradise, among all the animals; in stretching out his arm, he made them die; or else they would file by two by two lined up by size from elephants and lions to weasels and ducks, like the day when they entered Noah's ark. In the shadow of a cave, he would throw javelins at them that never missed; others would come; it was unending; and he woke up rolling his eyes wildly. (*3c* 636; cf. Genesis 8.16–19)

Flaubert's tale takes on the flavor of the Bible, which Alfred Maury indicates is appropriate for Christian legendry. Maury describes medieval monks in the thrall of illusion telling the story of a favored saint, wrapping the tale with biblical colors and linking it more or less accurately with tradition. "Such must have been the way the life of a saint was written, in those times of profound ignorance and tenebrous piety" (Maury 91). Despite his yearning, Julien refuses to hunt, in hopes of nullifying the terrible prophecy about his parents. Hunting was, however, an important part of his make-up and his thirst grows.

Then comes the time when Julien can resist no more, and he goes off into a supernatural world where, on this second surrealistic hunt, he is surrounded by animals but unable to kill. Even the wild bull is unscathed despite being hit by a lance. Both Raitt and Biasi have noted that during the first hunt where he kills animals that are generally benign, in the second where he cannot kill, his prey is quite dangerous (Raitt 47). The only corpse left after the second hunt is a long-dead, rotten partridge that he finds (*3c* 641), a Christian symbol of utter spiritual ruin.[16] The reader moreover quickly perceives that Julien is driven not by sport and enjoyment of the hunt, but by a lust for blood and death.

116   *Flaubert's Talking Heads in* Trois Contes

"His thirst for carnage filled him again; since there were no animals, he would have happily killed men" (*3c* 641). Wild with frustration, he returns in darkest night to the chateau and finds another man in his bed with a woman whom he thinks to be his wife, but is in fact his mother. Enraged, believing his bearded father is a lover who has cuckolded him, he kills both parents as the bearded black stag bells in the distance. In opposition to Julien's raging passion for blood, on two occasions the narrator envisions his body in the shape of the cross, and we know that "the cross is the symbol of salvation" (Maury 62). He is tragically aware that he has however murdered his own parents, so he must carry the burden of both matricide and patricide.

In part iii of "La Légende," after Julien grows up and, later, as a great hero eventually culminating in the murder of his mother and father, he moves away from his life at the apex of society. Leaving everything behind, filled with remorse, he penitentially brutalizes himself and welcomes the abuse of others as though it were deserved punishment. Biasi's convincing analysis of the symbolism of sandals left at the top of the stairs in the story's part ii underlines the importance of Flaubert's subtle use of detail and links sandals to the egregious bloodletting of the hunt, to the murder of the parents, to the saint's will to absolute repentance and destitution, and to his future beatification.[17] Subsequently, yearning to die and thus free himself from guilt, he peers into a fountain. He sees that the image of his father mirrored in the water in fact reflects himself. To commit suicide would destroy his father's son, thus his father's sole seed, making it impossible to kill himself. It would be a conscious, second patricide. Flaubert's use of implication has developed into a particularly effective aesthetic device.

The budding saint continues to wander in part iii until he is drawn to the banks of a dangerous river. He builds a hut of clay and timber and settles in, determined to pay for his sins with a life of service by helping his fellow man cross the river safely. First, he builds a walkway across the mud flats, almost losing his life in the process. Then, after repairing the remains of a boat that he found, he transports anyone who asks, taking nothing but the scraps of food and clothing that his passengers deign to leave.

The disembodied voice later calling Julien from the other side of the river prepares for the hallucinatory Jesus, whose body is being destroyed by leprosy. Despite the scaly pustules, noisome breath, running ulcers, and the gaping hole replacing his nose, Jesus holds himself with authority. He is dressed in rags that look like a shroud, "his two eyes redder than hot coals" (*3c* 646–47). At the leper's demand, Julien gives Him food and drink and finally not only opens his bed but joins Him, warming Him with his own body, "mouth to mouth, chest to chest" (*3c* 648). The allusion to Elisha's life-restoring treatment of the little boy seems clear (2 Kings 4.32–35; Lasine 127). Julien's total self-abnegation as he

Flaubert's *Talking Heads in* Trois Contes   117

hugs the leper and takes him to his bed echoes Félicité's love for the wormy, stuffed Loulou. The reward is at least equally dramatic, for Jesus carries Julien off to heaven (*3c* 648).

Though "Hérodias," the last tale of Flaubert's trilogy, has a number of historical anomalies,[18] it offers color from the wide variety of mid-eastern landscapes teaming with animals and people that mass in pages of the tale. Set in a citadel atop a cone of igneous rock, surrounded by four deep valleys and houses huddled against its base, it contains a brutal society ruled by animalistic lust and avaricious ambition. When the tetrarch, Hérode-Antipas, begins his day by looking off into the distance, he quickly concentrates on the Arab king's tents, whose daughter he had married, then rejected in order to marry his brother's wife, Hérodias, of whom he is now weary. Hérodias' former husband is currently arming himself secretly, and the ruler is uneasy. With good reason to feel threatened, Antipas hopes for Roman support to sustain him. And, as if these troubles were not enough, Antipas holds in his dungeons Iaokanann, or John the Baptist, whom he considers a violent madman and, as well, a prophet to be feared. His most dangerous adversary remains his wife, Hérodias, however. Her animosity is so great that she is willing to use her own daughter, Salome, as a tool of vengeance.

The tetrarch takes advantage of his birthday to invite the most important people of the region to a celebratory feast, hoping to find safe passage through the dangers that surround him on every side. When the Roman proconsul Vitellius and his son Aulus arrive, the festival begins, but only after Aulus disappears in the kitchen to assure himself of the choicest morsels and to abuse the help sexually. The powerful Roman guests soon investigate the subterranean storehouse of weapons and a hundred or so white horses that Vitellius envies. Only these gorgeous animals appear to know what it means to play, seemingly more human than the guests and hosts. Back above ground, still snooping for Hérode the Great's hidden treasures, the proconsul demands that they open one of the underground pits, where Iaokanann has been incarcerated. The prophet with long hair and wearing an animal's pelt takes advantage of the moment to scream imprecations from his lair at this society that has turned from God. To the amusement of his audience, the words of this first prophecy culminate with the condemnation of the adulterous Hérodias and Antipas. "Your incest has already been punished. God has afflicted you with the sterility of a mule" (*3c* 665). The prophetic utterance is given double force by the translator's faithful reformulation into Latin for the visitors. Flaubert describes the bedlam resulting from the inclusion of Galileans, priests, soldiers, and quarrelsome Sadducees and Pharisees to these officials in the revelry. Antipas seems the most human of all the characters in the story and its bestial world, but only because he is weak and afraid, which helps orient readers toward what is truly important. This is a society without virtue, without compassion

118 *Flaubert's Talking Heads in* Trois Contes

or kindness, without real love. Only the lust for power and pleasure dominates. By implication or explicit comparison, almost all the characters emphasize the imagery of the preceding tale, "La Légende de saint Julien," and reveal their animal natures.

Phanuel, a passing Jew whose significance will grow in the Christian community, brings the second prophecy: that very night an important man will die (*3c* 667). Antipas fears that he will be the one. The true victim will, of course, be John the Baptist, whose story is told in Matthew 14 and Mark 6 of the Bible. In Flaubert's version, after Salomé's dance "[t]he head came in," and the executioner displays it for all to see (*3c* 677). Despite the prophet's death, Phanuel and Iaokanann's two friends are encouraged by John's third prophesy from God announcing the coming of Christ to the dead. The next morning, the two men leave with Phanuel, each of the three taking turns to carry the prophet's heavy head toward Galilee. As Alfred Maury explains is the case with Christian legendry, and as Flaubert applies these insights to his triadic *Trois Contes*, each of the tales makes free with detailed historical truth, opening the door to a world of faith in a popular, legendary religion.

II

While the relationship of each of the cycle's three stories, "Un Cœur simple," "La Légende de Saint Julien l'Hospitalier," and "Hérodias," to the others is both clear and easily demonstrated as one reads the volume from beginning to end, it is also true that one can envision the tales as discrete wholes. Each tale can be isolated from the others, as indeed has happened when studied in numerous classrooms. Each is a good story that reads lyrically as one would expect of the best nineteenth-century literature. And each has been the subject of numerous scholarly / critical studies that leave little doubt of their high artistic quality.

The tales could also be mentally arranged in a metanarrative as an image structure, one above the other as though they were very closely related, if not repeated with variations, rather like Mandelbrot's mathematical, self-similar fractals.[19] Though they are different, their similarity is striking. Each deals with sanctity, for example (Biasi, "Introduction" 41). Each begins with disorder and follows the exemplary lives until the saints arrive at the point where they have completely surrendered and demonstrated their utter self-abnegation. In an excellent study of *Trois Contes*, Carla L. Peterson points to the similarity of the governing pattern of each of the three stories. "First, the stories may be read as repetitions of one another. [... F]inally, each individual tale is a synecdoche, as it can be seen to tell the story of the volume as a whole."[20] As she puts it, "[E]ach part, each tale, is equal to the whole, to the entire volume" (255). Although two of the stories are also formally divided into three parts, the five chapters of "Un Cœur simple" are fundamentally triadic,

Flaubert's Talking Heads in Trois Contes   119

as shown by the three phrases in Loulou's repertory: the first part of Félicité's story is capped by her love for a "Charming boy," the second dominated by her role as "your servant, Sir," and the third by the depth of her commitment to her faith: "hail, Mary!" (*3c* 613). Each of the main characters are exiles, forced by need, fear, or authority to leave their homes. They are regularly compared and contrasted to animals.

Three separate prophecies likewise dominate "La Légende de saint Julien," as do the three in "Hérodias." Those themes or images that are repeated in each of the tales, like the terminal sunrises, the number three,[21] the doves,[22] the dragons,[23] the flaming eyes of each of three prophets,[24] the allusions to Scripture, or the textual prophesies, these and many more emphasize the commonalities of the three tales, all of which highlight their relationship each other and to other hagiographic accounts. There are, of course, many definitions of sainthood, but the one that seems most appropriate for *Trois Contes* was proposed by Aimée Israel-Pelletier: "the process of sacrificing worldly pleasures and happiness for a transcendent goal."[25] Each of the three stories relates to the Word of God that is announced prophetically. In the first two stories the prophecies are delivered by animals, while in the third, although Iaokanann is a human being, he is "laid out on the ground beneath his long mane tangled up with an animal's hair" (*3c* 663). Antipas commands John to be still, but the prophet responds, "I will scream like a bear, like a wild donkey, like a woman giving birth!" (*3c* 665), implying his own primal nature. Of course, all of the characters have noticeable traits of animals. Even in the case of Félicité, who seems able to control the animals in her world, when Mme Aubain would say, "'My Lord! how like an animal (*bête*) you are!' she responded: 'Yes, Madam'" (*3c* 615). The only thing that distinguishes the three principal characters from the natural kingdom is their expressions of faith, as one would expect on taking a cue from Maury's history of the Church.

Perhaps the most interesting indication of the profound unity of the three tales comes in the titles. They have caused much confusion, but only because it is easy to think that they were chosen to highlight the saint involved in the story. As is often the case, however, one must consider every element in Flaubert's creations from several points of view. Shelly Thomas suggests, for example, that one need only turn the titular crystals around and recognize that they signal, not the saint, but one who pursues the source of the prophetic voice of God.[26] As Maury argues, and as I summarized above, it is not uncommon for saints to become hunters (*chasseurs*, which can mean either *pursuers* or *hunters* in English), avidly seeking the Divine Being they worship (178). In the first two tales, much as Maury explains in his general study of saints' tales, "Saints will have been transformed into hunters" (178), that is, they pursue (*chassent*) God. Just as Félicité pursues Loulou frantically when the parrot wanders away, so Julien's *chasse* (hunt) ends when he hears

120   *Flaubert's Talking Heads in* Trois Contes

the terrifying prophecy of his destiny as the enormous black stag dies. Likewise, Hérodias, whose name is associated with that of the huntress Diana,[27] obsessively pursues John the Baptist, not in search of God, but to assassinate the prophetic voice of God, who she feels has insulted her.

Although Flaubert's individual tales can easily stand alone, a list of themes and images repeated in each of the three creations would be lengthy and clearly mark their lineage and close relationship. In addition, as Issacharoff says, "Because of the recurrence of the symbolic elements, it is obvious that *Trois contes* does not constitute three autonomous tales."[28] Each of the tales marks a character who is elected, chosen for sainthood, and the reader follows the unrolling of his or her destiny. The question of *Trois Contes'* unity has frustrated many Flaubertians, and the issue arises repeatedly in the secondary literature.[29] One scholar believes that the author could not have had three tales in mind from the beginning (Biasi, "Introduction" 10), a real possibility judging from Flaubert's letters, but the truly important factor is the definitive triadic version that was finally published under the author's direction. In that regard, the three stories work together to present a unified whole. *Trois Contes* would suggest for some, and certainly for the author of *La Tentation de saint Antoine* where the Trinity is so important, the possibilities of the number three. Each of these stories was projected for something well short of a novella in length,[30] yet Flaubert wanted, indeed given his financial straits, needed a volume that would sell well. These pecuniary concerns, however pressing, were only one more reason, in addition to his aesthetic sensibilities, to structure the three coincident stories into a mutually reinforcing complex. The resultant Trinity guarantees the importance of each part and of the whole. Indications leave little doubt that at some point early or late, Flaubert had a comprehensive unity in mind. Indeed, the sense of the work leaves an over-riding perception that the three stories have many common elements and on several levels.

Each of the talking heads that incarnates the spiritually prophetic voice of God suffers from degradation and abnegation. Loulou is still alive when he enunciates his structurally determinative repertory. The sixteen-point stag is dying when it utters its prophecy, and when Iaokanann makes his important forecast of the coming of Christ to the underworld, he is dead. The rather imposing parrot, Loulou, is reduced to a seemingly small, worm-eaten, avian head sticking up from the street altar outside Félicité's window (*3c* 622); the prophetic stag collapses from an arrow in its forehead (*3c* 632); after calling Julien three times, Jesus puts his leprous body in the saint's bed (*3c* 647–48); and saint John the Baptist, who has been limited for the most part in the story to his disincarnated voice, appears as a severed head at the banquet (*3c* 677), having nonetheless descended to speak in another world.

A major factor in the artistry of Flaubert's cycle is the fact that each story repeats the images and patterns of the others to reinforce a single,

Flaubert's Talking Heads in Trois Contes   121

overriding, aesthetically satisfying image where the three become one, a Trinitarian cycle. Together the three images create a representation of sainthood that rises above any particular period. It would be difficult to elicit moralizing for good or ill, since the virtue is balanced throughout with evil. There are examples of good in Félicité, in Julien, and in Iaokanann, but the results do not bring nice solutions, at least not until God reaches out and saves his elect. Prior to that point, the saints are increasingly deficient, misused, and abused.

III

Each of the stories is positioned on a line of descent toward death, strengthening their fundamental unity. Félicité's room is up above the main part of her house, Julien's activity is generally at ground level, whereas Iaokanann ends his account in a subterranean realm. In fact, all of the details are important in strengthening the connective links and order of the three tales, but the most important comes from Flaubert's acquaintance with his friend Alfred Maury and the latter's major study of 1843 on religious legends. As I have noted above, Maury is an important source for information about *Trois Contes*. It remains to be pointed out that Maury's *Essai sur les légendes pieuses* provides a crucial explanation for the order Flaubert chose for the three tales that became a second metanarrative, this one sequential. Although Flaubert in his role as a literary archeologist chose to organize his cycle regressing from present to past, the dominant images from Holy Spirit to the Son to the Father follow the biblical chronology of God's primary activity in the world.

Maury wishes to explain the history of the supernatural legends that have grown up around the Christian religion through the ages. For him, Christianity was from the beginning involved in unremitting conflict between faith and reason. The religion began during Jesus' ministry. It was initiated, took root, and spread by faith. Almost immediately, however, it was attacked by reason. As Maury remembers early in his study (viii), Saint Paul repeatedly castigated direct observation and reason (viii; e.g. 1 Cor. 1.19). Furthermore, Jesus blessed those who believe without having seen (John 20.29). Maury goes on to insist that initially, Christianity was preached to men who did not seek to know anything; they only wanted to satisfy their deepest need for love, to love and to be loved (viii–ix). Accepting his friend's historical argument, Flaubert follows saints' tales back through time, choosing to place one of his tales in each of the periods when Christian faith was vigorously combatting reason. Whether during the first century with Iaokanann, or the twelfth with Julien, or the nineteenth with Félicité, he has settled on a period when a reinvigorating faith was combatting if not overcoming reason.

122   *Flaubert's Talking Heads in* Trois Contes

Maury describes his understanding of humankind at the time of Jesus:

> In the infancy of humanity, a human being doubtless lived nothing but an external, animalistic life. His principal satisfaction came from satisfying physical needs, acting on penchants and passions. For a long time, like animals, he must have lived out his natural role as though irresistibly and instinctually, without paying attention to his actions, impressions, or thoughts. Abstract and metaphysical ideas were beyond his still feeble, impotent intelligence. Or if an idea occasionally came along and suddenly struck and grasped his attention, it had nothing but a vague and indefinite impact, and its fugitive appearance was quickly effaced by the prompt return of material ideas growing from sensations. (Maury 45)

At first, such bestial people could be touched by an uncomplicated Gospel, and in his explanation, Maury's argument incorporates those images that give life to Flaubert's stories. The historian stays above the details of the narration, yet moves from contemporary reality to the medieval period, then to the beginnings of Christianity. In antiquity, he says, human beings, with only an unclear sense of a spiritual dimension, were governed by their lusts. Once sated, they moved on to other desires. Maury would have his readers believe that they were beasts subject only to their passions, bowing before nothing but animalistic force, incapable of understanding anything but vague impressions of metaphysics. Mercy was lacking in the conceptions of the day. One was either entirely victorious or defeated. Morality was subject to authority and power. Spirituality was only a means of explaining the inexplicable. Even Flaubert's Vitellius is disgusted by such creatures.

> Their god could easily be Moloch, whose altars he had seen on the road. The sacrifices of children came back to his mind, with the story of the man whom they had mysteriously fattened. Repugnance was aroused in his Latin heart by their intolerance, their iconoclastic rage, their brutish obstructionism. (*3c* 674)

According to Maury, Christianity was based on an exceptional man and a new teaching of love. It required not awesome theology or doctrine; it was a religion of faith. The events of the Messiah's life took place in a world defined primarily by simplicity and ignorance. When Christianity appeared, it was preached by simple men to those who were even more simple, men who had never felt an insatiable need for novelty or even hungered for knowledge. They had but one need, a need that Christianity taught and explained: absolute, sacrificial love. This sentiment was the new Law (Maury 120). Consequently, Flaubert's Iaokanann screams his harsh prophecies and sermons of doom at them, for only fear can

Flaubert's Talking Heads in Trois Contes   123

break through the wall of self-centered hostility and superstition in order to open the way for this kind of spiritual love.

Little by little, the miraculous life and teachings of Christ were subordinated to reason, logic, and science, which became the constant companions of the religion. "Science, that is to say reason, which is its foundation and essence, became [...] one of the noblest of God's attributes. It served to interpret the law and to penetrate mysteries that the latter created" (Maury vii-viii). Rather than being subjected to the law of faith and love, theology soon turned into "nothing more than a trembling slave delivered over to the caprices of reason" (Maury xvii). Despite the attractively revolutionary substance of the new system founded on faith, logic soon intervened. Interpretations of biblical healings were revised to signify symbolic liberation from sin (Maury 65). Rationalists argued that the healing of a blind man was nothing but opening his mind to Scripture, rather than a true physical healing (Maury 67). Maury believed that on investigating Church literature and numerous pious fictions that have grown up subsequently, it was possible to trace the activity of reason in the lives of naïve and credulous believers culminating in the destruction of Christian faith. In spite of itself, faith was overwhelmed, a change that the Church accepted only with great regret. "Reason [...] was gradually substituted for the simple, ignorant faith of the first days" (Maury xx).

By the ninth century, according to Maury, the Church recognized that reason was winning over the spiritual reality, slowly pushing aside the core teaching of faith, and the institutional Church began opposing reason vigorously. Flaubert's second tale about Julien grows from the medieval period when the Church was aggressively attacking the societal efforts to reduce faith to common sense. Many monks were set to writing supernatural tales, stories about particularly admirable believers like Flaubert's St. Julien, who had miracles working in their lives. Maury speculates that a medieval author would attribute stories both from the Bible and from other saints' tales to the saint he was writing about. Because Jesus was a perpetual example of moral perfection, looking to His life as described in the Gospels was far more effective than what could be gleaned from the sages of the past. Jesus, the Christ, was a living model, in whose life could be discovered subjects for meditation and rules of conduct (Maury 1–2).

The medieval religious orders illustrated the faith with stories and stained glass windows, all to encourage unsophisticated believers, for whom miracles existed (Maury 104). The legends are to be explained by popular conceptions, taught figuratively, which transformed spiritual attacks into struggles or actual battles, but which superior believers had overcome by triumphing over Satan (Maury 146). Naturally, subject to popular understanding, the tales changed through time. Flaubert's Julien was prophetically signaled as a chosen-one, for his world is one

124 *Flaubert's Talking Heads in* Trois Contes

where miracles take place. It is a world where a man whose blood lust could not be satisfied would begin to submit to God while on supernatural hunts. After becoming guilty of patricide, his repentance leads him to understanding the need to submit "to serving others" (3c 645), to love no matter what, and to bow totally to the will of God.

In representations like that of the stained glass window of Rouen, and in Flaubert's somewhat different version, we can follow the miracle of Julien's contrition, penance, and salvation, and, simultaneously, see how legends are born. Flaubert invites our admiration of his talent as the creator of saints' tales in the nineteenth century: for his own and Félicité's day in "Un Cœur simple," when faith was seemingly almost impossible, for Julien's medieval period, and for Iaokanann at the time of Christ in "Herodias." After considering the sources of Saint Julien, Biasi suggests that Flaubert has simply invented "another variant of the tale."[31] Debray-Genette makes the further statement that "'Un Cœur simple,' like 'Saint Julien' and 'Hérodias,' is a tale from the past" (274–75).

Historically, similar efforts invented and added extra-scriptural miracles to the life of the Virgin-Mother (Maury 37–40), though she had a very small role in the belief system of the early Christian church. The Middle Ages were nonetheless a "period of naïve and credulous simplicity" (Maury 43), during which the windows and friezes on the churches aided belief. "From seeing something painted, represented, people ended naturally by accepting it. Then what people saw [...] was more powerful than the intelligence" (Maury 104). "First, they offered believers representations of martyrdom [...], so as to use a visual image to revive the still tepid and indifferent beliefs of the masses" (Maury 111). "In a word, all of these simulacra offered the least equivocal expression of the crassest anthropomorphism" (Maury 117). Deer also played large roles in medieval legends. People thought a deer was in many circumstances gifted with prophecy, particularly in bringing an unbeliever to the faith (Maury 169–76).

But reason, logic, science could not be ignored, Maury argues. Skepticism continued to undermine the miraculous events of the Christian tradition until the core of the religion's faith disappeared. There were no longer any miracles. By the fifteenth century, "theology, philosophy, the sciences, little by little purely rational methodology penetrated everything. [...] Reason is subsequently the only criterion of truth" (Maury xvi). If reason was incapable of explaining a particular event or act, it was branded an allegory, and if the report was contradictory, it was simply rejected (Maury xvii). Christianity was abandoned to the logical mind of man, rendering faith impossible. In rejecting faith, Maury argues that theology had finally rejected the religion itself. Christianity was only available to uncomplicated people and could only be accepted by those like Félicité, who are simple in heart and mind.

Flaubert's Talking Heads in Trois Contes   125

By the nineteenth century, Christianity has been limited to "simple hearts." The skepticism is so rampant that one can only hope that Félicité signals a new commitment to faith. Flaubert was clearly taken with his friend Maury's more or less historical interpretation, since it became an important organizing factor for his *Trois Contes*. In his stories, he wanted to present an implicit spiritual history of the Western world that was reflected in saints' tales. He begins with Félicité's story that could only happen either before reason had wreaked its destructive will on Christianity, or with a person who had escaped the sophisticated teaching of modern science and reason. "Today we try [...] to test everything on the basis of common sense. [...] Faith in miracles has disappeared" (Maury 234). Sincere believers needed, in short, the faith of a simple heart, someone who lived at a physical, animal level, who had an instinctual understanding of nature, able to react to stimulus without previous preparation and plans. Although Maury's essay called for a weak, ineffective mind, Flaubert understood that a lack of education did not mean a lack of wily insight. Abstract ideas made no impression at all or left the individual he was creating confused, with only vague, ill-defined concepts that rapidly disappeared in the midst of activity in the real world. Félicité was created to satisfy the needs of the cycle. Not stupid, she functions well with others at her level, whether children like Paul and Virginie, peasants like Robelin and Liébard, drunks like the marquis de Gremainville, or like her own family's Victor and the Leroux. She does less well in regard to the more sophisticated gentry, Mme Aubain, Bourrais, and Paul's wife, though her constant good will inevitably finds a way.

For Flaubert, one of Félicité's crucial traits would be her visual and aural sensitivity that harked back to people of the first century. Her priest's summary of sacred history, illustrated by luminous stained glass windows, made a powerful impression. "[S]he loved the lambs all the more tenderly because of the love of the Lamb, doves because of the Holy Spirit" (*3c* 601), though she understood nothing about established doctrine. Otherwise, however, this was her world. "Sowing, harvest, wine presses, all these familiar things that the Gospels talk about were in her life" (*3c* 601). God Himself had sanctified them (*3c* 601). What she learned, as Maury would have explained, was love, a law that she followed in everything she did. Maury reminds his mid-nineteenth-century readers, who might doubt that anyone could believe such fantasy, of the enormous numbers of their contemporaries that accepted the claims of Mesmer's "magnetic fluid," to his mind an equally unlikely reality (Maury 6).

Flaubert and Maury investigate changes taking place in saints' tales back through the history of Christianity. The deleterious effect of reason on faith was obvious in the nineteenth century. Despite the attractively revolutionary core of the ancient system founded on faith, emphasis on

126 *Flaubert's Talking Heads in* Trois Contes

the demands of logic had intervened. Interpretations of biblical healings had been recast in other terms (Maury 65). Rationalists explained away miracles (Maury 67). Still, to find a suitable hero, around whom a saint's tale could be created, Flaubert needed only consider the people unencumbered by systematic thinking who surrounded him in the French countryside. Félicité was not alone.

Serving as an implied frame subject to an implied narrator, Maury's argument allows Flaubert's cycle of stories to lead readers back through history from the naïve possibilities of an uneducated peasant, to a saint's tale exploiting many of the medieval period's markers, to the third tale about Iaokanann that might have been possible at the time of Christ. As pointed out previously, each of the stories is positioned on a descending trajectory, ending in death and suggesting the spiritual, spatial, and temporal analogical regression through time to the earliest days of Christianity. Félicité's room where the Holy Spirit comes for her is on the second floor, Jesus comes for Julien on a river bank, whereas Iaokanann ends his account in a subterranean world where the pre-Christian believers awaited the Messiah. Félicité's behavior is explained by the law of love that she follows in everything she does (Maury 234). Love is not particularly apparent until Julien recognizes his river ministry, and one is forced to assume that Iaokanann's love was displayed in the underworld.

Flaubert was not attempting to teach morality or theology or secular virtue. It seems clear that he was instead doing everything in his power to create a work of art by exploiting the generic saint's tale. His use of Maury's historical interpretation served merely as a useful chart for arriving at his artistic destination. For readers who take the time to revel in the motifs and patterns of *Trois Contes*, there is also a strong movement from first to last that portrays the history of saints' tales. Flaubert, the literary archaeologist, drives from modern civilization, where reason so dominates that miracles seem impossible, into a past that he knew well from his historical and religious studies. He demonstrates the birth of religious tales, illustrating Maury's analysis of how such creations came into existence. In each case, readers are implicitly invited to hold the story up to the probable reality, while recognizing that each tale and the three tales as a whole illustrate the biblical aphorism: "For Him to increase, I must decrease" (John 3.30; *3c* 651, 678).

There have been a few scholars who have pointed to the movements, from the style of realism, to that of saints' lives and legendry, to that of history. In a letter of 1 June 1856, Flaubert himself projects the sequence of "the Modern, the Middle Ages, and Antiquity" (*Corr* 2.614). Or, as Jasinski said, "From the modern day saint, passing by the medieval saint, one goes back to saint John the Baptist, that is, to the very origins of Christianity."[32] There is, as well, the terminal order moving from the Holy Spirit in "Un Cœur simple," to Jesus in "Saint Julien," to God the Father for whom the Baptizer speaks, which completes the Trinity. From

Flaubert's Talking Heads in Trois Contes   127

last to first, they feature the Holy Spirit, the Comforter sent after Jesus's departure during the time of the Church, Jesus of the New Testament, and the Father God of the Old Testament. In the conclusions, Loulou hovers over Félicité, Jesus carries Julien off to heaven, and the Christians take Iaokanann's head toward Galilee. This brief list merely begins the list of images whose significance changes from the first tale to the last in important, sequential ways. For one more example, Félicité is recognizably human, Julien's humanity struggles against his periods of brutality, and Iaokanann is little removed from savagery.

As readers regress from modernity to antiquity, they watch the gradual decline into brute bestiality, where characters are virtually indistinguishable from creatures of the natural kingdom. Step by step, using Maury's essay as an armature to undergird his stories, Flaubert tears aside the civilization surrounding Félicité, then he casts down reason serving as a first principle, until he can focus on a humanity that little differs from animals, and reveals the birth of Christianity and saints' tales. The prophets are exemplified in Loulou's small skull, the deer's traditionally marked forehead, and Iaokanann's massive cranium, and the talking heads speak volumes through the stories, confounding saintly Félicité, extraordinary Julien, and savage Iaokanann, all of whom were called of God. They bring the different tales together, demonstrate the creation of the genre, and portray sainthood, as they push backward through time to illuminate a series of memorable personages transformed by the Spirit, the Son, and the Father. Most of all, models of both short story and saints' lives function implicitly to allow readers the experience not of Christian theology, not even of history, but of an extraordinarily complex cycle or, to use Flaubert's words, to experience "the goal of art, that is, beauty."[33] As La Varende said of Flaubert, *Trois Contes* is "the flower of his work."[34]

Notes

1 As James Baltzell puts it, "[T]he short story is a genre which the French have rarely seemed to take seriously"—quoted from Michel Viegne, *L'Esthétique de la nouvelle française au vingtième siècle* (New York: Peter Lang, 1989) 1. In fact, in Balzac's time, contemporary (romantic) literature was widely discredited: L. Cassandra Hamrick, "La Crise d'identité littéraire en 1837 selon la presse périodique," *Autour d'un cabinet de lecture*, éd. Graham Falconer (Toronto: Centre d'Etudes du XIXe Siècle Joseph Sablé, 2001) 69–90; and James Smith Allen, *Popular French Romanticism* (Syracuse: Syracuse University Press, 1981) 131–44. Balzac's disdain for such creations liberally exposes "creators" like Étienne Lousteau in *La Muse du département* and Lucien de Rubempré in *Illusions perdues*. Lousteau, for example, uses his journalism to pay for his pleasures: "His serials, his articles, and the two short stories that he wrote each year for the daily papers were the tax imposed on this happy life"—Balzac, *La Muse du département* (1847), *La Comédie humaine*, Bibliothèque de la Pléiade, Vol. 4 (Paris: Seuil, 1966) 734.

128 *Flaubert's Talking Heads in* Trois Contes

2 For example, in Eri Ohashi's dissertation, he says, "In reality, analyzing *Trois Contes* with the aid of the notebooks, you understand that each tale has a different content, but that they retain a common structure"—"Analyse des manuscrits des *Trois Contes*: la transcendance des hommes, des lieux et des choses chez Flaubert," Littératures, Université Rennes, submitted Feb. 19, 2013, 109. <https://tel.archives-ouvertes.fr/tel-00790321>. For other examples, see below.

3 P. W. M. Cogman, "Gaps and Gap-Filling in Maupassant's 'Le Champ d'Oliviers'," *French Studies Bulletin* 60 (1996): 12.

4 Armine Mortimer, "Secrets of Literature, Resistance to Meaning," *Confrontations: Politics and Aesthetics in Nineteenth-Century France*, eds. Kathryn M. Grossman, Michael E. Lane, Bénédicte Monicat and Willa Z. Silverman (Amsterdam: Rodopi, 2001) 55–66.

5 Félicité's place in society is not established at the beginning of "Un Cœur simple." Nor has Julien settled in, since he seems torn between differing goals. And the third tale introduces the titular character, Hérodias, still struggling to realize her ambitions, though Iaokanann, one of her enemies, is festering in prison. In addition to the way the latter tale begins *in medias res*, confusion is immediately introduced, for, as Raitt argues, Hérodias "gives her name to the story, even though she is by no means the focus of attention or the most prominent character"—A. W. Raitt, *Flaubert. Trois Contes* (London: Grant & Cutler, 1991) 64.

6 Michael Issacharoff, *L'Espace et la nouvelle: Flaubert, Huysmans, Ionesco, Sartre, Camus* (Paris: José Corti, 1976) 31.

7 William J. Beck, "Félicité et le taureau: Ironie dans 'Un Cœur simple' de Flaubert," *Romance Quarterly* 37 (1990): 293–300.

8 The passages regarding the whipping are in *Trois Contes* 604, 605, 616. All further references to *Trois Contes* will be to this Pléiade edition, *Flaubert: Œuvres*, Vol. 2 (Paris: Gallimard, 1963) 575–678, preceded by *3c*. The reference to Hans Peter Lund, is to *Gustave Flaubert, Trois Contes* (Paris: P. U. F., 1952) 60.

9 Jacques-Bernardin-Henri de Saint-Pierre, *La Chaumière indienne* (Paris: B. Le Francq, 1791) 28–29.

10 L. F. Alfred Maury, *Essai sur les légendes pieuses du moyen-âge* (Paris: Ladrange, 1843) 123. Flaubert had known Maury's work since the 1840s. For a more detailed account of Maury's life and his relationship with Flaubert, see Florence Vatan, "Lecture du merveilleux médiéval: Gustave Flaubert et Alfred Maury," *Savoirs en récits I, Flaubert: la politique, l'art, l'histoire*, éd. Anne Herschberg Pierrot (Saint-Denis: PU de Vincennes, 2010) 87–107. Maury's *Essai sur les légendes pieuses* first appeared in 1843; the novelist used it while creating *Salammbô*—P. W. Wetherill, éd., "Introduction générale," *Trois Contes*, by Flaubert (Paris: Classiques Garnier, 1988) 44, 55, 92n.1. A second edition was published in 1896. In a letter of 30 September 1875, Flaubert asks his niece Caroline to set the book aside to bring to him in Paris and leaves no doubt of his familiarity. All references to Flaubert's letters are to Jean Bruneau's edition of the *Correspondance*, 5 vols., Bibliothèque de la Pléiade (Paris: Gallimard, 1973) 4.963, and will be preceded by *Corr.*

11 Allan H. Pasco has buttressed William J. Beck's arguments in "Flaubert's 'Un Cœur simple': The Path to Sainthood?" *Xavier U Studies*, 7.2 (1968): 59–67, and added further bibliographical references to the controversy surrounding "Un Cœur simple" in: "Ironic Interference and Allusion: 'Un Cœur simple',", *Allusion: A Literary Graft*, rpt. 1995 (Charlottesville, VA: Rookwood P, 2002) 22–38. For further bibliography, see Raitt 82–86; and Wetherill 146–54.

Flaubert's Talking Heads in Trois Contes 129

12 William J. Beck, "Flaubert's Félicité," *Explicator* 35.4 (1976) 4.

13 Raymonde Debray-Genette, *Métamorphoses du récit: Autour de Flaubert* (Paris: Seuil, 1988) 187.

14 Shoshana Felman, "La Signature de Flaubert: 'La Légende de saint Julien l'Hospitalier'," *Revue des Sciences Humaines* 181 (1981): 49.

15 Stuart Lasine, "Matters of Life and Death: The Story of Elijah and the Widow's Son in Comparative Perspective," *Biblical Interpretation: A Journal of Contemporary Approaches* 12.2 (2004): 117. Animal imagery marks an important opposition throughout *Trois Contes* to those few characters who exemplify humanity.

16 Jean Chevalier, and Alain Gheerbrant, *Dictionnaire des symboles: Mythes, rêves, coutumes, gestes, formes, figures, couleurs, nombres* (Paris: Laffont, 1969) 592.

17 Pierre-Marc de Biasi, "Un Conte à l'orientale: La Tentation de l'Orient dans 'La Légende de saint Julien l'Hospitalier'," *Romantisme* 11.34 (1981): 59–66.

18 Pierre-Marc de Biasi, "Introduction," *Trois Contes* (Paris: Librairie Générale Française, 1999) 37–38; Raitt's related discussion focuses on the novelist's commitment to art rather than history (61).

19 Joseph Frank calls the structure I have in mind a spatial form—*The Widening Gyre: Crisis and Mastery in Modern Literature* (Bloomington: Indiana UP, 1968): 8–9—though I prefer broader implications of the term "image structure." It might be described as a central symbol or complex composed of elements which may be connected to other elements and may be replicated. When such structures are repeated in literature, they generally move from the specificity of the story to a more general thematic or symbolic level.

20 The quotation, from 244, occurs in the midst of Peterson's argument relating the stories' thought to Flaubert's enormous knowledge of the Bible and of third- and fourth-century theology, particularly the Trinity and the various theories of history in his own day— Carla L. Peterson, "The Trinity in Flaubert's *Trois Contes*: Deconstructing History," *French Forum* 8.3 (1983): 243–58. See, also, Issacharoff 21–59; Wetherill 125; and Diana Knight, *Flaubert's Characters: The Language of Illusion* (Cambridge: Cambridge UP, 1995) 64.

21 As examples, by no means a complete list, I think of the three phrases of Loulou's repertory, the three prophesies regarding Julien, the three times Jesus called the saint to his boat, the three objects of Julien's pursuit (animals, men, and himself, though he decides not to commit suicide at the last moment)— *3c* 603, 625, 632, 646.

22 Jacques Neefs, "Le Récit et l'édifice des croyances: *Trois Contes*," *Flaubert: La Dimension du texte*, ed. P. M. Wetherill (Manchester: Manchester UP, 1982) 124.

23 Félicité sees Saint Michel killing the dragon in the stained glass (*3c* 601); Julien killed the dragon of Oberbirbach (*3c* 635), and Iaokanann softens his voice to announce "the newborn [putting] an arm into the dragon's cave" (*3c* 664).

24 "Sometimes the sun entering through the dormer window struck his glass eye, and made a big, luminous ray shine, which made her go into ecstasies" (*3c* 619); "the flaming eyes" of the big deer (*3c* 632); Iaokanann's "blazing pupils" (*3c* 654). In another passage, we see the latter's "face [...] where two coals gleamed" (*3c* 665). Biasi considers the flaming eyes, but only as they function in "La Légende de saint Julien"—"La Pratique flaubertienne du symbole," *Gustave Flaubert e il pensiero del suo secolo*, ed. Giovanni Bonaccorso (Messina: UP Messina, 1985) 261–63.

130   *Flaubert's Talking Heads in* Trois Contes

25 Israel-Pelletier, *Flaubert's Straight and Suspect Saints* (Amsterdam: John Benjamins, 1991) 122.

26 Shelly Purcell Thomas, "Thematic Progression in *Trois Contes*," *Romanic Review* 80.4 (1989): 541–47. While she accepts the double cone that Yeats first suggested, she is troubled by the inconsistencies that appear in John R. O'Conner's attempt to apply it to *Trois contes*. Thomas appropriately demonstrates "how the progression in the degree of sainthood is inversely proportional to the regression in the reception of the prophetic word" (547). Given Flaubert's near certain recognition that Hérodias was associated with Diana (see below, n27), Thomas's insistence on prophetic reception should not be ignored.

27 Maury 376; Jacob Grimm, *Teutonic Mythology*, trans. James Steven Stally-brass. Vol. 1 (New York: Dover, 196) 1.285–88.

28 Issacharoff 58. Similarly, Théodore de Banville says, "The *Trois Contes* are not detached tales; they are on the contrary unified by a tight relationship which is the exaltation of charity" (quoted from Biasi, "Introduction" 41).

29 Little has changed since Raitt's summary of the disappointing results of this controversy (76–81). Biasi says briefly, criticism of the unity of the *Trois Contes* has not always elicited clear answers ("Introduction" 41). Maurice Bruézière reproaches *Trois Contes* "for having no profound unity"— "Notice," *Trois contes* (Paris: Classiques Larousse, 1953) 14. Michel Tournier occupies the middle ground: "[T]he presence of God is the common trait of the three tales—all things considered, so ill-assorted"—"Préface," *Trois Contes* (Paris: Gallimard, 1973) 14.

30 For "Un Cœur simple," Flaubert told Tourgueneff on 3 Oct. 1875 that it would be very short, at most thirty pages (*Corr.* 4.972). "La Légende de saint Julien" was also projected as a little piece that would be no longer than thirty pages in a letter to Sand, 16 Dec. 1875 (*Corr.* 4. 996). In his follow-up letter to Sand, he repeats his estimate of thirty or so pages: Bruneau dates it: "end Dec. 1875" (*Corr.* 4.1001).

31 Pierre-Marc de Biaisi, "Le Palimpseste hagiographique: L'Appropriation ludique des sources édifiantes dans la redaction de 'La Légende de saint Julien l'Hospitalier'," *La Revue des Lettres Modernes* 777–81 (1986): 86.

32 René Jasinski, "Le Sens du *Trois Contes*," *Essays in Honor of L. F. Solano* (Chapel Hill: U of North Carolina P, 1970) 119.

33 Letter to Sand of 3 April 1876, *Corr.* 5.31. Curiously, though Flaubert continued to complain about how hard it was to write, he also repeated that he had turned to the short story because it was easier than working on *Bouvard et Pécuchet*. Still, he never deviated from his stated goal of creating art, despite using genres that were little used for such lofty goals. As he says in another letter, to Tourgueneff, "It seems to me that French Prose can attain a beauty that people cannot imagine? And yet, there is in this world nothing important but that" (5.60; 21 June 1876).

34 Jean de La Varende, *Flaubert par lui-même* (Paris: Seuil, 1967) 54.

8 The Power of Ambiguity in Balzac's Open Closures

Balzac always wanted more, whether in his love life or his finances or his creative works. This drive to extremes impelled him to force his creations to represent a larger vision than the genre or the basic meanings the words would allow. It is particularly evident in his short stories, and, for this chapter, three that he collected in *La Comédie humaine* offer excellent examples: "Gobseck" (1835), "Le Chef-d'œuvre inconnu" (1845), and "L'Auberge rouge" (1831). The list could easily be extended. Balzac often reworked previously published texts to more fully plumb their connotative potential. When variants for these publications are extant, scholars can gain a fuller understanding from the writer's revisions of what he was attempting as he expanded their import.[1] "Gobseck," for example, was first published in 1830. It was a superb character study of a greedy, though incongruously charitable usurer, perhaps based on a personage whom Balzac might have known. The novelist had a considerable number of acquaintances among the potential sources for the money he always needed. His full characterization of Gobseck gives him a believability that stands up well against Shakespeare's Shylock or Molière's Harpagnon, not to mention scores of other, well-rounded examples that have been elucidated in European literature.[2]

Five years after the initial publication of "Gobseck," however, Balzac made a radical change by adding a coda that turned this almost real personage into an image that can be read as pointedly identifying a major flaw in society's extreme commitment to money. Castex explains that Balzac's miser, Gobseck, is "the symbol of money, of its power, which made of him the very figure of destiny [...], an image of the epoch's aborning capitalistic energy."[3] The scholar uses the word "mythic" in detailing what happens to the foodstuffs that the miser accepted in payment for various debts and in describing the pile of fireplace cinders beneath which is hidden a quantity of gold and silver (2.1011). Balzac has completely recast his original image with more information in the text he added, giving it a decidedly negative turn. Cash, whether coins or paper, silver or gold, can have a useful function, but when such fungible means of conducting business (cf., 2.995) are turned into values in and for themselves, they represent amassing material goods for their own

132   Power of Ambiguity in Open Closures

end and, finally, become nothing but putrefaction and ashes, as the last version of "Gobseck" illustrates. In the character of Gobseck, Balzac incarnates his basic criticism of this inherently crass, sterile, materialistic society. By walking away from virtue, France has turned its back on the traditional values that give real prosperity, whether joy, compassion, love, peace, or friendship. While there was little reason in Balzac's versions preceding that of 1835 to believe that the author was playing on two possible meanings of *papa* in *"ego sum papa"* (father / pope 2.990), readers are meant to understand in the later, definitive version that this creature has become not just a father but, in fact, Pope Gobseck, the representative of a new religion of gold. The final characterization fulfills the potential of such comments as, "gold is the spiritualism of your current societies" (2.976). With the addition, Balzac brought new depth and expanded breadth of meaning to the societal implications of what was in earlier versions but a description of character, however brilliant.

As Balzac demonstrates, there are many ways of opening a fiction to a more complete or, indeed, a more profound story. Among his interesting tactics, the author's stories exploit the constant, running references to contemporary society. The regular incorporation of real persons into his fiction emphasized histories that are pertinent to his fictive creations. As Balzac insisted, his goal in writing *La Comédie humaine* was to "write the history forgotten by so many historians, that of manners" (1.11). Not only did he wish to describe his world realistically, he worked to understand and explain his tumultuous surroundings with an overview that brought everything together in a coherent whole, what he called a "seminal" or "generative idea" ['une idée mère'].[4] His famous, reappearing characters were in fact just one of many means of holding his work up as a social mirror and insisting on its realism and significance.

"Le Chef-d'œuvre inconnu" ['The Unknown Masterpiece'] (1855) raises editorial problems that must be dealt with before beginning an analysis of the story. René Guise, the Pléiade editor, reproduced the last version of the story published in *Le Provincial à Paris* (1847) with one exception. Although recognizing that Balzac was responsible for these changes, Guise nonetheless does not include the new title of "Gillette" (10.1408). He concludes that this variant was only for the new publication, and not for the preceding "corrected" Furne edition of *La Comédie humaine*. Although Guise is a superb editor, his justifications for denying Balzac's title change are unconvincing (10.1409), as, indeed, he subsequently decided. He argues several years later that Balzac's new title of "Gillette" (1847) is of a piece with the author's other changes.[5] Poussin's mistress has from the beginning of the last, definitive version of 1847 successfully resisted total commitment to art and aesthetic theory by representing the true love of a live woman, the kind of love that stands in conflict with Frenhofer's pathetic, Pygmalionesque behavior as though his painted creation were alive. As the reader soon learns,

Power of Ambiguity in Open Closures 133

Poussin follows Pygmalion's similar route of turning away from the real and preferring art or the artificial.

At the beginning of "Gillette," Balzac regressed historically to an earlier era before the nineteenth century, inventing an episode in the life of one of France's great renaissance painters, Nicolas Poussin. "Toward the end of the year 1612" (10.413), the narrator says, providing the date we expect of an authentically historical work. He goes on to describe the setting, just across from the Ile de la Cité in the heart of "Old Paris" (10.413), and to introduce the famous French painter, Nicolas Poussin, as a young man. While there are many realistic elements in the characters and setting, Balzac's tale itself was largely imaginary, for its purpose was to consider not a historical reality but the tension between love, if not life, and art. In the story, Poussin has the opportunity of making the acquaintance of Master Frenhofer, a painter he admires. Soon it develops that Frenhofer has put the final touches to what he considers his own masterwork. He would be willing to show it (or her, as Frenhofer terms it) to the young Poussin, who is wild to learn anything at all that might increase his artistic ability, if Poussin would allow him to compare his lovely mistress, Gillette, to the painter's canvas of Catherine Lescault.

Gillette has already learned that when she models for her lover, he no longer sees her with tenderness, but rather objectifies her as a potential work of art. Nonetheless, her love makes it impossible to refuse to do as Poussin (and Frenhofer) wish. The Faustian bargain is clear: Poussin will expose Gillette to Frenhofer's examination having nothing to do with love (perhaps not even with art), so that the young painter may then be the first to study Frenhofer's most recent masterwork. In exchange, Frenhofer's foreign eyes will see and compare God's work in Gillette with his personal, painterly rendition of Catherine Lescault. The results are, on at least one level, catastrophic (Whyte terms it an "ocular rape" 103). Gillette is real; the painting of Catherine is but an unsuccessful expression of life. Poussin learns nothing, for the painting is a failure. Frenhofer has over-painted his work, leaving but one marvelous fragment visible, in the midst of a jumble of caked-on color. The next day, Frenhofer is dead, an apparent suicide, and all of his paintings are lost in a conflagration that destroyed his studio. The lovely Gillette lives, though her betrayed love for Poussin has cooled.

Readers are left with many questions at the end of the story. Did Frenhofer commit suicide? Were his other paintings true masterpieces destroyed in the holocaust? If he set the fire, why did he deprive mankind of his achievements? What was his state of mind when he incinerated his masterworks and died? We can answer none of these questions with any assurance. We do have a resolution to the central opposition between Gillette's love and Poussin's art, however. We know from the painter's biographies that Poussin failed to learn his lesson and commit himself more fully to love, as his mistress wished, since Gillette does not appear

134 *Power of Ambiguity in Open Closures*

in his later life. Even if he mended their relationship after this disturbing betrayal of her lovely body to the gaze of another man, thus selling her for his own gain, we can easily divine that he continued to sacrifice his love for art. Only then do we recognize, and regret, that love lost the battle for Poussin's heart.

Outstanding writers regularly use a tale's terminal confusion or ambiguity to force readers to seek an underlying but inexplicit image. The conclusion of "Gillette" implies that Poussin has continued to put his mistress in second place, and he has lost her. She is pointedly not in the last pages. Those readers who challenge the story's ending in the hope of a better understanding have no choice but to recognize Gillette's absence from the conclusion of Balzac's story, but also from the history of the great Poussin's later life. If Balzac's account is factual, if Poussin's biographies are accurate, if history is true, the tale's conclusion goes beyond the bounds of both fiction and history itself into an unknown "reality." By bringing in a famous person and describing something that might have happened as the truth, the novelist's creation exists somewhere between the real and the imaginary. Without question Balzac's representation implies the failure of art, since Frenhofer's botched painting is by no measure worth Gillette's love for Poussin. Perhaps Frenhofer also concluded that his art was no match for life, and he gave up trying, destroying his legacy as a lost cause. Structurally, by implication, the tale nevertheless continues beyond the conclusion and tells what Armine Mortimer calls a "second story" with a new, open conclusion that has different implications.[6] Gillette's love will die, and Poussin will lose her, since love is a fragile relationship that never survives being relegated to any inferior commitment.

Not all readers would accept without significant hesitation the author's open conclusion suggesting that in the implied second story Gillette's love lost out to art, though the hesitation is consistent with the tenor of this revolutionary period at the turn of the sixteenth century, just as it was at the beginning of the nineteenth century when Balzac was writing. Revolutions generate uncertainty. They impose equivocation that is marked by confusion, and it is not surprising to find themes and images of indecision, doubt, and ambiguity again filling the pages of literature in the period of the Restoration, when Balzac creates an even more complicated set of allusions in the sequential narration of "L'Auberge rouge" ['The Red Inn'] (1832). The story, like Denon's "Point de lendemain," considered above in Chapter 2, builds a confused pattern of multifaceted implication until the reader seizes the terms of antithetical innocence and culpability to personally improvise a resolution. In "L'Auberge rouge," however, the terminal ambiguity is never resolved as it is in "Gobseck" or "Gillette." Readers of "L'Auberge rouge" are left wondering amidst a series of unresolved and contradictory declarations of culpability: is Taillefer indeed guilty of murder? Is the narrator's

Power of Ambiguity in Open Closures   135

suspicion of the banker's guilt an entire misconception? Along the way, if the banker is indeed responsible for the after-dinner mysteries of the Auberge rouge, the text asks readers to come to terms with whether Mademoiselle Victorine Taillefer's relationship to her father means that any suitor who marries her and her fortune must unequivocally share her father's guilt. Readers may leave the story confused and dissatisfied, or they may reconsider what they have read, looking for other indications of a conclusion. Balzac's use of allusions to Rabelais and Goethe shift the reader's attention away from the father and murder to whether the main narrator and the reader should rather have spent his time cultivating his love for Victorine.

For those who appreciate clarity and precision, "L'Auberge rouge" does not begin in a promising way. Though eschewing the fairytale tag of "once upon a time" ['Il y avait une fois'], an anonymous, main narrator serves to open the account and sets the scene for the embedded story told by Monsieur Hermann. The main narrator does not recall the year, seems unsure of the setting (11.89), and prefers to retain the imprecision of the atmosphere (11.90), while he does remember attending a party for a "good heavy-set German," who was the "head of I don't know what fairly important bank in Nuremberg," and named Hermann, "as," he says, "are almost all Germans that authors put on scene."[7] The main narrator's mention of Hermann's name is hardly reassuring, given his later admission that he invented another name. All these reiterations of the narrator's faulty memory immediately bring the textual reality into question. As is often the case in Balzacian fiction, the reader is introduced in the opening pages to the major image, for whenever the author repeats an image, a name, a word, or a phrase in such close proximity, it is but another way of telling the reader to pay attention. This is a story that begins and ends in vagueness or, indeed, like "Point de lendemain," in uncertainty.

The host's daughter announces at the end of the dinner that Hermann is going to tell a terrifying story, inspired by two fashionable writers of the day, Sir Walter Scott and E. T. A. Hoffmann. Physical appetites sated, everyone is ready to sit back and enjoy a good story. Suddenly, however, even before the storyteller begins, the main narrator notices the man across the table from him whose face had turned sallow, perhaps darkened by a shadow. "You would have said the deathly pale visage of a dying person" (11.91). Could he be suffering from too much to drink? Is he facing a disaster, like bankruptcy? The narrator's neighbor explains that he is certainly not bankrupt; he is rather the enormously rich Frédéric Taillefer. She goes on to remember what readers learned about this recurring character in *Le Père Goriot*: the merchant / banker long refused to recognize his daughter, so that he could leave his vast wealth to his son. Eventually, the son died in a duel, and his father has little choice but to re-establish relations with the girl, who thus becomes

136   *Power of Ambiguity in Open Closures*

one of the best prospects for marriage in Paris. The aged financier will have no more children to share the inheritance. Suddenly this object of the narrator's observations loses his troubling appearance, smiles, and once again becomes a well-fed guest happily digesting his dinner, ready to hear an engaging story with the rest. The narrator feels ashamed of his previously unsympathetic consideration that revealed his faulty "divinatory knowledge *in anima vili*" (11.92).

Hermann begins his tale. It was back toward the end of October of 1799, which was just a few days before 18 Brumaire, when Napoleon would stage his coup and take power. The revolutionary violence was by no means over then. Hermann adds that two young men in French uniforms left Bonn one morning to arrive at the end of the day near the town of Andernach on the Rhine. They were happy with themselves, with their medical training, and with the adventures they have had in Germany. They even have a little money in their pockets, real money in a period when the revolutionary *assignats* had become worthless. Just at the moment when Hermann mentions the name of one of the boys, Prosper Magnan, Taillefer suddenly grabs a pitcher across from the narrator and, with trembling hands, pours himself a glass of water. Downing it with one swallow, when queried, he denies feeling indisposed, despite a perspiring brow making him appear feverish. Hermann continues with his story: the two travelers decide to spend their last night of freedom from military obligations in the local Auberge rouge, an inn whose name exudes the color of wine, blood, and passion that was perfectly appropriate in a tale that would satisfy the demand for something terrifying. Hermann tells that a diminutive man named Walhenfer arrived. Unfortunately, the inn was full. The newcomer would have to sleep on a chair in the common room and share the fish dinner destined for the soldiers. While they ate, the innkeeper locked everything but an already barred window for the night.

The scene shifts back to Paris and the banquet, where the distressed Taillefer gulps yet another glass of water.

In Andernach, continuing the story within the story, the innkeeper joins the soldiers and Walhenfer after dinner. Conversation begins. Prosper talks of home, wondering what his mother is doing. His companion teases him with the guess that she's dreaming of buying the property next door, thus satisfying the family's long-held desire. Prosper's companion, whom Hermann has arbitrarily decided to call Wilhem, generously offers the late arrival his bed. Expressing his gratitude, the traveler admits that he is happy to be away from the boatmen, with whom he's been traveling, but who seem suspect to him. He explains that he has just sold his business and is carrying a hundred thousand francs in gold and diamonds in his suitcase (seven or eight hundred thousand euros in today's money) that he keeps near him. Finally, the group begins to move toward sleep. Prosper, however, lies awake ruminating about what he

Power of Ambiguity in Open Closures   137

could do with a hundred thousand francs. He could buy the property next door for his mother, for example, and he could court a well-off young woman in his hometown of Beauvais. Little by little he begins to imagine the crime. He could use one of his surgical instruments to cut off the traveler's head, then run away to Germany. Of course, he reprimanded himself. Even "[t]he thought of it was doubtless already a crime" (11.102).

At this point in the appalling tale, the first narrator watches M. Taillefer wipe his forehead and drink a little more water (11.102). As Dorothy Kelly aptly points out, the carafe's stopper that Taillefer fingers can be seen to symbolize Walhenfer's head that will soon be on the floor in Hermann's account (38).

In the Auberge rouge, Prosper gets up and begins in the darkened inn to prepare to commit the murder. He takes the bars out of the window and opens it. He rummages in his bag and finds a scalpel. He actually goes to the side of Walhenfer's bed before being overcome with horror at the realization of what he is considering. Flinging down the instrument, he jumps out of the window, hoping to wear himself out with a long walk. When he later returns after thanking God for sparing him from committing such an unspeakable crime, he shortly falls into a deep sleep.

"Would you like some water, Monsieur Taillefer?" asks the Parisian host on seeing the banker reach for the carafe, which is now empty.

The next morning Prosper awakens in Andernach, only vaguely cognizant of his surroundings, until he perceives Walhenfer's shocking, decapitated body still on the bed and the pool of blood between his mattress and the dead German's head. Overwhelmed by feelings of guilt, he faints and falls onto the bloody floor. "It was already [...] punishment for my thoughts" (11.105). Later, he regains consciousness seated on a chair in the common room, surrounded by Republican (French) soldiers and drenched with blood.

Back at the Parisian banquet, as Hermann tells the horrifying tale, Taillefer pulls out his handkerchief and wipes his forehead. His face is thoughtful and sallow. Only the narrator watches, for the others are focused on the storyteller, listening avidly.

In Andernach, Prosper is surrounded by his surgeon-major, his papers, his medical bag, and the sharp instrument used in the murder. Sentinels are stationed outside beneath the windows, and one can hear the sound of their rifles and of the crowd of locals attracted by curiosity to the crime scene. Prosper seems completely befuddled, in a fog that is interpreted as cowardice by an irate soldier and the crowd. Unable to sustain interrogation, he is led off to prison. Hermann mentions in an aside that Prosper told him about his mental and physical state, while he personally was also there with him behind bars. Having previously raised a small troupe to oppose the French, Hermann was betrayed, imprisoned, and was awaiting his own fate. This gave him the opportunity

138   *Power of Ambiguity in Open Closures*

to converse with the young soldier, and he was immediately struck by his fellow prisoner's pitiable state. "[H]is face had a look of candor and innocence that struck me deeply [...H]e seemed like a victim and not like a murderer" (11.107). Hermann became convinced of his jail mate's innocence, though Prosper fears that he might have committed the crime in a somnambulant state.

Of course, if Prosper is innocent, his companion must be guilty. After all, as Hermann points out, Wilhem is gone, having left without awakening Prosper. Furthermore, Walhenfer's suitcase with the gold and diamonds is also missing. Were Prosper the killer, one would think the wealth-laden suitcase would still be present. The young man feels nonetheless culpable, since he was drenched in blood and not only considered committing the assassination, he almost did. As he confessed to Hermann,

> [H]e still felt crushed by remorse. He had certainly raised his arm to cut off the merchant's head. He was trying to be truthful, and he knew his heart was not pure, after having committed the crime in his imagination [...] 'I feel like I lost the virginity of my conscience'. (11.108)

The lesson is clear. For Prosper, any sin committed in the imagination is as much a sin as if it were done in reality. At his trial, they asked him about the open window, about how he got out, about what he was doing. Nonetheless, though they asked many questions, nothing pointed to his innocence, but rather the answers directed them to the circumstantial evidence that could indicate his guilt. The boatmen were sure he buried the loot. He himself defended his comrade, whose name was not Wilhem, the narrator suddenly remembers, but rather Frédéric. Prosper did not even declare his own innocence, and he was condemned.

Though the conjunctions of the events of the story and Frédéric Taillefer's dinner-party behavior are circumstantial, the narrator cannot help but draw the conclusion that the banker is greatly affected by the story being told. The financier has shielded his eyes with his hand. Nevertheless, the narrator believes that dark flames could be seen through his fingers. Shortly the banker regains his calm demeanor, and the narrator wonders whether his suspicions could possibly be wrong. Could the man be innocent of the crime? Or was the source of his great wealth Walhenfer's gold and diamonds? Prosper had asked Hermann, who was convinced of his innocence, to attend the execution and to take a letter to his mother. The narrator eventually traveled to tell Madam Magnan, but she had died of consumption during the preceding winter. The young lady who originally asked for the story stops Hermann from telling the end, since it is clear that Prosper was going to be executed, and she does not want to confront such a conclusion. For the reader,

Power of Ambiguity in Open Closures 139

it is another indication of inconclusiveness. Furthermore, as Prosper Magnon was executed on circumstantial grounds, so the narrator judges Frédéric Taillefer on the basis of similarly uncertain evidence.

The financier's currently calm demeanor on being served a cup of coffee encourages the narrator once again to decide that his suspicions are surely unfounded. Taillefer denies ever having been in Germany, when queried by the narrator's neighbor, and the doubts are once again quickened by the host's reminder that as a supplier for Napoleon's armies, he was definitely at Wagram. Unable to stop wondering about the banker's guilt, the narrator pursues him through the rest of the evening. "Would you be [...] Monsieur Frédéric Taillefer, whose family I knew very well in Beauvais?" he asks (11.114–15). Taillefer acquiesces, and then, complaining of the heat, "His face suddenly revealed horrible suffering, and he went out abruptly" (11.115).

At this point, the part of the story that has elicited most of the interpretation in the critical literature is complete. Readers do not know and will never find out whether Taillefer was a vile assassin. The rest of the text has little effect, and indeed one has to wonder whether Balzac has made a terrible mistake in releasing another shallow crime tale into the market. What is worse, perhaps, is that the author's suspicious narrator is incapable of solving the mystery. He is certain that he has identified the murderer, but his proof is circumstantial, thus quite unsatisfactory. The evidence suggests but does not resolve the assassin's identity. Perhaps identifying the assassin is not in fact the subject of the story. Perhaps readers should remember the initial indication of uncertainty as a major theme, if not the very subject of the tale.

The narrator's dinner companion remonstrates with him for jumping too rapidly to conclusions. He should leave things in the hands of human and divine justice. "If we escape one, we will never avoid the other!" she says (11.115). The narrator laughs off her admonitions and—a third twist in Balzac's story—he eagerly uses the arrival of the lovely Victorine to change the subject. Without knowing her identity, he had fallen in love at first sight with her several days before. Just when his companion tells him she is Taillefer's daughter, they hear "violent but stifled cries that seemed to come out of a neighboring apartment and echoed faintly in the gardens" (11.115–16). The host comes to speak a word to the young woman, who leaves immediately, doubtless, to join her father. The other guests wonder about the banker's malady. The hostess explains: "The doctors don't know how to cure it. It seems that the suffering is atrocious [...]. This poor man claims to have animals gnawing on his brain in his head: there are shooting pains, sawing, horrible throbbing inside each nerve" (11.116). For thirty years, he has been regularly afflicted near the end of the fall (and we remember that the murder took place about then) (11.117). The hostess repeats, as we have already learned from the narrator's observations, that in the course of an attack the pain periodically

140 *Power of Ambiguity in Open Closures*

comes and goes, allowing him to eat and drink, before the bout recommences. His physician says it is a nervous affliction, though Taillefer attributes it to a splinter of wood in his head, the result of falling on a boat while he was in the army, and Moïse Le Yaouanc takes him at his word.[8] The dinner guests propose several diagnoses: tetanus? a variety of cerebral gout? In 2005, one of my physician friends said the symptoms given in the story could indicate a particularly acute migraine headache, though to confirm his diagnosis, he would want to spend some time with the patient.[9] Anne-Marie Meininger remembers, as well, that Monsieur Brousson, the doctor who reminds the hostess of the diagnosis, bears a name that Balzac almost certainly constructed on that of the period's famous Dr. F. J. V. Broussais. This shrewd insight may indicate that for Balzac Taillefer's unnamed but terrible malady was caused by acute inflammation, "an inflammation of the nerves" (11.116), the core symptom of Dr. Broussais' medical theory and of crucial importance to migraines.[10]

As the third-level story continues, the narrator's love for Victorine blooms unabated, and she seems to share his affection, though he is repelled at the thought of allying himself to the daughter of an assassin. Revolted by this horrible crime, to which Taillefer's apparently guilty behavior at the dinner appears to link him, he tries to quell his affection by leaving town and traveling. On returning to Paris, however, his passion is renewed, and he wonders whether it is possible to marry Victorine honorably, especially since his suspicions remain acute. "There is certainly a pool of blood on Mademoiselle Taillefer's land; the estate she inherited from her father is a vast *hacelma*" (11.121). Meininger explains that the italicized word refers to the Hebrew *haceldama*, which "signifies *field of blood*," a word given to the potter's field bought with the thirty pieces of silver Judas received for betraying Jesus (11.1256n3). The narrator wastes himself in casuistry. Even if he had not known that the father had previously done everything in his power to distance himself from his daughter, can visiting the sins of the father on such an extraordinary daughter of grace, talent, and accomplishments be justified? Rather than dealing with the doubts himself, the narrator invites a group of acquaintances to dinner in order to help him decide whether he should marry the possibly tainted, young woman.

Those who know Balzac will remember his admiration for Rabelais and the thematic similarities with Panurge's quest for the answer to a similar question: should he marry? And if he does, will he be cuckolded? Pantagruel repeatedly makes his opinion clear: "Everyone must be the judge of his own thoughts and take counsel of himself."[11] Only the individual in question can decide about marriage, and only being actively engaged in marriage will answer his fear of future cuckoldry. Panurge's inability to understand these truths grows from his acute self-love and makes him the object of Pantagruel's continuing mockery. Panurge asks

Power of Ambiguity in Open Closures   141

guidance of the Virgilian lottery (activated by a toss of the dice) and a dream. Nothing satisfies him, so he leaves on a quest, raising the issue with numerous people. In the midst of his travels and frustrated queries, Pantagruel convinces him to have a dinner where he can consult with some highly regarded authorities like a religious scholar, a physician, a lawyer, and a philosopher. The lawyer is unable to come, having been arrested for questionable verdicts. The results of the dinner are no better. Panurge is quite right to find all the answers unsatisfactory for, even when given, they show no more than the personal bias of whomever is concocting the response.

Although the main question that occupies Balzac's narrator is whether he should marry Victorine, the answer is likewise left to his friends, chosen for an allusive dinner that, like the guests at Rabelais' similar repast, represent humankind in general: "two Englishmen, an ambassadorial secretary and a puritan, a former minister who has matured in politics, young men who are still innocent, a priest, an old man, then my former tutor" (11.118–19). The narrator thinks about other difficulties related to the girl, which seem endless, all based on events and facts that may be imaginary. Remaining convinced himself of Taillefer's guilt, he goes on to conclude that the money Victorine has inherited has been corrupted by her father's apparent crime. His friends accept his conclusion of the banker's culpability. What can he do? If he marries her, should her fortune be returned to the murdered man's family? In the amount stolen? In the sum to which it has grown? To whom can he return it, since they could never find the industrialist's heirs? The questions seem overwhelmingly important, and he fears "that my scruples are degenerating into monomania" (11.118). Does he have the right to reveal this "secret" he has "discovered" to the daughter, to add a decapitated head to her dowry, to destroy the illusion she has of her father, in effect, and since the father has recently died, to kill him a second time, telling her "[a]ll your money is stained"? (11.121) If they marry, could he do something else with her fortune? Establish funds to have masses performed for Prosper's soul? build a hospice? fund a prize for virtue? live a life of poverty? None of these ideas seem compelling, since such institutions as he might establish often fund scoundrels. What should he do? Not surprisingly, the notary follows the Rabelaisian model and recuses himself from the deliberations. He has a contract to write (11.119).

At this point, whether one accepts Taillefer's guilt or not, the answer seems indisputable. There is no convincing reason for the narrator to turn away from Victorine. In a Judeo-Christian culture, God does not wish the sins of the father to be visited upon the child, and He promises to break any such limitations for those who love Him (Ezekiel 18.19–20). Even if Taillefer were guilty, the young woman seems an appropriate candidate for being freed from the culpable association. She was long separated from her father and, moreover, she is presented as a fountain

142   *Power of Ambiguity in Open Closures*

of virtues. In the period of the story's setting, there is even less reason for the narrator's concerns, since, through the course of the eighteenth and nineteenth centuries, young people were increasingly granted the right to choose their betrothed, a fact that is widely reflected in the literature,[12] thus marking their independence from parental influence. The obsessive narrator is, however, incapable of accepting her for what she is and arriving at his own decision.

As only Panurge can respond effectively to the question of his personal matrimony, so also Balzac's monomaniacal narrator. His friends are quite right to focus on the central matter of marriage, though, content to quibble over minor matters, they are not united in a desire to provide a definitive answer. The lawyer considers the source of other fortunes. The priest distracts the narrator and wonders whether the narrator should be content with the "legitimate" goods inherited from the mother's side? His drunken former tutor asks whether the subject is appropriate for discussion. One suspects that he followed the Rabelaisian admonition that wisdom is to be found in the command, "Trinch!" ['Drink'], thus arriving at his wise position (883). As Rabelais shows, others cannot provide useful responses, and as Balzac's text thus insists by means of the allusion, the only sensible and correct answers must come from within oneself. Finally, the seventeen friends to whom Balzac's limited narrator accords "the utmost in honesty, delicacy, and honor" split nine to eight on the essential question of whether he should marry the girl, which with the narrator's implicit vote makes the divide an even nine to nine. "How can one resolve the dilemma?" (11.121). The only answer was long ago suggested by Rabelais: like Panurge, as Pantagruel insists repeatedly, the narrator should himself decide. And to Panurge's second question, as to whether he would be cuckolded, it will depend on the narrator himself. If he divests himself of the fortune and forces Victorine to live in penury, it is possible that "[s]he will be stolen by a slender, dashing, jauntily mounted officer, [...] who will have a nicely curled mustache, will play the piano, and praise Lord Byron" (11.122).

Similarly, the reader must decide the outcome of these multiple mysteries at every level of the intertwined stories for him- or herself. The evidence is neither clear nor certain. While one might conclude that the cranial pain is the result of Taillefer's guilt, which is the shared conclusion of legions of scholars, there is no certainty, at least no absolute certainty. On thinking through the story once again, readers may remember (though the narrator has forgotten) that Taillefer's attack began before the onset of Hermann's story. Even then, "his face [...] had become sallow, streaked by purplish tints. You would have said it was the deathly pale head of a dying person [...]. His dull eyes remained fixed on the sparkling facets of a crystal stopper" (11.91). Only after the onset of Taillefer's discomfort does Hermann take a pinch of snuff and

Power of Ambiguity in Open Closures   143

begin to tell his gory account. The suggestive names and origin may be nothing but a coincidence. Indeed, on seriously considering the paucity of real rather than coincidental and circumstantial evidence—the likely migraine linked imprecisely to the chronology of Hermann's story, the given and family names of Frédéric Taillefer, and the connection with the village of Beauvais—could a conviction be obtained in a court of law? Indeed, even if the father is guilty, should the wealth be considered tainted without proof, and should his virtuous daughter be penalized?

As the allusion to Rabelais filled out the story of Victorine and the narrator, so another allusion emphasizes the Rabelaisian insight. Despite Balzac's claim that "almost all Germans put on stage by authors" are named Hermann, as the benighted main narrator says (11.89), it is simply not true. Nonetheless, whenever Balzac brings attention to a name, the reader must likewise heed its import. Given Goethe's pervasive renown in the early nineteenth century, there is one character that comes principally to mind: Hermann, a young farmer who met the lovely Dorothea while wandering afield in revolutionary turmoil. It is a story that Goethe told in his long poem, *Hermann und Dorothea* (1797). The young woman has just assisted another in childbed, and Hermann is overwhelmed by her courage, compassion, and beauty. Dorothea likewise enthralls Hermann's family friends, the minister, the pastor, and the doctor, not to mention all those female acquaintances who have been captivated by her humane ministry. Her outstanding attributes are enough to convince Hermann to disagree with a talkative neighbor, who believes that, in a time of tumultuous war, it is best not to marry. In addition, the young woman has, like Victorine, a negative burden from the past: she was betrothed to another now-dead young man. Should Hermann turn from her because of her former attachment? Hermann's love is profound, however, despite his father's preference for a young woman with a good dowry, and he vows that he will either marry Dorothea or remain single, thus without heir, until the end of his days. Fortunately, his mother has as well been favorably impressed by Dorothea, and she urges the father to be more open to his son's deep affection for his choice. Hermann's father finally agrees to accept the recommendations of his friends, who are both very favorably impressed by the young woman. The new betrothal takes place, but only because Hermann knew the importance of his affection, only because he knew his own mind. The thematic and onomastic allusions in Balzac's story elicit reverberations of Rabelais and of Goethe, their opposing illustrations of marital decisions thus highlighting the narrator's spineless indecision.

"L'Auberge rouge" seems an irresolvable dilemma for the reader who is insensitive to Balzac's use of allusions to Rabelais and Goethe's stories, as he delves into the tale of the terrible murder and of the narrator's conflicted love. Such readers are left in the midst of uncertainty, abandoned to their own means, wondering amidst a series of unconvincing

144 *Power of Ambiguity in Open Closures*

declarations of culpability whether Taillefer was indeed guilty of murder and whether the narrator's suspicion of the banker's guilt was an entire misconception. The story becomes a simple crime tale of little weight, though it sets a far more important puzzle that remains unsolved. Does Taillefer's guilt or innocence matter? Is it not uniquely the narrator's indecisiveness that has real human significance? Whether the banker is guilty or not, the reader is asked to come to terms with Mademoiselle Taillefer's relationship to her father. Does it mean that any suitor who marries her must unequivocally share the father's guilt? Indeed, why does the narrator want to torture himself by asking about Taillefer's hometown? One of the men listening to the narrator shrugs: "You fool, why did you ask if he was from Beauvais!" This question and its implications cannot be resolved by anyone but the narrator, though the reader has to wonder: why ask a question which could ruin your life, especially since it has no real relationship to Victorine's suitability for marriage or to the central and very personal issue of whether the narrator should in fact marry her?

Balzac opened the story with his allusions to a larger human context and to a conclusion of considerably more importance for Victorine and the narrator than whether or not her father / banker did or did not kill a man decades ago. Just as Rabelais' Panurge and Goethe's Hermann must decide for themselves when confronted by choices of extreme personal importance, so also the narrator and the reader. Balzac avoids the ambiguity by demanding that the reader evaluate Panurge, who is pathetically unable to make up his own mind, before observing Goethe's Hermann who does so by standing up against differing opinions. The reader is invited to return to the reading experience he or she has just had and find the references to these two allusions scattered subtly through the account. Like the new conclusion added to "Gobseck," this lengthy coda opens a new, larger significance. But unlike those previously explored tales by Denon and Barbey, or Balzac's own "Gillette," the story implies a significant twist that recasts the future. The narrator's indecision does not direct the reader forward, especially since his inability to come to a position will almost certainly cause him to miss out on this life-changing possibility of marriage. In the end, Taillefer's guilt or innocence should have but minor importance for the narrator's life, especially when there is no objective means of coming to absolute truth. The narrator should be posing different questions. Is Victorine worthy of his love? Does she love him? Does he love her sufficiently to spend the remainder of his life with her? While he proves that he can ask others such questions, he also proves that his friends can provide no trustworthy answers. He is the only one who can decide whether or not he should marry Victorine, and he alone can treat her so that she does not become the prey of another man. The narrator must make up his own mind about whether or not he should marry and whether he should marry Victorine. We do

Power of Ambiguity in Open Closures   145

not know what he will decide. Any implications for the future reside in the lessons the reader has learned from observing the paralyzing performance caused by unrelenting equivocation. We do, however, understand that, for every human being, major decisions must to a large degree be self-motivated.

"L'Auberge rouge" is a sequential story that moves rapidly through the crime, even making the narrator's tergiversations seem sensible and necessary, at least until the reader arrives at the inconclusive end. Only by slowing and reconsidering the tale and its context does one recollect and wonder why the narrator needs anyone else to make up his mind. Important changes have taken place in what was once an unalloyed patriarchal society and, while the father remains important, young people have much more autonomy. At the conclusion of the story, although the narrator is challenged by the suggestion that he knows too much, in reality the conclusion drives the reader to experience an unresolved adventure similar to that of the narrator. Carefully embedded in the account are allusions that encourage the reader to create a parallel narration of evaluation and judgment. As only the narrator can decide on his marriage, so also the narrator can decide on Taillefer's guilt, and on the conclusion that will impact the narrator and Victorine's life. The story's end drives home the dismal future of hapless equivocation. Of course, as France was slowly moving away from a series of inadequate governments and toward its own Industrial Revolution, such vague hopes and hazy fears for the future were everywhere. Balzac impressively makes his small story of a narrator who, incapacitated by uncertainty, mirrored the major problems and opportunities affecting the future of France.

Notes

1 Pierre Laubriet's impeccable consideration of the text: *Un Catéchisme esthétique:* Le Chef-d'œuvre inconnu de Balzac [In Appendix: a critical edition of two early versions of the story 201–39] (Paris: Didier, 1961) 9–200.
2 For a comparison of two of Balzac's misers, see Eric Le Calvez, "Gobseck and Grandet: Semes, Themes, Intertext," *Romance Studies* 23 (1994): 43–60.
3 Honoré de Balzac, "Gobseck," *La Comédie humaine,* éd. Pierre-Georges Castex. 12 vols., Bibliothèque de la Pléiade (Paris: Gallimard, 1976–81) 2.955. For a more detailed analysis of "Gobseck," see my, *Novel Configurations: A Study of French Fiction,* 2nd ed. (Birmingham, AL: Summa, 1994) 51–71; and Owen Heathcote's insightful "From Cannibal to Carnival: Orality and Violence in Balzac's 'Gobseck'," *Modern Language Review* 99.1 (1996): 53–54.
4 Honoré de Balzac, "Etudes sur M. Beyle (Frédéric Stendhalh [sic])," *La Revue Parisienne* (25 septembre 1840), (Œuvres complètes de Balzac, ed. Maurice Bardèche, vol. 24 (Paris: Club de l'Honnête Homme, 1971) 253. All other references to Balzac will be to the Pléiade edition.
5 René Guise, "Lire 'Le Chef-d'œuvre inconnu'," *Autour du "Chef-d'œuvre inconnu" de Balzac* (Paris: Ecole Nationale Supérieure des Arts Décoratifs, 1985) 9–13. See also the subsequent arguments that refer to this position, in

146 *Power of Ambiguity in Open Closures*

general to maintain the old title: see, for example, William Paulson, "Pour une analyse dynamique de la variation textuelle: 'Le Chef-d'œuvre' trop connu," *Nineteenth-Century French Studies* 19.3 (1991): 404–16. Likewise for Peter Whyte, "'Le Chef-d'œuvre inconnu' de Balzac: esthétique et image," *Text(e) image*, ed. Margret-Anne Hutton (Durham: U of Durham, 1999) 96n7, 102–06. Nonetheless, as David A. Powell argues with a clear consideration of the various emphases of the story, "For [...] Poussin, choosing to seek the absolute in art is renouncing Gillettte and love"—"Word and Image in Balzac's 'Le Chef-d'œuvre inconnu'," *Interfaces* 29 (2009–10): 254; and as Eric Ganz correctly says, Balzac changed the title in 1847 in order to make sure that the story was focused on love—"Balzac's Unknowable Masterpiece and the Limits of the Classical Esthetic," *MLN* 90.4 (1975): 504–16. Sigbrit Swahn also insists on the importance of Balzac's last textual changes: "'Le Chef-d'Œuvre inconnu,' Récit Hoffmannesque de Balzac," *Studia Neophilologica* 76.2 (2004): 206–14.

6 For Armine Kotin Mortimer's superb work on concluding overtures, see, especially, "Second Stories, *Short Story Theory at a Crossroads*," eds. Susan Lohafer and Jo Ellyn Clarey (Baton Rouge: Louisiana State UP, 1989) 276–98; "Second Stories: The Example of 'Mr. Know-All'," *Studies in Short Fiction* 25 (1988): 307–14; and "The Devious Second Story in Kleist's *Die Marquise von O...*" *The German Quarterly* 67.3 (Summer 1994): 293–303.

7 Balzac, "L'Auberge rouge," éd. Anne-Marie Meininger, *La Comédie humaine*, Bibliothèque de la Pléiade, 11.89. For Dorothy Kelly's excellent analysis of the murder, see, "Balzac's 'L'Auberge rouge': On Reading an Ambiguous Text," *Symposium* 36 (1982): 30–44.

8 11.117. Le Yaouanc, *Nosographie de l'humanité Balzacienne* (Paris: Maloine, 1959) 179.

9 I am grateful to N. Dean Weaver, M.D., for sharing his knowledge and experience.

10 Meininger's perception is found on 11:1254n1. For the details on Dr. Broussais, see, *Encyclopedia Britannica*, 11th ed. (New York: Encyclopedia Britannica, 1910) 4.656.

11 Rabelais, *Le Tiers Livre des faites et dicts héroïques du bon Pantagruel*, *Œuvres complètes*, eds. Jacques Boulenger and Lucien Scheler, Bibliothèque de la Pléiade (Paris: N. R. F., 1962) 454. Pantagruel is repeatedly clear: see, for another example, "Are you not sure of what you wish? That is the principle factor" (361). I am grateful to my colleague E. Bruce Hayes for his assistance with Rabelais.

12 See my *Revolutionary Love in Eighteenth- and Early Nineteenth-Century France* (Aldershot: Ashgate Publication, 2009) 33–65.

9 Maupassant's Exploding Closures

Maupassant, a prolific master of the short story, left many examples of ways that brief narrations could be structured to engage, hold, and challenge readers. At the time he was writing, not everyone agreed that he was particularly expert. After reviewing the collection of tales published under the title of *La Maison Tellier* in 1881, Emile Zola, for example, felt that his young colleague needed to write "a long novel to show his capabilities,"[1] a position that has more to do with Zola's failure to comprehend the unique qualities of the short story than with the short-story genre or Maupassant's astonishing abilities. Edith Wharton spoke to the issue.

> It is sometimes said that a "good subject" for a short story should always be capable of being expanded into a novel, [...] but it is certainly a misleading [principle] on which to build any general theory. Every "subject" (in the novelist's sense of the term) must necessarily contain within itself its own dimensions.[2]

Henry James was even more to the point:

> [I]f the tales [by Maupassant] deserve the first place in any candid appreciation of his talent, it is not simply because they are so much the more numerous: they are also more characteristic; they represent him best in his originality, and their brevity, extreme in some cases, does not prevent them from being a collection of masterpieces.[3]

Whether Maupassant exploited allusions, mise-en-abyme, open or closed conclusions, image and sequential structures, or whatever else in his published stories, it was done with sure competence. As one of many examples, I think of "Madame Parisse" (1886), where he paints a trite if not grotesque comic tale of modern adultery to draw parallels with Homer's tale of Menelaus and Helen,[4] or one might cite "Le Protecteur" (1884), where the character Jean Marin has reached a position of success by holding firmly to the coattails of an accomplished friend and now government minister. Recognizing his enormous debt to his friend and

148   *Maupassant's Exploding Closures*

to society, he decides to be helpful to others, indeed to help anyone at all who comes across his path. After writing several letters of recommendation for a passing acquaintance and discovering to his chagrin that he has created a false portrait, he categorically decides that it is wrong to write letters of recommendation. While this decision may for a moment seem entirely appropriate, on reflection it is not acceptable because it is a mistake to write letters of recommendation but because Marin agreed to write for someone he did not know. On reconsidering the protagonist's history, the reader is forced to reorder the events of the story to conclude in retrospect that, however well meaning, if not incapable, Jean is a fool.

Maupassant excels at such surprise endings as in the celebrated "La Parure" (1884), where the reader learns that the misplaced and arduously replaced necklace is only worth 500 francs. Or in "Tomboctou" (1883), the seemingly inconsequential story that leaves the reader puzzled as he follows the narrator through his adventures early in the war of 1870, until suddenly, at the end of the account, he realizes that the enormous man could always buy drink for himself and his friends because he had an income source from the sale of human meat, for which there was a generally ignorant but ready market. Many of Maupassant's concluding sentences, like the "No, that can't be what happened" of "La Main" (1883 1.1122), compel the reader to turn from the story's obvious conclusions and consider other possibilities. The ending of "Confessions d'une femme" (1882) even more explicitly obliges the reader to reorient his or her expectations when the narrator learns that her husband had meant to kill the man he thought erroneously to be her lover: "And at that moment, I understood that I would be unfaithful to my husband" (1.472). Though highly appealing, few of Maupassant's stories are philosophically profound and certainly not revolutionary. Many readers have, however, been permanently marked by his touching excoriation of war in "La Folle" (1882).

Numerous tales resolve in ways that require final reflection to evaluate the implications of the sweep and scope of what preceded. All of his tales open windows onto the human character, some with a smile, or a laugh, others with a frown if not tears. Maupassant's technical toolbox included most of the devices discussed in previous chapters, though as the critic André Vial argued, he excelled in exploiting the conclusions of his short stories. Indeed, "In the enormous majority of [Maupassant's] tales, the privileged instant is placed at the end" (Vial 444). These endings may be no more than the terminal implication of "Suicides" (1880), whose narrator found a newspaper article by a man whose lackluster life led him to consider suicide, and who picks up the revolver on his table. "I cock it... " he writes (1.180), the terminal ellipses leaving very little to the imagination. More often, the conclusions are designed to discomfit readers by disorientation, leading them to reorder the events and assumptions of the story to encompass a different motive and meaning.

Maupassant's Exploding Closures   149

Of course, stories must always to some degree engage readers, or the story would not attract a continuing audience. Great stories can appeal to generations, if not centuries, of readers.

"L'Aveu" of 1884 suggests a reversal of the roles a reader might expect and then opens a continuing story. It begins with two peasant women carrying buckets in a pasture, a mother and daughter from the affluent, peasant Maliverne family. They come to a cow and kick it up for milking. Finally, with the buckets full, they began to walk back. The girl, Céleste, stops walking and begins to cry. She can't carry the bucket. The mother wants to know what is wrong with her (2.192), and the girl covers her eyes with her apron. She thinks she's pregnant, she says, sobbing. Dumbfounded, the mother sets down her load. She can think of nothing to say. "Where?" "In Polyte's coach." The mother tries to understand. This sort of thing happens, and is not too bad if it is with a boy of means, who would bring some advantage to the family that is after all established, respected, clever, and powerful.

"And who done it t'ya, bitch?" "Polyte" (2.194). The mother begins to beat the girl with her fists, hitting her in the head, the back, all over, for she knows that the boy has nothing. The daughter falls to the ground, between the pails, which protect her a little. "Tramp!" The mother wants to know why she would do that with a mere coachman. "I di'nt pay for the ride," she explains, and the light shines. Céleste goes to the market twice a week with produce: chickens, cream, eggs in two big baskets. The girl had been paying six sous for herself and four for the produce. Eventually, she complains about the price. He says that he wouldn't charge if she would be open to a "bit o' fun." When he would see her he would say, "For Saturday, right?" Then, every time she got a ride from him, he would say, "Ain't it for today, the fun?" And they'd both laugh. Then she began to calculate what she has already paid. She tried to bargain. He agreed to lower the price for the fun. In the last two years she has paid him 48 francs. Sooooo, she soon pays the non-cash price. Three months later she suspects the pregnancy. Her mother tears into the sobbing girl again, "Bitch! trash!" Then she pauses to ask whether Céleste had told Polyte. No, she did not. The two women agree not to say anything. If he knows she is pregnant he might begin charging her again, and if he does not know, she may get another six or eight months of "free travel." "For sure, I won't say nothing," the girl promises (2.197).

The conclusion is open, but the implied second story is clear. The agreement will continue until the coachman can see that she is pregnant. Then there may be a new arrangement. But that is for the future. For the moment it is more important that the mother's attitude has changed. Both are now aware that this is a practical matter. Although the mother would doubtless not have agreed to her daughter's prostitution at the beginning, now confronted with the reality of pregnancy, she wants to squeeze as much benefit as possible from the situation. The variance is

150   *Maupassant's Exploding Closures*

explained in the differing socio-linguistic filter. Now the curse words that the mother liberally applied to her daughter are not just true but accepted. The mother agrees to the business arrangement despite its demeaning significance. In fact, she accepts that the epithets she has been using on her daughter are correct. The girl has become a prostitute, a "tramp," a "bitch." But business, after all, is business. She agrees that her daughter will continue to sell herself for a few sous every week. Such a small amount of money is far more important than morals for Maupassant's peasants, even for those who are reasonably well off.

Indeed, Maupassant is particularly skillful in regard to open structures like those just considered in Balzac's work. In Maupassant, the open stories offer a powerful technique for expanding their reach and suggest, not a continuation, but an actual second story. Vial, for example, believes like legions of other critics that the novel genre is anchored in "plurality and diversity" (453), while its briefer cousin, the short story, commonly suppresses time and presents "a unique, immobile image that can turn itself into a three dimensional space" (455). Still, while Maupassant seems to have preferred image structures over the sequential, he regularly exploited narration as well, allowing it to unroll within the text and, not infrequently, to continue on into an implied future, actually creating another story in the reader's mind. "Le Horla" (1887), like "Boule de suif" (1880), comfortably exploits narration, though doubtless Maupassant's mastery is equally evident in stories like "La Dot" (1884). There the relatively new bride goes on her honeymoon to Paris, where she is deserted by her husband, who absconds with the dowry. She goes weeping to her cousin, who decides to stay home from work to "comfort" the distraught girl, obviously sensing an easy, though inexplicit, conquest.

Maupassant demonstrates another side to his talents by employing the folklore that plays an important role in "Les Epingles" (1888). The cultural thrust of the story is worth exploring, especially since the knowledge on which Maupassant bases his allusion has faded into the past. Two young men are chatting. One complains that some women "played an abominable trick on him" (2.1088). Earlier in the year, tired of a dull life governed by entrenched habits, he had opted for a change. He went to Dieppe, leaving his mistress behind in Paris. "You can't spend all your time strolling on the boulevards" (2.1012), he explains. He meets a young woman vacationing on the beach and begins an affair. After all, her husband is horrible. Fortunately, the spouse only joins her on Sundays, and the narrator has a good time with her during the rest of the week.

The narrator's Parisian mistress, whom he terms "my habit" (2.1011 and *passim*), is unable to leave the capital city. It is not that he does not love her, for he does. He has known her and her husband for years, and she is very important to him. Likewise, her husband "is a fine man,

Maupassant's Exploding Closures   151

whom he likes a lot [...], a good guy, a true friend" (2.1011). Eventually, he returns home to Paris, as does his new mistress, whom he terms his "minister" (her husband is a chief clerk). This opens complications in his schedule. He is not one to make changes for no reason, so he now has two mistresses in the same city. Since they almost met each other, he assigns to each her days. "I don't know how to break things off. I collect [mistresses]" (2.1012). Things continue for a while uneventfully, though pleasurably. One day his young "minister" left one of her pins in a wall hanging near his mirror. The small straight pin (*une épingle*) was of the old-fashioned kind with a round, black head. His more mature "habitual mistress" saw and collected it, leaving one of her own in its place. The "minister" responded by leaving two crossed pins, and his "habit" a third, one on the other (2.1015). Aware of each other because of the interaction through reciprocal placement of pins, the two women soon establish regular correspondence. One day, the appointed mistress does not come. The narrator goes to her place and finds her reading a novel. She doesn't offer a convincing excuse. The next day the other does not show up either, and he soon finds her at home, reading a novel and giving the same inadequate explanation.

Growing increasingly frustrated over the next three weeks without his regular visitors, able to see his mistresses only in their homes where there is little privacy, he eventually understands that they are in collusion. They have not broken with him exactly; they are all still friends, very close friends, but then on the same day they send him letters bringing the sexual relationships to a conclusion. The women who communicated with pins are now writing each other letters and thereafter meeting in person. The narrator feels he has paid a high price for their intimacy. When his friend says, "Well, well. And doesn't that give you an idea?" (2.1016), he remains confused. Clearly, he does not understand what if anything is being communicated. The friend has no doubt of what is going on, however, for those like Yvonne Verdier who know the symbolism and can "read" the pins, "these details constitute a language, a language of seamstresses regarding pins and needles, which can be deciphered when they are again put in the ethnographic context of peasant society at the end of the nineteenth century."[5] "You big booby," he says, "[don't you understand that] the idea is to have them double up and start over?" ['l'idée de leur faire repiquer des épingles doubles?'] (2.1016). "Repiquer," of course, suggests "pricking or beginning again," "starting out once more." "Epingles doubles," referring to duality, can also refer to a hairpin or a bobby pin doubled over and a safety pin.

The French ethnographic tradition of pins and needles long pointed to the female side of sexuality, as Bernadette Bricout and Yvonne Verdier have argued.[6] Pins and needles were of course tools that women learned to handle quite early. Ethnographers would argue that in folk tales and in the broader society, pins and needles were often linked to a parallel

152   *Maupassant's Exploding Closures*

sequence of female sexual development. Verdier writes more specifically that at first the instruments reflect the girl enjoying her good looks. She is "tirée à quatres épingles" ['well turned out'] (179). When at about the age of fifteen, the girl goes to a local seamstress for a year or so of apprenticeship, not so much to learn to sew, but to "take the rough edges off" ['dégrossir'] (178), and while ending her adolescence in this quasi-finishing school, she learns the skills and insight she will need later. During this period, she may have some early amorous experience despite a vigilant chaperone, and she uses pins to arrange her attire temporarily. At about the moment when menses arrive, she advances to more sophisticated sewing with needles. This, of course, signals the time for serious romance if not a permanent attachment.[7]

Verdier points out that straight pens served early on for the girl's personal adornment, temporarily repairing any holes in her garment, where the needle was employed only later and came to stand for the subsequent period, after she had served her seamstress apprenticeship and was prepared for the life of a woman, wife, and mother (178–79). The physical structure of the needle is not without consequence; "[p]ins and needles must not be confused. The development of femininity is established by pricking" and marked by blood at menstruation, the breaking of the hymen, and childbirth (179). In short, the broad cultural meaning, illustrated by fairy tales and cultural understanding of the period regarding the *épingle*, or straight pin, is related to pre-pubescence, during the period when a local seamstress teaches the girl to sew and prepares her for the time of needles and maturity, one more step on the way to womanhood (179–206).

Monjaret's discussion of "the way of pins" (*la voie des épingles*) and that of "needles" (*la voie des aiguilles*) is grounded ethnographically in popular versions of *Little Red Riding Hood*. The later, written developments by Grimm and Perrault mute the sexuality and elide the paths of pins and needles that are both common in the oral, peasant tales, though Verdier mentions their decision to use the sexually suggestive color red. In many earlier folk versions, Little Red Riding Hood is asked where she is going. After mentioning her grandmother, she goes on to discuss the way she plans to walk. "I prefer the way of pins [*le chemin des épingles*], with which you can make yourself pretty, to the way of needles [*le chemin des aiguilles*], with which you have to work," she says in a version from the Forez region.[8] The way of pins symbolizes the spirited social life of an adolescent seeking a husband, while the way of needles turns more toward sexual maturity in domestic life and its realities (Monjaret §40–45). But whichever way the girl chooses, the provocative and opportunistic wolf is always there, and sooner or later will bring the expected conclusion (Monjaret §45).

While an ethnographer would apparently have no trouble deciphering Maupassant's tale of a confused man at loose ends, it poses difficulties

Maupassant's Exploding Closures   153

for those not versed in peasant traditions. Once put into a context that is today obscure or barely decipherable but, according to specialists, well understood in the nineteenth-century countryside (Monjaret §1–3, 67), a surprising message was apparently sent to the boulevardier. The women he has "collected" have established their mutual presence and acknowledged the love triangle. Not antagonistic rivals for his affection, they have joined forces and intermingled pins, seemingly proposing a new novitiate in the possibility of group sex, thus their intent to keep the triadic arrangement at the level of extra-mural and extra-marital play, a team sport. While ethnographers insist that pins must be kept separate from needles, the narrator's mistresses have intermingled and grouped their pins in preparation for the next development. Although critics must be aware of how problematic such an interpretation must remain, the author seems to have unified the image system, proposing another way for the "naïve" narrator. If his friend was right and he does not know enough to gather up the comingled pins, thus accepting the invitation, his future will not explode in the new experience of an informal *ménage à trois*.

In another, late tale, Maupassant traces his fragmentary thoughts in variants, as he built a more complexly enigmatic but fascinating short story entitled "Le Champ d'oliviers" (1890), a story that Robert J. Niess calls the author's "last true masterwork."[9] In preliminary versions of the tale, there were no mysteries, for Maupassant explained everything. Subsequently, on returning to the manuscript in the definitive version, he concludes with a bloodbath that can scarcely avoid puzzling the reader. The truncated final version makes sense to those ignorant of what preceded only if the text succeeds in encouraging the reader to fill in the dots and compose the enigmatic story of the priest's death and the son's condemnation. Perhaps only then will the reader recognize that the priest has found a way to have his son justly executed for murder.

The title "Le Champ d'oliviers" hints at the issue of religion that shows up in the first few lines, so that one may divine from the beginning that there is more involved than the tale of a parish priest. Some will remember that it was on the Mount of Olives that Christ memorably taught and beneath an olive tree that he later experienced his greatest sorrow and his only weak moment (2.1190). The priest thinks of the surrounding olive trees as he murmurs repeatedly, "Oh! God, help me" (2.1192). The story concerns a popular priest and curé, Father Vilbois, and opens when he comes back from fishing. Several of his parishioners hurry to the shore to give him a hand, though he is obviously in excellent physical condition. As a vigorous man, he has no difficulty handling the boat. The catch is respectable: three sea bass, two eels, and five sunfish. One of the locals takes the fish, and they head off to the priest's *bastide* (the local term given for small cabins designed for solitary enjoyment, though the name was taken from a series of forts and fortified cities built from

154   *Maupassant's Exploding Closures*

the twelfth century through the fourteenth century). He has rented the place in the midst of a grove of olive trees to enjoy time alone and skills like shooting that have less to do with his vocation than with personal pleasure. He himself has the appearance of the dignity and strength one might find in a military officer rather than a village priest.

Little by little we learn his history. He actually chose the parish he would serve, and he regarded it almost as if he were an owner. He has been in Garandou for twenty years, and thinks of it as *his* village… *his* church. He plans to die there. He has been a priest since he was thirty-two. This evening in July, he is happy. He has a good catch; he likes the fact that he is respected because of his physical prowess, a little point of vanity that he allows himself. Once he had been a socialite, a baron, before he became a priest in reaction to a disappointing love affair. Actually, it took longer than that. He had started law school, but when his father, then mother passed away, he decided to simply enjoy his wealth and social standing as he finished his studies. Handsome, intelligent though perhaps limited in his beliefs, traditions, and princi-ples, people liked him. Then he met a young actress, Rosette, and fell in love. Absolutely crazy with passion for her, she became his mistress. For four years, she seemingly reciprocated his affection as his grew in intensity. Indeed, despite his family name and station, he would have married her, had he not discovered that she had long been betraying him with the friend who introduced them. What made it even worse was that she was pregnant. The thought that it might be his child drove him to distraction, arousing all his aristocratic prejudices, and, had she not sworn that it was not his child, he might have killed the squalid woman and "this ignoble creature" that she carried (2.1182). He threw her out, and moved toward the south of France until he found a village where he stayed for eighteen months, desperately seeking peace. "He lived with the devouring memory of the traitorous woman, of her charm, of her ability to completely engulf even occupy him, of her unquestioned be-witchment, and with memory of her presence and her caresses" (2.1183). His confused thoughts are easily recognized as the evidence of the slow death of an obsession. Slowly, his old piety came back, and the religion that had once seemed a refuge from the mysterious life to come now represents protection from a life of misconception and torture. He still knew how to pray, and he abandoned himself to the mystical love of God that vanquished the other human passion. He became a priest, who was rigid, but kind, and his family connections got him posted to the little village on the sea.

As Father Vilbois comes up to his little *bastide*, he immediately disap-points the maid who takes care of him. She is ready to serve him a good dinner of rice and chicken, but he wants to have one of the fresh sea bass he just caught. As she turns back toward the kitchen separated from the house, she remembers to tell him that he has had a visitor, a rather

Maupassant's Exploding Closures   155

disreputable looking man. She is habitually fearful, imagining that they will one day be assassinated, and Father Vilbois laughs, not taking her seriously. The vagrant approaches, and the priest agrees that the man does indeed appear unsavory. With a blond beard, his hair sticking out beneath his old, misshapen hat, covered by a long, brown overcoat, he walks with the soft, rolling movement of someone wearing peasant espadrilles. "Well, do you recognize me?" the new arrival asks. He goes on to show the curé a photograph taken of him many years before, in the days when he was involved with his treacherous mistress. On her deathbed she told this disreputable vagabond, her son, that Vilbois was his father. Moreover, on comparing the photo with the young man in front of him, the resemblance is such that the priest is forced to agree. The tramp is certainly his child. He remembered his outrage at the woman and understood how she could have lied for her own protection. "And his own son was born, had grown up, had become this sordid marauder, who smells of vice like a ram smells of goat" (2.1189). They go for a walk as the priest attempts to come to terms with this new revelation, and a short, desperate prayer rises from him. When he learns that his son has not eaten since yesterday morning, however, he is filled with pity and reaches out to the filthy offspring, which encourages the young man. By laying out a generous repast, the priest imitates the way the father in the parable welcomed the prodigal son's return (Luke 15.11–32). In this case, the biblical model fails as a predictor, for the garrulous newcomer has not come in repentance, as was the biblical case, but to exploit his father. The tramp becomes more cynical as the meal progresses. "Ah, well, really! I begin to think that we will reach an understanding" (2.1191), he says. With the fish and the chicken there is plenty to eat. Marguerite, the maid, is waiting, and five minutes later they are eating the preprandial soup. Since the kitchen is outside the *bastide*, the priest summons her by sounding a gong.

If one can believe the intruder, he bears the name of Philippe-Auguste, a name composed of the given names of his putative fathers, one of whom, the priest, abandoned him before he was born, and the other, a senator who finally recognized and rejected him as the child of his rival. As the meal continues the newcomer becomes more talkative and more offensive. Marguerite brings the fish, but she is angry, for she does not trust the tramp. Father Vilbois sends Marguerite for two bottles of good wine. The marauder is delighted. "It's been a long time since I've eaten so well" (2.1193). Marguerite senses that the tramp represents a significant danger, and she does not wish to leave, though the priest insists, and she returns to the kitchen. The priest's anxious questions continue amid an undercurrent of prayers and the contextual olive trees surrounding his *bastide*, reminding readers of the Garden of Gethsemane (2.1192). What does he most want to know? Everything... It is as though he is once again Rosette's lover, and he learns that the woman

156   *Maupassant's Exploding Closures*

who betrayed him was able to live with his rival for thirty years. The son admits that he made their life difficult. "I always spoiled everything," he says (2.1194).

Philippe-Auguste drinks more and more. His long fast sends the alcohol straight to his head, and he becomes drunk. Father Vilbois fills his son's glass yet again, hoping that he will hear more of the truth. When Marguerite brings the chicken and rice, she is outraged by the young man's drunkenness. The tortured priest sends her away. He is filled with questions. "What did your mother say about me? [...] How did they act toward you?" (2.1195). As a boy, the "prowler" (2.1195) was well treated until Father Vilbois' rival, Senator Pravallon, recognized that he was in fact the priest's son, at which point the boy's situation turned decidedly worse. He committed what he views as a few little pranks, and his step-father and mother had him put away in a house of correction (2.1195). It was a good way to get rid of him. The priest can discern his mistress' manipulative cunning in Philippe-Auguste's feminine features. As the "marauder" continues to brag about his errancy, the priest recognizes his own propensity to jealous anger and violence. The bastard offspring has then combined the passions of the father with the sly perversity of the mother. His psychopathic nature could not be more obvious.

As the vagrant throws glass after glass of wine down his throat, he becomes increasingly inebriated and garrulous. One of his "farces" killed an entire family, which cost him several years of detention. But the vagabond wants to tell what he did after being released from prison. He says he got vengeance on Pravallon, the rival. The senator had offered him a thousand francs to disappear, despite the fact that the young felon could see much more money in the drawer that his step-father was keeping for himself. Furious about what he interprets as selfishness, the vagrant knocked Pravallon down and used a hot poker to mark him front and back with crosses. The young scoundrel thought he would escape punishment, for he did not believe Pravallon would admit to what was done to him. The perversion of the Christ story becomes inescapable. Where Jesus' sacrifice required only one cross to bring peace to the world, the evil Philippe-Auguste produced many crosses on his foster father's body and will doubtless commit numerous future crimes to satisfy his selfish, repeated need for vengeance. Many for one, rather than one for many.[10] He brings the priest into his saga: "I got even for you, Papa" (2.1196), he says, and the priest's terrified eyes are glued on his repugnant son.

> All the ardor of his passionate heart and violent blood extinguished by the priestly calling reawakened in an irresistible revolt against this miserable creature who was his son [...] and against the fatal destiny that welded this rogue to his paternal foot like a galley slave's ball and chain. (2.1201)

Maupassant's Exploding Closures 157

He decides that he'll bribe his mendicant offspring to leave the country for a place of his choice, though the small payment will stop if he disobeys him. The drunken tramp stutters that the priest should watch out, that he now is in charge, which simply infuriates the priest and makes him want to deal violently with the vagrant. He pushes the table into his son's chest, screaming, "Watch out, watch out, I'm not afraid of anyone…" (2.1201). The drunk wobbles on his chair, realizing that he is in danger. He reaches for a knife and the priest pushes the table so forcefully that his son falls flat on the ground. The light is extinguished. And the silence of the tomb engulfs them. Neither moves. For a long time, perhaps even an hour, it is quiet, until the priest's gong sounds, and Marguerite comes running, pausing only to bring her kitchen light. She sees two bodies on the floor and slips on a red liquid, before she realizes that something terrible has happened, and she flees into the night, barging against the trees as she runs terrified across the countryside to get help in the village. In the dark, the little pink *bastide* seems black. The arrival of the villagers carrying lanterns turns the *bastide* pink once again, while the local police have their revolvers out and support Marguerite who is hardly able to stand. There is blood all over. It has flowed across to the tramp passed out on the floor, bathing one of his legs and one of his hands. "Father and son slept, one with his throat cut […], the other drunk" (2.1204). The police quickly chain the tramp, who awakens, stupefied, understanding nothing. After two previous crimes, his companions informed on him. This time the evidence falsely accuses him. "Why didn't he run away?" the mayor asks. "He was too drunk," the policeman replied. The crime scene seemed easy to interpret. "Everyone agreed, since no one would have thought that Father Vilbois had perhaps committed suicide" (2.1204).

And the story ends, leaving a little mystery that most readers would quickly solve. The textual details leave little doubt. The priest's life suddenly became unbearable torture. His former love has been rekindled despite the unquestionable reality of his fornication in the fruit of his illicit affair. His priestly veneer is shattered by the passions aroused from the past, negating the validity and power of his sacerdotal transformation, and he reacts with his old, prideful violence. In effect, the son destroys what he has become. One might even say that the son has killed the father. Recognizing his offspring as a psychopath, the priest surely believed that for the good of society, his child should be incarcerated if not executed for his crimes. What better solution than for the priest than to kill himself in such a way that the offspring would be blamed? He would no longer have to confront his own sin, and the son, a self-confessed murderer, would deservedly be removed from the world.

More interesting than divining the motives for this suicide is the question of why Maupassant not only wrote the conclusion summarized in the last paragraph of his early version published in *Le Figaro*, but

158   *Maupassant's Exploding Closures*

why he later deleted it, thus leaving his reader to deal with the definitive version as best he could. On considering the newspaper passage where the author spells out the priest's thoughts, and the eventual results for the son, it is difficult to justify the deletion, for it is as well written as one would expect from the pen of this author. I take and translate the passage published in the early *Le Figaro* version from Forestier's notes in the Pléiade edition:

Somewhat reassured by the presence of the guns and axes, Margarite then told that an evil-doer had just assassinated her master, and had almost killed her, since she had come in just at the instant when the crime took place.

They took every precaution on approaching the house that was surrounded and invaded like a fort captured by assault, and they discovered, in fact, Father Vilbois in the dining room with his throat open and lying on his back in a sea of blood that was already beginning to coagulate.

At the other end of the living space, a man was in a deep sleep. The Arlésienne [maid] cried, "No, he isn't sleeping... kill him... kill him... there is the knife..."

And she pointed to a bloody knife on the table cloth near a plate almost full of blood that must have spurted from the wound.

The assassin still seemed asleep. They got him up, shook him, hit him. He opened his eyes and appeared to understand nothing, because he still seemed completely drunk.

They showed him the dead man with the horrible wound that made a red hole between his chest and his head. He was very afraid.

The mayor and the police arrived and, after the usual considerations about the position of the body, the supposed sleeper, the place where the instrument of the crime had been found, and the fall of the lamp that suggested a short struggle, they took down the servant's first deposition.

She said and affirmed under oath, that she had come in at the moment when the man was still leaning over the priest, and that he had immediately rushed toward her with his knife raised. She owed her salvation to the fact that she threw her light at him and ran away as fast as she could. In fact, they found the servant's little kitchen light near the place where the vagabond was sleeping or pretending to sleep. The proof seemed established.

But they got lost in conjectures about why the murderer remained at the scene of the crime rather than fleeing.

A voice said:

"He was too drunk to run."

. . . .

Maupassant's Exploding Closures   159

Philippe-August was judged at Aix-en-Provence and condemned to death. Right up to the end, he protested his innocence with such desperate energy that he shook his judges' conviction.

But the charges against him were overwhelming, aggravated especially by the maid's testimony.

To defend himself, he told a bizarre story, from which it followed that the priest was his natural father. They didn't believe him, for it occurred to no one that Father Vilbois might perhaps have cut his own throat.

The accused having run out of arguments called for the testimony of an honorable senator, Count Pravallon. But the information furnished by this witness on the accused's antecedents was so deplorable that they decided to condemn him.

He was guillotined in the public square. (2.1706–07)

While we do not know when the manuscript was originally written, or when the passage quoted above was deleted, except that the deletion took place after its first publication in *Le Figaro* between February 19th and 23rd, 1890, and its republication in early April of the same year in *L'Inutile Beauté*, we can safely assume that it was Maupassant who cut the explanation offered in the newspaper version. The resulting ambiguous ending is very Maupassantian. It remains only for us to try and grasp with some clarity why the writer would prefer the excised version that ended with an unexplained, overturned table in the midst of a flood of blood.

On considering the story, Maupassant wished to underline the priest's character. A noble from a long line of warriors and priests, it is reasonable to assume that he might have an underlying proclivity for violence in his blood if not in his early education. His pride at his physical abilities is perhaps understandable, as well, and one can sympathize with both his extreme love for an entrancing but treacherous woman and his dismay when she betrayed him with a friend. It cannot have made him feel any better to learn that the traitorous couple lived together for a further thirty years, apparently without betrayal. The priest must have felt a twinge if not an overpowering surge of jealousy. In the end, there seems a shallowness about the priest's character that may be responsible for his inability to cope with the original cuckoldry either then or when he eventually meets his son. Still, Father Vilbois is faced with a difficult situation. His psychopathic offspring would make his situation impossible in such a small community. There would surely be more "pranks" like the one that previously resulted in several deaths. The priest already feels shame for his affair with a lower-class actress, and guilty remorse grows when the passionate memories are resuscitated. Furthermore, though his little character weaknesses, his little vanities, are only human and have been accepted as endearing idiosyncrasies during the years that he had served the village, they can hardly be cited as virtues. In short,

160 *Maupassant's Exploding Closures*

for the psychopathic marauder to become a continuing burden in his parish life would have been impossible, and his rage at this emotion laden, unwonted intrusion is rekindled.

The priest's character is not clarified by making the reader review the indications of his life and personality. The difference between the early and definitive versions of the short story comes from the degree that the reader's imagination is able to make the priest's anguish come alive in all its breadth and depth. Maupassant trusted the portrait that the reader would create more than what he could write, for his own newspaper description was too limited. When the reader is forced to put together Father Vilbois' personality, his fury at the horrendous situation, his responsibility for the monstrous offspring he has loosed on society, and his growing sense of indelible guilt, the priest's inability to control the filial jailbird is inescapable and grows in importance. With this realization, the reader may gain a stronger impression of the desperate decision the father makes. To what degree is Vilbois' untoward love affair to blame? Is the priest hoping to be free of the unhealthy relationship by dying? Certainly it is a possibility. Most importantly, however, Father Vilbois finally takes responsibility for his past and his present. He must control his son, though he is apparently unable to do so. The attempt to bribe the vagrant offspring was tried previously by the senator, his rival, and it failed. More people will die, for the son has no conscience and is unable to appreciate the value of human life. In the end, one can perhaps admire the priest for having confronted and remedied the results of his past. To die becomes the unique chance to dominate the son and thus rid the world of the noxious offspring, and it both punishes him for exposing the father's latent passions that had been suppressed beneath priestly trappings and preemptively avoids the trouble to come.

On carefully considering both what happens on the level of plot and the character traits governing father and son, the two conclusions seem equally clear and well designed. Though the maid does not tell the truth in the newspaper version, she doubtless believed what she said. Her lies are what one would suspect of a terrified but simple woman. Indeed, all of the long preliminary conclusion deleted by Maupassant, where most of the i's are dotted and the t's crossed, seems well written, perfectly in character, and an acceptable if not particularly powerful conclusion. It would satisfy any reader with high closure tendencies. By excising the lengthy explanation, what changes is the fact that, without the eliminated coda Maupassant wrote for the first draft, the reader is required to take part in the creation. Maupassant obliges all readers to conceive or to "write" the ending.

Many stories have what P. W. M. Cogman calls "gaps,"[11] though few work so well aesthetically as this one. It seems certain that Maupassant was attempting to lure his reader further into the story and the creative process. He apparently thought this was the most effective way

Maupassant's Exploding Closures 161

to make an impression on his readers and to give his fiction further life beyond the words of the tale itself, especially since we know that he wrote many stories to impel a similar kind of cooperation from his reader (see, e.g. "Hautot père et fils" 1889). We learn from Maupassant's other conclusions that he did not suffer from a need for high closure. He was perfectly comfortable with and indeed relished ambiguity; he did not expect to have to provide and explain all the details. He regularly made sure that the most important details were included somewhere in the story, but he often left it for the reader to sense the clues and create a meaningful conclusion, to close on the adventure he offered. A number of Maupassant's stories have left professional readers in a daze, unable to do their critical work. Scholars have obviously had difficulty with "Les Epingles," for example. The story is too closely attached to the author's much discussed sexual deviancies to go unexplained and unanalyzed, yet it has been left with little critical commentary. In short, the author of "Les Epingles" demanded too much of his readers.

This was a period when readers were expected to bring insight, technical skill, and cultural and educational background to the reading experience. Symbols had become an important part of creation and explication, and connotations a matter of course. All are somewhat equivocal, though in masterpieces the analogical systems have powerful sway. Mallarmé was developing poetry influenced by hermeneutics, a philosophy of difficult interpretation, and designed for hyper-sophisticates. The poet obviously had little patience with those who could not see through the shifting veils of meaning. Readers from the 1880s through the beginning of the First World War were expected to read knowingly and well. As just one example, Proust explicitly and implicitly wanted this sort of reader. Consequently, he had absolute disdain for lazy readers like his character Charlus.[12] While Maupassant was not always so demanding, he also wrote his stories for insightful collaborators. By deleting the lengthy explanation in "Le Champ des oliviers" that he published at first in the *Figaro*, he left unsaid what would come of Father Vilbois or Philippe-August, but also demonstrates his trust that the reader would join him in creating an aesthetic resolution for the horrible crimes depicted. Though the story explodes after the son destroys the father's priestly vocation, the latter is avenged in the conclusion. Nonetheless, by committing suicide, a mortal sin since the time of St. Augustine, he compounds his guilt with the perhaps justifiable murder of his son by setting up his execution. Still, the son had gleefully confessed the deaths to his priestly father, without asking for absolution. Thinking back to the unexplicated, multiple crosses Philippe-August burned on his foster father, one might say that Father Vilbois' behavior in "Le Champ d'oliviers" reestablishes the singular need for a single cross. Father Vilbois becomes an inverted Christ figure who sacrificed himself, not to save others, but instead to condemn his son.

162　*Maupassant's Exploding Closures*

Notes

1　Emile Zola, "Alexis et Maupassant," *Œuvres complètes*, Vol. 14 (Paris: Cercle du Livre Précieux, 1962) 623. As Vial shows, Maupassant was pleased to comply with a novel: *Guy de Maupassant et l'art du roman* (Paris: Nizet, 1954) 12.
2　Edith Wharton, "Telling a Short Story," *The Writing of Fiction* (New York: Charles Scribner's Sons, 1925) 41.
3　Henry James, "Maupassant," *Partial Portraits* (New York: Macmillan, 1894) 264.
4　See, Louis Forestier's analysis of "Madame Parisse," *Maupassant: Contes et nouvelles*, 2 vols. Bibliothèque de la Pléiade (Paris: Gallimard, 1974, 1979) 2.1542–43. He summarizes the newspaper material that encourages readers to interpret the story as a parody, or as a straightforward allusion to the story of Paris and Helen of Troy, or, as Forestier says, "sentiment as far from Zola as from Feuillet" (1543).
5　Yvonne Verdier, "Le Petit Chaperon rouge dans la tradition orale," *Coutume et destin. Thomas Hardy et autres essais*, ed. Yvonne Verdier (Paris: Gallimard, 1995) 178; see, also, an early version, "Le Petit Chaperon rouge dans la tradition orale," *Le Débat* 3 (1980): 31–61. Mary Donaldson-Evans, in fascinating articles tracing the motif of sewing and seamstresses in the art and literature of France, also suggests an alternative interpretation of the women taking vengeance on Maupassant's narrator—"Pricking the Male Ego: Pins and Needles in Flaubert, Maupassant, and Zola," *Nineteenth-Century French Studies* 30.3–4 (2002): 254–55; "Maupassant épinglé?" *L'Angélus* 11 (déc. 2000-jan. 2001): 3–11. For Micheline Besnard-Coursodon it is simply a matter of abandonment—*Etude thématique et structural de l'œuvre de Maupassant: Le Piège* (Paris: Nizet, 1973) 259–61.
6　Bernadette Bricout, "Les deux chemins du Petit Chaperon rouge," *Frontières du conte*: Textes rassemblés par François Marotin (Paris: Éditions du CNRS, 1982) 47–54; and Verdier, *Coutume* 171–206, and her article in *Le Débat* 31–57.
7　Verdier 179; Anne Monjaret, "De l'épingle à l'aiguille: L'Education des jeunes filles au fil des contes," *L'Homme* 173 (2005): 119–47. The relationship of red to blood does not convince Monjaret, who sees no justification for the red of *Little Red Riding Hood*. For her, the Grimm and Perrault versions "denature" the popular versions of the tale (Monjaret §24, 27–29, 36).
8　Bricout 50; Verdier, *Coutume* 178; *Débat* 32. See, also, the versions inventoried in Verdier, *Coutume* 199–206, Débat 57–61, and P. Delarue and M.-L. Tenèze, *Le Conte populaire français: Catalogue raisonné des versions de France*, 4 vols. (Paris: Maisonneuve & Larose, 1997) 1.373–83.
9　Robert J. Niess, "Two Manuscripts of Maupassant: 'Le Retour' and 'Le Champ d'oliviers'," *French Studies*, 8.2 (1954): 149.
10　Robert M. Fagley has considered the tale as a retelling of Christ's arrest, judgment, and crucifixion while drinking the "cup the father has given [him]" (John 18:11). Jesus, of course, is in submission to His Father, while all obedience has been evacuated from the story of Philippe-Auguste: *Bachelors, Bastards, and Nomadic Masculinity: Illegitimacy in Guy de Maupassant and André Gide* (Newcastle upon Tyne: Cambridge Scholars, 2014) 167–68, and, as well, the results of illegitimacy in interclass relations. The mother, "a child of Parisian gutters" ['enfant des trottoirs de Paris'], has become a lower-class manipulator of noble men, while the father's passions of rage or love were scarcely contained. Father Vilbois became so enamored of her that he actually considered marriage, whereas the rival Pravallone stayed with her unmarried to her death (168–72).

11 P. W. M. Cogman, "Gaps and Gap-Filling in Maupassant's 'Le Champ d'oliviers," *French Studies Bulletin* 60 (Autumn 1996): 9–13. Balzac called such empty spaces or absent links that nonetheless signify "lacunae of its construction": see Allan H. Pasco, "Unifying Units," *Balzacian Montage: Configuring* La Comédie humaine (Toronto: U of Toronto P, 1991) 46–73.

12 Marcel Proust, *A la recherche du temps perdu*, ed. Jean-Yves Tadié, 4 vols. Bibliothèque de la Pléiade (Paris: Gallimard, 1987–89) 2.856. See Allan H. Pasco, "Proust's Reader," *Inner Workings of the Novel: Studying a Genre* (New York: Palgrave Macmillan, 2010) 141–50.

10 Conclusion

Reading great short stories is more than a spectator sport. They demand that the reader wrestle with the implied concepts and implications to gain the prize. Whether long or short, true or false, stories are important to human beings. When well told, they can be particularly effective, able to stimulate the audience and create exceptional, lasting moments. As the media has shown in this current period of emphasized "narration," the pretense of truth, as long as it is verisimilar, can be as effective as actual truth. In all cases, the skill of the telling has enormous significance. A good story always has suitable characters and interesting episodes, and while the lesson often seems negligible, stories occasionally teach material of great importance. What matters is that we recognize humankind acting out whatever "reality" is being unfolded before our eyes or ears. Whether put, take, lift, or release, and when, where, how, and why they do it, what they say or do matters in making any kind of a lasting impression. Equally significant for aesthetic pleasure is the way of the telling, the arrangement of the characters and their words in the narrative, and, most important, whether there is a meaningful concept or idea holding it all together, whether the work is more than a mere entertainment. Skillful writers choose those tactics that will most effectively set off the story. Certainly, many devices can be exploited to make an impression. It is even possible to use the genre itself. As previously mentioned, according to Hugo, "An idea never has more than one form that is appropriate."[1]

Once an acceptable definition of a genre exists, it is possible to explore the kinds of experiences that the genre type can effectively render. The preceding pages have been particularly engaged with masterpieces capable of stimulating readers to elucidate exceptional experiences. Chapter 1 defined the short story as an *artistically designed, short, prose fiction*. This formulation describes legions of tales from across the ages, irrespective of quality. Some stories are old; some recent; some very brief; some pushing the limits of 40,000 words; some aesthetically pleasing; others not. Trained readers would find rather few examples in the enormous short-story repertory that are compelling, for most do not exploit the potential of the analogical levels of human thought that go beyond the literal meaning of the stories' words. Only a limited number bring the reader into the reading experience and engage him or her as a co-creator.

Conclusion 165

Within the mix, however, are occasional, perhaps even rare, masterpieces that have exploited all the tools of the writer's craft to unify and illustrate the main idea or concept and, thus, are able to make a deep impression on those who have a sure sense of the language and know the genre, as well. The preceding pages have examined outstanding examples of short-story masterpieces of nineteenth-century France, the period when short stories bloomed in full maturity. And, as suggested, each of the terms of the suggested definition demands consideration and opens the opportunity for controversy. There is little lasting interest in pedestrian short stories, that is, in stories that do not encourage readers to go beyond the literal meaning of its words and, using Edith Warnton's expression, to cast a "spell."[2] My example of the best of denotative tales is "Point de lendemain," a beautifully written puzzle that highlights the uncertainty of the period and plays on readers' common desire to understand mysteries. Still, even in stories like Denon's masterwork, there is somewhat more than the literal resolution of the problems posed: for example, why was the narrator invited to the woman's reunion with her husband? or, in other cases, is the criminal caught? does the sailor return safely to shore? does the settler shoot the marauding bear? does Sally marry John? does the child come to harm?

Of course, no story can divest itself of lexical or situational connotations. Virtually at a first reading, many cowboy tales bring the excitement of the uncivilized West to the experience, just as pornography plays on the eternal interest of sex, as tales of "rags to riches" stimulate associations with the desire to succeed, as thrillers project the shivering implication of danger or evil. Many examples of general types entail an inescapable aura, perceptible whenever type is suggested. In general, though, such popular fiction seldom accomplishes much more than to echo the faint resonance of its literary ancestors. Masterpieces do more. Some writers are able to take the associative meanings that waft from the faint implications and residual associations and create significance that goes well beyond superficial dictionary definitions of words in order to entrance experienced readers. Their creators were clearly cognizant of the multi-faceted potential of their words, whether literal or analogical, and they arrange them in special, focused ways to create coherent patterns of mental or spiritual meaning that successfully exude evocative ideas. They take the values of the words, whether denotative or connotative, and create complexes of significance that one recognizes as especially worthwhile and well executed, perhaps even beautiful. Words have extra-dictionary associations whether the writer wants them to or not, and superior artists use those analogical images. I think of the passionate implications that accompany the color red in "L'Auberge rouge," or the excitement that accompanies the political and social movements represented by the Prussian officers in "Mademoiselle Fifi," or the fear that may be produced by "Le Horla" or "La Main." The genre provides an encompassing form, and great writers not only fill

166   Conclusion

it in, but also use its history and traditions to go beyond it. In the cases like "Claude Gueux" and *Trois Contes*, the conceptual fable itself is a part of the story's meaning.

A useful definition of a genre provides the means of identifying a particular kind of literature, and offers the reader a sense of expectation regarding the work's form, since it is well established that we best grasp what we are prepared to understand. In the case of short stories, my definition offers a description of what the genre entails, its general extent, and its limits, but it falls short of providing a means of appreciating the value of specific examples. A generically limited object is especially interesting, however, when it tantalizingly becomes something more, an image or sequence that rises above the basic form of the thousands of short stories that conform perfectly to the definition. In fact, most examples of the genre are simply trifles circumscribed by boundaries established by tradition. Concepts of genres have defined quantities that are mentally inclusive and exclusive, sufficient to serve as a means for identifying them. Genres can then be measured, for they have (somewhat elastic) limits. Unlike novels, which must be free to exploit their lengthy liberty, at least according to Henry James,[3] short stories are and must be constrained. It is paradoxically in exploiting brevity to overcome the physical limitations that they achieve impact and lasting life.

Outstanding short stories almost always imply an expanded scope, another continuing or different analogical idea. This special quality may be nothing other than extreme focus, or what Edgar Allan Poe termed "the unity of effect or impression."[4] Another way of posing this requirement is to say that every element in a short story must serve the tale's effect, while the more lengthy novel can afford a few loosely connected asides and redundancies. Short-story masterpieces push the essence of the work beyond the genre's limits, or, as Warnton put it, "The real achievement, as certain tales of Flaubert's and Turgenev's, of Stevenson's and of Maupassant's show, is to suggest illimitable air within a narrow space" (55). But it would be impossible to improve on Poe's statements: "In the whole composition there should be no word written, of which the tendency, direct or indirect, is not to the one pre-established design" (606). "Every word *tells*, and there is not a word that does not *tell*...." (607). The writer has no choice but to assume that the reader will not only understand, but also remember every word. Short-story masterpieces have no leeway.

To reconsider the definition of the short story briefly, the first term is *artistic*, that is, a writer arranged the work in search of beauty, so that all the pieces fit together meaningfully, while corresponding to other instances of the type. Beauty and meaningfulness are co-dependent terms. An exceptional example of the genre can carry an aura that reaches beyond reason to touch our spirits and minds. Not every reader is capable of sensing this extra-literal reality; not everyone

Conclusion   167

has the cultural background and sensitivity necessary to peer beneath the surface. Novels can and often do educate their readers; short stories seldom have the space. Even well-trained literary critics, with a clear knowledge of the tradition, of the form, of the available strategies and techniques, and of the language, may fail to sense the larger, implied message if their professional preparation or natural perceptions are not fully developed or if, like Homer, they nodded. Despite outstanding minds and excellent training, readers may be ignorant of the legendary information that the Virgin Mary was thirteen when she was visited, for example, like Barbey's teenager who thought she had been touched immaculately and impregnated. Little else would signal the story's blasphemy. Others might be unaware of the Latin meanings of the homonym for "Carmen" and not focus on the red color that accompanies the gypsy's passionate character even before her dress is mentioned. To derive the full value of short-story masterpieces, it pays not to be a lazy reader but rather to read both thoughtfully and in depth, remaining open to the author's clues. Because of the genre's brevity, the key may reside in one single coded reference, allusion, or analogy, perhaps in nothing but one word.

The second term of the definition, *design*, is closely related, in that the author's choice of vocabulary and imagery and arrangement are essential to the communication of significance. Particularly sensitive or well-prepared readers will be able to grasp that the cultural shadow accompanying this common feature of short-story masterpieces is the requirement to maximize the potential of words and forms, to exploit every element, every possibility in the creation of intense focus on the central idea. Today most have forgotten the long history of the generic fable embedded in Hugo's "Claude Gueux." Whether perceived or not, it is real, and it brings with it the possibility of insisting on a moral position without inflicting tedium on the reader. The forgotten implications of Maupassant's "Les Epingles" create confusion. Flaubert's use of the religious story seems less to communicate a moral than to raise its aesthetic quality. Hundreds of saints' tales that have come down to us are little more than artless recounting. By taking the genre and perfecting it, Flaubert was able to demonstrate that modern readers could be gripped by generic forms that had been poorly exploited in the past. In the process, he demonstrated that subject matter was of little aesthetic importance. What mattered was its ability to fulfill readers' structured sense of beauty. In Flaubert's and in Hugo's stories, shadow-like genres rise from the text and from the past both to serve modern needs and to offer aesthetic pleasure. As Hugo started with a news story, so Flaubert began with generally undistinguished tales of saints, in the effort to infuse fixed, traditional, narrative forms with art that in and for itself could grip the reader and stimulate a lasting lesson, perhaps even civic action in their readers.

168   *Conclusion*

The third term of the definition, *brevity* likewise imposes a rigid limitation on short stories. Possibly, the author may only have in mind the length limit imposed by a periodical, not perceiving the exciting potential that such a limit provides. Whatever the intentions, brevity is a physical attribute that resists length. Only when the author succeeds in exploding the brief, literal, denotative form can he or she effectively steer the reader's creativity toward an idea, a concept, an attitude, or an insight that goes beyond the surface text. Such a mental reality provides the thrust that exposes the power and, often, the real subject of a masterpiece. Baudelaire understood that "the short story [...] has the enormous advantage over the novel of vast proportions that its brevity adds to the effect's intensity."[5] He may also be correct in ascribing the short story's power to this very attribute: "Since the time consecrated to reading a short story is much less than that necessary to digest a novel, nothing is lost in the totality of its effect" (ibid.). As always, of course, when Baudelaire is speaking of artistry, he is referring to creators who have exceptional aesthetic abilities similar to his own.

When the short story's "totality of [...] effect," is well exploited, it leads to intensity. With Barbey's character Don Juan, it may arise through the implication of the blasphemous reality underpinning the personage the author has created. Or, it may occur in the sudden realization that Huysmans' "Un Dilemme" turns on a false dilemma, thus encouraging the reader in the formulation of what the nineteenth century considered a true dilemma and the condemnation of bourgeois greed. It may be the stimulus for the reader to continue the story beyond its denotative limits, by implication seguing into another story entirely, as short fictions by both Balzac and Maupassant regularly illustrate. In one way or another, the best short stories overcome brevity to create an expanded, indeed expansive image of more import than what the little tale normatively projects. Shortness provides the foundational setting that analogically promotes another reality. There are numerous ways of overcoming the limitation of brevity, thus raising the original story into a creation of importance.

And there is the genre's fourth term of *prose*, the pedestrian means of communicating, made exceptional by careful selection and arrangement. Only a bourgeois gentleman could find it astonishing to discover himself speaking prose. It is the common vehicle for communication, occasionally dressed up to make an impression on others. Its everyday, utilitarian nature suggests nothing so much as an absence of pretense in the real world. Of course, that makes it perfect as a means of encouraging an audience to accept a false reality. It is so common as it is normally used for no other reason than that it is the way humans talk as they live their day to day lives. Lacking any particular orientation, it is so recognizable that it rings true, encouraging readers to accept its basic vision as real and thus believable. It appears to be free of the artifice and intent marking poetry, though its appearance may be deceptive.

Conclusion 169

The fifth term of the definition, *fiction*, is important simply because the short story is an art form, a created object. There are certainly times when the reader remains unable to distinguish whether the action recounted is true or false. I have mentioned Marguerite de Navarre's *Heptaméron* and the anonymous *Lettres portugaises* as problematic cases, but, in fact, the evaluation of their factual truth has no importance to the genre, though, of course, fiction cannot succeed if it fails to remind the reader at some level of human experience or potential. Truth requires verification through factual recording or through the possibility of replication, which has nothing to do with meaningful beauty, the *raison d'être* of the masterpieces analyzed above. To serve as the conveyance of stories having an aesthetic goal, language must be carefully selected, with full understanding of its various levels of meaning, and then situated in a context that enhances the thrust of its constituent images. While stories may be important whether they actually happened or not, fiction has the privilege of arranging unimportant prose in ways that become aesthetically engaging as they make a difference to each one of us.

When confronting any story, the reader is required to be sensitive. The prose of short stories does not usually employ a persistent rhythm, though occasionally, for passages emphasizing a particular point, the rhythmic movement of the line may have noticeable impact. Medieval fabliaux, Baudelaire's prose poems, or Pushkin's *Eugene Onegin* prove that stories can be told lyrically. Still, occasional poetic rhythms are never the primary device in short stories. When poetic melodies become a dominant, we have simply moved into another, if not a hybrid, genre. I think of the insistent outrage of the words in the conclusion of "Claude Gueux" or the breathless beat of "Le Horla" as the narrator watches his servants burn. In general, however, rhythm is exclusionary, proclaiming its poetic rather than prosaic reality. When rhythm becomes dominant throughout the work, we have moved from the short story to poetry. Prose in the hands of great writers depends especially on the connotative associations that words have on levels other than rhythm and can be arranged in such a manner as to make alternative or expansive meanings possible.

Short stories use numerous strategies working in conjunction to transmit meaning in a way that can give power and thrust to increase impact and duration. None of the definitive elements work alone, as pointed out in Chapter 1. Any element can work meaningfully in other genres. The five qualities that work together to define short stories are of little help in considering their value. That requires a different kind of judgment. The artistically designed prose fictions that were considered in earlier chapters show various ways prominent authors of nineteenth-century France exploited them to gift the world with exemplary short stories. "Point de lendemain" provides a good example of a masterpiece that, despite a passing reference to Psyche and Amour and another to Molière's *L'Ecole*

170   *Conclusion*

des femmes, makes little or no use of connotations. While its central theme of uncertainty has a great deal to do with the unrelenting tumult of the period, it gains and keeps the reader's attention on the level of the obvious, salacious meaning of the language and the brilliantly rapid pace of the narration. Those few analogical references that the reader could take as an invitation to interpret on another level are limited to the simplest links, for example, that the name of "Arnolphe" equals "cuckoldry." The work succeeds because of the riveting narration enticing the reader from one conquest to another without, as the story says, any moral. Denon has then created an amusing, beautifully written entertainment, where every integrated part works to highlight the whole, with no pretense to a larger significance, other than its intent to discuss an intense sexual encounter. At the end, all questions are answered and closure is complete. While the characters are assumed to continue their lives, the reader expects no meaningful plot twists or surprises.

Huysmans' "Un Dilemme" is likewise closed and doubtless doubly tragic when, at the conclusion, it seems that young women like Sophie have no hope. The text regularly compares the bourgeois Le Ponsart and Lambois to beasts of prey, and when they "chassent" [evict or pursue] Sophie from her apartment, readers should be reminded of the hunt, perhaps even to imagine baying dogs. The girl's helplessness is underlined by her last name, Mouveau, which suggests a bovine etymology and the fact that she is both prey and malleable. According to her bourgeois persecutors, like Saint Sophia, Huysmans' Sophie is helpless, even after she consults her friend, Madame Champagne. Although Sophie is destroyed, unlike her patron saint, or more pertinently like Le Ponsart, she does not face a true dilemma. If she had been more experienced or astute, she could have side-stepped Le Ponsart's strategy and joined Madame Champagne, forcing Jules' relatives through public embarrassment to reform their ways. Only divine power could control the ancient Emperor Hadrian, while Huysmans heroine is tricked by despicable men lacking any real power. Gentle Sophie has a special glow as she is clumsily victimized by Maître Le Ponsart. Though abused, poorly educated, modest, and only moderately attractive, we understand how Jules could have loved her, and we see her virtues, if only because the connotations emanating from Lambois and Le Ponsart are so negative.

I suspect it is due to a frustrated desire for justice that readers may search back through the story's events and details that create the image of the bourgeoisie and realize that, though Huysmans could not bring himself to give Sophie an unadulterated victory, he does leave indications that society was changing. Viewed realistically, it is possible that Mme Champagne would not have won in returning with Sophie and the baby to Beauchamp, but the fact of Le Ponsart and Lambois' fear of exposure may point to a better future. In short, good readers will go beyond the conclusion's defeat and find Mme Champagne's explicit, though

Conclusion 171

unfulfilled plan to force a different conclusion. The story is incomplete, or almost incomplete, which is one of the ways that artists try to force their readers into going beyond the denotative limits of their creations. As he hoped elsewhere, Huysmans has successfully used the short story's "form as a frame in which to insert more serious work."[6] He has used a plot, but the plot is of negligible importance when confronted by the image of Sophie's bestial destruction by heartless bourgeois and the growing public awareness of such social exploitation. For those readers who grasp the old men's degradation and the condemnation of bourgeois greed in the sub-text, there seems to have been progress in society: a sense of justice may have become a major force.

Close readers who remain aware of the image of satanic evil implied early in Barbey's *Les Diaboliques* will perceive Satan's activities as he destroys one person after another. The vision created by the cycle is quite civilized, and does not resemble imagined horrors like Stevenson's Dr. Jekyll and Mr. Hyde, Mary Shelley's Frankensteinian creature, or any of the odd werewolves, vampires, or zombies that populate horror stories. Barbey relies on the foundational preparation of Christianity that had for centuries promoted belief in an invisible hell and its satanic minions. According to the Bible and the Church, the devil is real, but in the modern world, Barbey understood that he was neither dressed in red nor equipped with a pitchfork. Rather he manipulated humans for his own malignant purposes in a very real, modern society. In one story after another, Barbey creates a mosaic of bits and pieces that he uses analogically to structure the malevolent but shadowy creature behind the scenes pulling strings and giving cohesion to the volume. As the details, themes, and images are repeated in ways that give meaning to the whole, the reader recognizes that this Satan is not a cartoon figure. His destructive force is powerful and final. It encourages characters to indulge in the pleasures of sin, thus bringing themselves to the damnation of uselessness. Lover, diabolique, and victim are always joined by illegitimate sex that leads inevitably to perdition. Once the reader partners with the author and recognizes the web of satanic associations, the stories each create an image of absolute, irrevocable loss, an image that differs in each of the stories, but has the same analogical underpinnings. The image of sin is made tangible.

Allusion is a powerful tool, especially so in the short story, and Barbey multiplies his allusions to the Bible, to legendry, and to history. Some may not remember either that the legendary Don Juan was condemned in Molière to die, or that Herod was eaten by worms for his blasphemous delight in being taken for God (Acts 12.23–24). Making sense of Marmor de Karkoël's quandary may well escape readers who neither recall the controversy that Jean-Baptiste Villèle stirred up around primogeniture fifty years before the publication *Les Diaboliques* nor Madame de Stasseville's son, mentioned only in a passing reference,

172   *Conclusion*

to whom Madame de Stasseville could easily have left her fortune. All the necessary information is indicated, however, and available to good readers of the period. Furthermore, the outcome of Marmor's life leaves little doubt, but we must recognize the details of a number of passages that reveal the evil mystery lurking beneath the cards of "Le Dessous de cartes d'une partie de whist." For well-prepared readers who read closely, the image of conquest and murder is clear. Although the text casts a bright light on the reality subsumed by the first level plot, it is all too easy to become fascinated by the luxurious description of a dying class and pass over the crucial clues pointing to an evil, vicious force. Barbey demands close reading to unravel the sinister implications of his stories.

Mérimée's *Carmen* raises the reader's interest with a completely different strategy. The author introduces a traditional narrator who promises to tell a "little story,"[7] and who, immediately, takes us into the tale of his youthful experience of Spain, gypsies, and bandits. The subject matter was of enormous interest to the French of the day, for they were extremely attracted to exoticism. The Romantic suggestion of intense passion also appealed to cultural preoccupations. The narrator implies that he will tell the truth about what happened to him in his youth. From the standpoint of the short story's form, the fact that this narrator comes back in the end as a mature man is more important, for it unveils an effective passage of time, one of the genre's rarely exploited possibilities. As is usually the case with such structures, another story is indicated by the frame, and the reader is invited to enter the narration and fill in what has not been mentioned. In this case, the reappearing narrator of the conclusion has changed significantly. Apparently because of his experiences during his youth, his interest in Bohemia has continued, but his awareness of the dangers has increased. Older now, rather than becoming involved personally, he remains on the outskirts, parading limited knowledge, yet unwilling to get too close.

Hugo chooses other sources for his allusions, and he uses them in a different way. He alludes to the fable genre in order to emphasize an idea. Utilizing the age-old form of the fable allowed him considerable freedom without losing the advantages of the genre. While short, thus with the potential impact of a brief form, it could be expressed in prose or poetry using human or animal characters. As Edith Wharton put it, great short stories have the power of "a shaft driven straight into the heart of human experience" (36). Hugo's fable is directed, picking up power from the related tradition existing shadowlike in the background that undoubtedly affected readers of Hugo's day. Through the course of the story, the fable gains consistency and substance, clearly arranging all the story's strands into a focused sequence. As classical tragedy was a "shadow" genre for the drama [*drame*], so the fable was a "shadow" genre for Hugo's short story. He brings together all the parts of his short

Conclusion 173

story leading up to the end, oriented precisely toward a conclusion for which the fable was invented, that is, toward a moral precept.

Flaubert's three major allusions to the Bible and saints' tales have a different function. While displaying his mastery of the generic lives of the saints, he takes this rich mine of material to create a kaleidoscope, rather than a lesson, and shows how the fragments remaining from the lives of three saints recreate each other and, as well, the three periods they represent to emphasize different sources: current reality, legendry, and history. As the reader moves from one of the tales to another, he engages in a bigger, retrograde narrative of the Church's history, but especially in Flaubert's proper artistry as he masterfully moves each suggestive part into new, dazzling configurations. Each tale is associated sequentially to the others. Each is a challenge, encouraging the reader's creativity. While there is a certain order leading from Félicité and the Holy Spirit, to Julien and Jesus, to Iaokanann and the Father, Flaubert saw to it that each tale could stand on its own artistic merits, nonetheless inviting the reader to consider and reconsider the lush, surrounding setting as his tales masterfully work together both as three and as one.

The most common means of overcoming the limits of the short story is the ambiguous implication of a continuing saga or of a completely different tale that grows out of what one is reading. Balzac was a master of the open conclusion. He used the technique to link a number of the creations of *La Comédie humaine*. Often, he leaves readers with no recourse but to turn helplessly away from the work with no resolution or, instead, to return and read more carefully, which can introduce another interpretive creation as a foundational means of further insight to lengthen the story analogically. Neither "Gillette" ["Le Chef-d'œuvre inconnu"] nor "L'Auberge rouge" include an explicit conclusion, for example, leaving both works open for the reader's terminal invention. While in neither case are readers left as free as at the end of either James' "The Turn of the Screw" or Frank Stockton's "The Lady or the Tiger," they are implicitly invited to create a probable ending. Balzac's stories often point to the inexplicit future of the text. We remember, for instance, that there is little doubt that Gillette and Poussin split up, thus tragically breaking a relationship of profound affection, just as the vacillating narrator of "L'Auberge rouge" will doubtless miss out on a deep and permanent love.

Balzac's "Gillette" leaves the negligent reader adrift. Again, I suspect that many readers are left frustrated by the conclusion. What is the point of the conflagration and Frenhofer's suicide? Why is the hero named Poussin? Did Poussin really debase his lovely mistress by having her strip so another man could "check her out"? What was the result? The answers are perfectly clear for those readers who know their history. Gillette's absence from Poussin's life lets us know that the girl's damaged affection for her lover was caused when Balzac's young painter,

174   *Conclusion*

essentially, sold her, turning her into a whore and himself into a pimp. The lesson is clear to close readers and confusing for those who raise a wall separating life from literature. By the mere fact of naming his character "Poussin," however, Balzac breaks out of a small work of art and enlarges it into a commentary on the sociological importance of love and art.

These structurally open works that imply another story and its implicit closure point to incompletion as a common trait in Balzac's writing. Close readers are expected in one of the stories in *La Femme de trente ans* to wonder why Julie d'Aiglemont dies shortly after finding a footprint leaving her daughter's bedroom. The answer is simple for those who know that this rebellious thirty-year-old mother has ignored her father's advice and subsequently broke her marriage vows with Charles de Vandenesse. She has thus turned against her family and is harshly punished in her daughters. Hélène, after murdering little Charles, goes off to be with a pirate, and Moïna has an incestuous affair with her half-brother. The lack of a clear explanation in the text leaves it for the reader to divine the motivations for the family's dissolution. A careful reading of the story unveils that when Moïna mocks her mother for her warning, Julie seeks peace in the garden and finds not sanctuary but proof that her son had just visited her daughter's bed.

Balzac's "L'Auberge rouge" provokes several kinds of frustrations. In the early part of the story, readers must realize that Taillefer was suffering from a physical attack, perhaps a migraine, before the beginning of Hermann's story. What the general narrator takes as proof of the banker's guilt may well have nothing to do with the events leading to Prosper's death. Indications of uncertainty begin early and increase in the end, when the point of the story seems to change. The main narrator, who has fallen in love with Taillefer's daughter, Victorine, begins to wonder whether he could ethically marry the girl. Allusions to Gœthe and to Rabelais flesh out his hesitations, insistently pointing out that he should make up his own mind, rather than allowing the opinions of others to decide for him. Balzac whose love of Rabelais was deep and long-lived may have thought that the mere suggestion of a dinner to ask friends whether marriage was appropriate would recall Panurge's quest for an answer to his similar question. None of the answers he received are definitive, however, unlike the resolution in Gœthe's *Hermann und Dorothea*. While Panurge simply cannot make up his mind, Gœthe's Hermann knows precisely what he wants and, thus, what he should do. He should marry Dorothea. Balzac's character confronts these similar events but cannot do as the author clearly expected of his reading audience. Pathetically, he is incapable of understanding the analogical lesson and making his own choice.

Maupassant also favored leaving fixed conclusions for the reader to create and, consequently, to take part in the experience of a new

Conclusion 175

adventure. When the main character of "Les Epingles" is confused, he models the reader, who like the main character has a choice. He can ignore the mystery and walk away, or he can pursue a resolution. More careful reading with the appropriate knowledge of rural folklore seems to provide the answer. As the early version of the abbreviated, definitive edition of "Le Champ d'oliviers" renders the events perfectly clear, Maupassant wanted his reader to be fully engaged, sharing the author's power to create from the religious and cultural background materials available. Frustration can be productive, if readers refuse to dismiss unanswered questions as auctorial clumsiness and actively take part in creating a complete image.

The pages deleted from Maupassant's early version of "Le Champ d'oliviers" are particularly important, for the two versions call for radically different audiences. The first invites a relaxed reading by a moderately engaged reader who goes no further than a general understanding of the events. The second, definitive version has elided much of the explanation, leaving only hints of the causes behind the bloody scene. It may frustrate the general reader, for it resists an explanation and seems incomplete. Of course, once the reader-cum-participant begins to challenge the text, refusing to shrug off the ambiguities and wonder what might have happened, the reality of the priest's solution gains clarity and purpose. The author leaves his story incomplete for no reason but to stimulate the close reader. In fact, of course, the creative thought will only occur if he or she has been actively lured into the tale and, in addition, has faith that the writer will not disappoint. Maupassant goes beyond a closed, denotative tale like "Point de lendemain" to create an undoubted, open-ended masterpiece. The references I made to the social context of Denon's tale cannot be ignored, but the turn of the century author made use of neither symbols nor allusions to overcome the generic limitations of his text. Instead he used the language of the day to paint a picture of a tantalizing but brief love affair. The story does include a conversational reference to Molière and the hint of a possible allusion to Psyche and Amour, but there the references to another level of related meanings stop, thus negating a more detailed after-story. At the end of Denon's curatorial version of the story, we know everything we need to know in order to draw the appropriate conclusions. Nothing further is either necessary or desirable. That is not the case with either Balzac's "Gillette" or "L'Auberge rouge." Comprehension requires bringing cultural information to the text in order to deduce the author's meaning.

While a run-of-the-mill work demands very little from readers, exceptional stories require more diligence and a significant dose of imagination. For authors of the nineteenth and early twentieth centuries, high expectations of the reading public were a matter of course. Good readers should add their own insight, background, and technical skill to the reading experience. Whether early or late in the century, sensitivity

176   *Conclusion*

to connotations, analogical meanings, and symbolism was required. Analogies can of course be abused, as they were in the hackneyed creations of many of the writers that Kenneth Cornell considered,[8] since readers rapidly tire of clanking knights galloping through bejeweled forests. But anything can wear out, and in the case of masterpieces, analogical references simply provide one more way to expand the form of the short story. As mentioned before, Mallarmé was but one example of an artist who was developing poetry for well-prepared readers. The poet obviously had little patience with those who could not see through the hermeneutic sophistication of meaning. Although he went further than most others, he was not alone. From the time of Chateaubriand, if not before, poets had sought spiritual realities that could touch the depths of their readers. The readers of great writers are expected to read knowingly and well; these authors seek a worthy audience. As mentioned in the last chapter, Proust and Gide, among others, explicitly and implicitly wanted sensitive, knowing readers.[9] While Maupassant was not always as demanding, he also wrote his best stories for the insightful collaborators among his reading public. Indeed, reading short-story masterpieces with appreciation requires a developed level of literary mastery.

If *"artistically designed, short prose fictions"* adequately defines short stories, there are of course many devices and strategies besides those possibilities mentioned in the above chapters for a writer to employ in pushing readers beyond the limits of the genre. Balzac's recurring play on historical reality, that I mentioned in regard to "Gillette," seems a ready possibility. He regularly mixed the names of actual people with those he created. While there is no need for replicative tests to justify its accuracy, although indeed a reviewer's pronouncement that an art object is "unrealistic" can be the kiss of death, the verifiable reality of art is seldom necessary. Though readers need something recognizable to establish context, it need be no more than the systematic logic of science-fiction or fantasy or the potential outgrowth of an organic or creative form. Readers will generally accept unrealistic items in a verisimilar complex, if they do not dominate. Remembering the sparseness of the "local color" used by Romantics to enhance realism, it is clear that it may take very little to establish a text's believability. Similarly, subtle clues suffice to engage collaborators in the fictive atmosphere, encouraging them to create for themselves, especially when the work is incomplete. Cutting the tales off without leaving a sense of the way the central idea works out can be very dangerous, if the artist seeks the reader's collaboration rather than frustrations. While I have resisted the suggestion that genres are limited to particular subject matter, it is true that many writers choose reality as their challenge. James and Maupassant insisted that it was the only possible subject.[10] Unfortunately, if Ovid's Aphrodite did indeed bless Pygmalion's heart-felt longing for a living breathing creation of his own design, the mythic artist was the only one. Art is not in that sense real.

Conclusion 177

As the short stories presented illustrate, artists who look upon the strictures of their chosen generic forms not as limitations but as qualities to exploit are much more likely to overcome and create truly outstanding aesthetic works. With consummate skill, their magic is manifest when they explore the implicit, the suggestive, the analogical, the inconclusive, the open, the allusive, and the expansive intuition that is much larger than the story itself. Like a jinni in a bottle or a small, clown-crammed circus car, the story-container explodes and produces a plethora of sometimes unexpected ideas. As Baudelaire rightly pointed out, the short story enjoys the benefits of constraint (2.119). For masters of the short story, less can be more, and, often, shorter is longer. A masterpiece is always more than the sum of its parts, and the moment the reader grasps an actual relationship between minimal exposition and maximal meaning, magic sets in and a story's artistry comes alive.

Notes

1 Victor Hugo, *Littérature et philosophie mêlées*, *Œuvres complètes*, ed. Jean Massin, 18 vols. (Paris: Club Français du Livre, 1967–70) 5.30.
2 Edith Warnton, "Telling a Short Story," *The Writing of Fiction* (New York: Charles Scribner's Sons, 1925) 38.
3 Henry James, "The Art of Fiction," *The American Tradition in Literature*, Vol. 2, ed. Sculley Bradley, Richmond Croom Beatty, and E. Hudson Long (New York: W. W. Norton, 1962) 659.
4 Edgar Allan Poe, Review of *Twice-Told Tales*, *The Literature of the United States*, Vol. 1, ed. Walter Blair, Theodore Hornberger, and Randall Stewart (Chicago: Scott, Foresman, 1953) 605. Fine writers, of course, share this opinion. Wharton writes, for example, "The least touch of irrelevance, the least chill of inattention, will instantly undo the spell" (38), or "When the reader's confidence is gained the best rule of the game is to avoid distracting and splintering up his attention" (39).
5 Charles Baudelaire, "Théophile Gautier," *Œuvres complètes*, ed. Claude Pichois, 2 vols. Bibliothèque de la Pléiade (Paris: Gallimard-Pléiade, 1975–76) 2.119.
6 Joris-Karl Huysmans, "Préface écrite vingt ans après le roman," *A rebours*, ed. Rose Fortassier, Lettres françaises (Paris: Imprimerie Nationale, 1981) 62.
7 Prosper Mérimée, *Carmen. Romans et nouvelles*, ed. Maurice Parturier. Vol. 2 (Paris: Garnier, 1967) 345.
8 Kenneth Cornell, *The Symbolist Movement* (New Haven, CT: Yale UP, 1951).
9 Marcel Proust, *A la recherche du temps perdu*, ed. Jean-Yves Tadié, 4 vols. Bibliothèque de la Pléiade (Paris: Gallimard, 1987–89) 2.856. For a similar expectation, see Gide's statement in "De l'importance du public": "The artist cannot get by without a public. And when the public is absent, what does he do? He invents one, and, turning his back on his own period, he expects what the present denies him from the future"— *Œuvres complètes*, ed. L. Martin-Chauffier, 15 vols. (Paris: N.R.F., 1932–39) 4.187. Or, to quote from several journal entries of 1902, "I read the way I would like people to read me: that is to say, very slowly, For me to read a book is to absent

178   *Conclusion*

myself for two whole weeks with the author"—Gide, *Journal: 1889–1939*, 2 vols., Bibliothèque de la Pléiade (Paris: Gallimard, 1951) 1.132—and "That a young man of my age and of my *value* would one day be moved in reading me and *remade* as I still am at thirty years of age in reading Stendhal's *Souvenirs d'égotisme*, I have no other ambition" (*Journal* 1.134).

10 James, "The Art of Fiction"; Guy de Maupassant, "Le Roman," *Romans*, Bibliothèque de la Pléiade (Paris: Gallimard, 1987) 703–15.

Works Cited

Allen, James Smith. *Popular French Romanticism*. Syracuse: Syracuse University Press, 1981.

Baldeshwiler, Eileen. "The Lyric Short Story: The Sketch of a History." May 202–13.

Baldick, Robert. *The Life of J.-K. Huysmans*. 1955; Rpt. Sawtry: Dedalus, 2006.

Balzac, Honoré de. "Etudes sur M. Beyle (Frédéric Stendhalh [sic])." *La Revue Parisienne* (25 septembre 1840). Rpt. *Œuvres complètes de Balzac*. Ed. Maurice Bardèche. Vol. 24. Paris: Club de l'Honnête Homme, 1971. 213–58.

———. *La Comédie humaine*. Ed. Pierre-Georges Castex. 12 vols. Bibliothèque de la Pléiade. Paris: Gallimard, 1976–81.

Barbey d'Aurevilly, Jules. "Le 'Procès' des *Diaboliques*." Ed. Andrée Hirschi. *Revue des Lettres Modernes* 403–08 (1974): 19.

———. *Les Diaboliques*. *Œuvres romanesques complètes*. Ed. Jacques Petit. Bibliothèque de la Pléiade. 2 vols. Paris: Gallimard, 1964, 1966. 2:9–264.

Bates, Herbert E. *The Modern Short Story: A Critical Survey*. Boston: The Writer, 1972.

Baudelaire, Charles. *Œuvres complètes*. Ed. Claude Pichois. 2 vols. Bibliothèque de la Pléiade. Paris: Gallimard, 1975–76.

Beardsley, Monroe C. *Aesthetics: Problems in the Philosophy of Criticism*. New York: Harcourt, Brace, 1958.

Beck, William J. "Flaubert's 'Un Cœur simple': The Path to Sainthood?" *Xavier U Studies* 7.2 (1968): 59–67.

———. "Félicité and the Bull in Flaubert's 'Un Cœur simple'." *Xavier U Studies* 10 (1971): 16–26.

———. "Félicité et le taureau: Ironie dans 'Un Cœur simple' de Flaubert." *Romance Quarterly* 37 (1990): 293–300.

———. "Flaubert's Félicité." *Explicator* 35.4 (1976): 4.

Benabou, Erica-Marie. *La Prostitution et la police des mœurs au XVIIIe siècle*. Paris: Perrin, 1987.

Berg, William J. *Imagery and Ideology: Fiction and Painting in Nineteenth-Century France*. Lincoln: U of Nebraska P, 2007.

Bernard, Claudie. "Rhétorique de la question dans *Claude Gueux* de Victor Hugo." *Romanic Review* 78.1 (1987): 57–73.

Berthier, Philippe. *Barbey d'Aurevilly et l'imagination*. Geneva: Droz, 1978.

180 Works Cited

Berthier, Philippe. *Les Diaboliques de Barbey d'Aurevilly: Une Ecriture du désir*. Paris: Champion, 1987.

———. "Les Diaboliques et la critique française." *Revue des Lettres Modernes* 403–08 (1974): 65–106.

———. "Les Diaboliques: table." *Barbey d'Aurevilly: L'Ensorcelée et les Diaboliques: La Chose sans nom*. Actes du Colloque du 16 janvier 1988. Paris: SEDES, 1988. 134–35.

Besnard-Coursodon, Micheline. *Etude thématique et structural de l'œuvre de Maupassant: Le Piège*. Paris: Nizet, 1973.

Biasi, Pierre-Marc de. "Introduction." *Trois Contes*, by Flaubert. Ed. Biasi. Paris: Librairie Générale Française, 1999. 5–45.

———. "La Pratique flaubertienne du symbole." *Gustave Flaubert e il pensiero del suo secolo*. Ed. Giovanni Bonaccorso. Messina: UP Messina, 1985. 249–70.

———. "Le Palimpseste hagiographique: L'Appropriation ludique des sources édifiantes dans la redaction de 'La Légende de saint Julien l'Hospitalier'." *La Revue des Lettres Modernes* 777–81 (1986): 69–124.

———. "Un Conte à l'orientale: La Tentation de l'Orient dans 'La Légende de saint Julien l'Hospitalier'." *Romantisme* 11.34 (1981): 59–66.

Bizet, Georges, adapt. *Carmen: Opera in Four Acts*. By Prosper Mérimée. Tr. Ruth and Thomas Martin. New York: G. Schirmer, 1958.

Blin, Jean-Pierre. "Nouvelle et narration au XXème siècle: La Nouvelle raconte-t-elle toujours une histoire?" *La Nouvelle: Définitions, Transformations*. Ed. Bernard Alluin and François Suard. Lille: PU de Lille, 1990.

Bonnes, Jean-Paul. *Le Bonheur du masque: Petite Introduction aux romans de Barbey d'Aurevilly*. Tournai: Casterman, 1947.

Bornecque, Jacques-Henry, ed. *Les Diaboliques*. By Barbey d'Aurevilly. Paris: Garnier, 1963.

Boucher, Jean-Pierre. *Les Diaboliques de Barbey d'Aurevilly: Une Esthétique de la dissimulation et de la provocation*. Montréal: P de l'U du Québec, 1976.

Bourgeois, Bertrand. "Quatre Ans seulement et pourtant: la distante proximité des deux versions d''Un Dilemme' de Huysmans." *Australian Journal of French Studies* 53.1–2 (2016): 109–22.

Bourget, Paul. "Mérimée nouvelliste." *Revue des Deux Mondes* 90 (15 Sep. 1920): 257–72.

Bowen, Elizabeth. "The Faber Book of Modern Short Stories." May 152–58.

Brady, Patrick. *Interdisciplinary Interpretation of Art and Literature: The Principle of Convergence*. Knoxville: New Paradigm Press, 1996.

Brereton, Geoffrey. *A Short History of French Literature*. London: Cassell, 1954.

Bricout, Bernadette. "Les Deux Chemins du Petit Chaperon rouge." *Frontières Du Conte*. Ed. François Marotin. Paris: Éditions du CNRS, 1982. 47–54.

Brombert, Victor. *Victor Hugo and the Visionary Novel*. Cambridge, MA: Harvard UP, 1984.

Brown, Susan Hunter. "Discourse Analysis and the Short Story." Lohafer and Clarey 217–48.

Bruézière, Maurice. "Notice." *Trois Contes*. Ed. Maurice Bruézière. Paris: Classiques Larousse, 1953. 5–14.

Butor, Michel. *Répertoire [1]*. Paris: Minuit, 1960.

Cégretin, Michel, ed. *Carmen*. By Mérimée. Paris: Bordas, 1980.

Works Cited 181

Charpentier, André. "Commencer et finir souvent. Rupture fragmentaire et brièveté discontinue dans l'écriture nouvellière." *La Nouvelle: Ecriture(s) et lecture(s).* Ed. Agnès Whitfield and Jacques Cotnam. Montreal: GREF, 1993.

Cheever, John. "Is the Short Story Necessary?" May 94–106.

Chevalier, Jean, and Alain Gheerbrant. *Dictionnaire des symboles: Mythes, rêves, coutumes, gestes, formes, figures, couleurs, nombres.* Paris: Laffont, 1969.

Clements, Robert J., and Joseph Gibaldi. *Anatomy of the Novella: The European Tale Collection from Boccaccio and Chaucer to Cervantes.* New York: New York UP, 1977.

Cogman, P. W. M. "Gaps and Gap-Filling in Maupassant's 'Le Champ d'Oliviers'." *French Studies Bulletin* 60 (1996): 9–13.

———. "The Narrators of Mérimée's *Carmen.*" *Nottingham French Studies* 27.2 (November 1988): 1–12.

Comeau, Paul T. "La Rhétorique du poète engagé du *Dernier jour d'un condamné* à *Claude Gueux.*" *Nineteenth-Century French Studies* 16.1 & 2 (1987–88): 59–77.

Corbière-Gille, Gisle. "*Les Diaboliques* dans le domaine anglo-saxon." *Revue des Lettres Modernes* 403–08 (1974): 114.

Cornell, Kenneth. *The Symbolist Movement.* New Haven, CT: Yale UP, 1951.

Cropper, Corry L. "Haunting the nouveau Riches: Bohemia in Mérimée's 'La Vénus d'Ille' and 'Carmen'." *Nineteenth-Century French Studies* 38.3 & 4 (2010): 183–95.

———. *Playing at Monarchy: Sport as Metaphor in Nineteenth-Century France.* Lincoln: U of Nebraska P, 2008.

Crouzet, Michel. "Barbey d'Aurevilly et l'oxymore: ou La Rhétorique du diable." Ed. Berthier, *La Chose sans nom* 83–98.

Culler, Jonathan D. *Structuralist Poetics: Structuralism, Linguistics and the Study of Literature.* Ithaca, NY: Cornell UP, 1975.

Cusset, Catherine. "A Lesson of Decency: Pleasure and Reality in Vivant Denon's *No Tomorrow.*" *The Libertine Reader: Eroticism and Enlightenment in Eighteenth-Century France.* Ed. Michel Feher. New York: Zone Books, 1997. 722–31.

Dacos, Xavier. *Prosper Mérimée.* Paris: Flammarion, 1998.

Dauzat, Albert. *Dictionnaire étymologique des noms de famille et prénoms de France.* Paris: Larousse, 1951.

de Negri, Enrico. "The Legendary Style of the *Decameron.*" *Romanic Review* 43 (1952): 166–89.

Debray-Genette, Raymonde. *Métamorphoses du récit: Autour de Flaubert.* Paris: Seuil, 1988.

Delarue, Paul, and M.-L. Tenèze. *Le Conte populaire français: Catalogue raisonné des versions de France.* 4 vols. Paris: Maisonneuve & Larose, 1997, Vol. 1.

Delon, Michel, ed. "*Point de lendemain*" suivi de Jean-François de Bastide, "*La Petite Maison.*" Coll. Folio. Paris: Gallimard, 1995.

Demers, Jeanne. "Nouvelle et conte: des frontières à établir." *La Nouvelle: écriture(s) et lecture(s).* Eds. Agnès Whitfield and Jacques Cotnam. Montréal: GREF, 1993. 63–71.

Demorest, D. L. *L'Expression figurée et symbolique dans l'œuvre de Gustave Flaubert.* 1931; rpt. Geneva: Slatkine, 1967.

182   Works Cited

Denon, Vivant. "Point de lendemain" (1812). *Romanciers du XVIIIe siècle*. Ed. René Etiemble. Vol. 2. Bibliothèque de la Pléiade. Paris: Gallimard, 1965. 383–402.

———. *Point de lendemain* (1777). Paris: Jacques Haumont, 1941.

Desan, Suzanne. *The Family on Trial in Revolutionary France*. Berkeley: U of California P, 2004.

Dickens, Charles. "Appendix I: Dickens' Prefaces to Collected Editions of *The Christmas Books*."*A Christmas Carol and Other Christmas Writings*. Ed. Michael Slater. London: Penguin, 2003. 265–66.

Diderot, Denis, and Jean Le Rond d'Alembert, eds. *Encyclopédie, ou dictionnaire raisonné des sciences, des arts et des métiers*. 17 vols. Paris: Briasson, 1751–65.

Diderot, Denis. *Supplément au voyage de Bougainville, ou Dialogue entre A et B. Œuvres*. Bibliothèque de la Pléiade. Paris: Gallimard, 1951. 963–1002.

Donaldson-Evans, Mary. "Maupassant épinglé?" *L'Angélus* 11 (déc. 2000-jan. 2001): 3–11.

———. "Pricking the Male Ego: Pins and Needles in Flaubert, Maupassant, and Zola." *Nineteenth-Century French Studies* 30.3–4 (2002): 254–65.

Du Camp, Maxime. *Souvenirs littéraires*. 2 vols. 1882. Paris: Hachette, 1906.

Dubuis, Roger. "Le Mot 'nouvelle' au moyen âge: De la nébuleuse au terme générique." *La Nouvelle: Définitions, Transformations*. Eds. Bernard Alluin and François Suard. Lille: PU de Lille, 1990. 13–26.

Dupâquier, Jacques. *Histoire de la population française*. 4 vols. Paris: P.U.F., 1988. Vol. 2.

Ejxenbaum, B. M. "O. Henry and the Theory of the Short Story." May 81–89.

Ellison, David R. "The Place of 'Carmen'." *Geographies: Mapping the Imagination in French and Francophone Literature and Film*. Ed. Freeman G. Henry and Jeanne Garane. Amsterdam: Rodopi, 2003. 73–85.

Engstrom, Alfred G. "The Formal Short Story in France and Its Development Before 1850." *Studies in Philology* 42 (1945): 627–39.

Erlich, Victor. *Russian Formalism: History—Doctrine*. 3rd ed. Paris: Mouton, 1969.

Eugenides, Jeffrey. NPR interview by Jennifer Kerrigan. October 1, 2017.

Fagley, Robert M. *Bachelors, Bastards, and Nomadic Masculinity: Illegitimacy in Guy de Maupassant and André Gide*. Newcastle upon Tyne: Cambridge Scholars, 2014.

Farrant, Tim. *Balzac's Shorter Fictions: Genesis and Genre*. Oxford: Oxford UP, 2002.

Felman, Shoshana. "La Signature de Flaubert: 'La Légende de saint Julien l'Hospitalier'." *Revue des Sciences Humaines* 181 (1981): 39–57.

Ferguson, Suzanne C. "Defining the Short Story: Impressionism and Form." *The New Short Story Theories*. Ed. Charles E. May. 218–30.

Flaubert, Gustave. *Correspondance*. 5 vols. Ed. Jean Bruneau. Bibliothèque de la Pléiade. Paris: Gallimard, 1973.

———. *Trois Contes. Œuvres*. Vol. 2. Bibliothèque de la Pléiade. Paris: Gallimard, 1963. 591–678.

Forster, E. M. *Aspects of the Novel*. Harvest Books. 1927. Rpt. New York: Harcourt, Brace, 1954.

Works Cited   183

Frank, Joseph. *The Widening Gyre: Crisis and Mastery in Modern Literature* (1945; rpt. New Brunswick, NJ: Rutgers UP, 1963.

Friedman, Norman. "Recent Short Story Theories." Lohafer and Clarey 13–31.

Furst, Lilian R. *The Contours of European Romanticism.* London: Macmillan, 1979.

Ganz, Eric. "Balzac's Unknowable Masterpiece and the Limits of the Classical Esthetic." *MLN* 90.4 (1975): 504–16.

Géal, François. "Mérimée et les gitans: Quelques réflexions sur le dernier chapitre de 'Carmen'," *Mérimée et le bon usage du savoir: La Création à l'épreuve de la connaissance.* Ed. Pierre Glaudes. Toulouse: PU du Mirail, 2008. 197–236.

———. "Le Poliglottisme, instrument de mystification et vecteur d'étrangeté, l'exemple emblétique de 'Carmen'." *L'Etrangeté des langues.* Ed. Yves Clavaron, Jérôme Dutel, and Clément Lévy. Saint-Etienne: PU Saint-Etienne, 2011. 105–16.

Genette, Gérard. "Genres, 'types,' modes." *Poétique* 32 (Nov. 1977): 389–421.

George, Albert J. *Short Fiction in France: 1800–1850.* Syracuse: Syracuse UP, 1964.

Gerlach, John. *Toward the End: Closure and Structure in the America Short Story.* University AL: U of Alabama P, 1985.

Giard, Anne. "Le Récit lacunaire dans *les Diaboliques.*" *Poétique* 41 (1980): 39–50.

Gide, André. "De l'importance du public." *Œuvres complètes.* Ed. L. Martin-Chauffier. 15 vols. Paris: N.R.F., 1932–39.

———. *Journal: 1889–1939.* 2 vols. Bibliothèque de la Pléiade. Paris: Gallimard, 1951.

Glinoer, Anthony. *La Bohème: Une Figure de l'imaginaire social.* Montreal: PU de Montréal, 2018.

Godenne, René. *Inventaire de la nouvelle française, 1800–1899.* Paris: Classiques Garnier, 2013.

———. *La Nouvelle française.* Paris: P.U.F., 1974.

Goethe, Johann Wolfgang van. *Hermann und Dorothea.* Wiesbaden: Verlag des Volksbildungsvereins, 1905.

Goyet, Florence. *La Nouvelle 1870–1925: Description d'un genre à son apogée.* Paris: P.U.F., 1993.

Gracq, Julien. "Préface." *Les Diaboliques.* By Barbey d'Aurevilly. Paris: Livre de Poche, 1960.

Gratton, Johnnie, and Brigitte le Juez, eds. "Introduction." *Modern French Short Fiction.* Manchester: Manchester UP, 1994. 1–21.

Greene, John Patrick. "Decor and Decorum in Vivant Denon's *Point de lendemain.*" *Dalhousie French Studies* 39–40 (Summer-Fall 1997): 59–68.

Grelé, Eugène. *Jules Barbey d'Aurevilly: sa vie et son œuvre d'après sa correspondance inédite et autres documents nouveaux.* 2 vols. Paris: Champion, 1904.

Grimal, Pierre. *Dictionnaire de la mythologie grecque et romaine.* Paris: P. U. F, 1969.

Grimm, Jacob. *Teutonic Mythology.* Trans. James Steven Stallybrass. Vol. 1. New York: Dover, 1966.

Grossman, Kathryn. *The Early Novels of Victor Hugo: Towards a Poetics of Harmony.* Geneva: Droz, 1986.

184 Works Cited

Grossman, Kathryn. *Figuring Transcendence in* Les Misérables: *Hugo's Romantic Sublime*. Carbondale: Southern Illinois UP, 1994.

———. *The Later Novels of Victor Hugo: Variations on the Politics and Poetics of Transcendence*. Oxford: Oxford UP, 2012.

Guise, René. "Lire 'Le Chef-d'œuvre inconnu'." *Autour du "Chef-d'œuvre inconnu" de Balzac*. Paris: Ecole Nationale Supérieure des Arts Décoratifs, 1985. 9–13.

Gullason, Thomas A. "The Short Story: An Underrated Art." May 13–31.

Gyp. *Les Femmes du colonel*. Paris: Flammarion, n.d.

Hamrick, L. Cassandra. "La Crise d'identité littéraire en 1837 selon la presse périodique." *Autour d'un cabinet de lecture*. Éd. Graham Falconer. Toronto: Centre d'Etudes du XIXe Siècle, Joseph Sablé, 2001. 69–90.

Hecht, Jacqueline. "Forum: From 'Be Fruitful and Multiply' to Family Planning: The Enlightenment Transition." *Eighteenth-Century Studies* 22.4 (1999): 536–51.

Hemingway, Ernest. *Death in the Afternoon*. 1932. New York: Scribner's, 1960.

Henry, David. *An Historical Description of the Tower of London and Its Curiosities*. London: J. Newberry, 1753. Google Books. Web. 23 Nov. 2013.

Hesse, Douglas. "A Boundary Zone: First-Person Short Stories and Narrative Essays." Lohafer and Clarey 85–105.

Hirsch, E. D. Jr., *The Aims of Interpretation*. Chicago, IL: U of Chicago P, 1976.

Horrocks, Gillian. "A Semiotic Study of 'Carmen'." *Nottingham French Studies* 25.2 (October 1986): 60–72.

Houppermans, Sjef. "La Description dans *Point de lendemain*." *Description-Ecriture-Peinture*. Ed. Yvette Went-Daoust. Groningen: Department of French, U of Gronigen, 1987. 36–47.

Hovasse, Jean-Marc. *Victor Hugo*. 2 vols. Paris: Fayard, 2001.

Hugo, Victor. *Œuvres complètes*. Ed. Jean Massin. 18 vols. Paris: Club Français du Livre, 1967–70.

Hunter, Adrian. *The Cambridge Introduction to the Short Story in English*. Cambridge: Cambridge UP, 2007. 10–15.

Huysmans, Joris-Karl. "Un Dilemme." *Œuvres complètes*. 18 vols. Paris: Slatkine, 1972. 12*. 10–11.

———. "Un Dilemme." *Revue Indépendant* 1 (1884): 371–98, 469–501.

———. *Un Dilemme*. Paris: Tresse et Stock, 1887.

———. *Lettres inédites à Arij Prins (1885–1907)*. Ed. Louis Gillet. Geneva: Droz, 1977.

———. *Lettres inédites à Emile Zola*. Ed. Pierre Lambert. Geneva: Droz, 1953.

———. *Lettres: Correspondance à trois*. Ed. Daniel Habrekorn. Vanves: Thot, 1980.

———. *Nouvelles: Sac au dos, A vau-l'eau, Un Dilemme, La Retraite de Monsieur Bougran*. Ed. Daniel Grojnowski. Paris: GF Flammarion, 2007. 145–200.

———. "Préface écrite vingt ans après le roman." *A rebours*. Ed. Rose Fortassier. Lettres françaises. Paris: Imprimerie Nationale, 1981. 51–66.

Ingram, Forest L. *Representative Short Story Cycles of the Twentieth Century: Studies in a Literary Genre*. The Hague: Mouton, 1971.

Israel-Pelletier, Aimée. *Flaubert's Straight and Suspect Saints*. Amsterdam: John Benjamins, 1991.

Works Cited 185

Issacharoff, Michael J.-K. *L'Espace et la nouvelle: Flaubert, Huysmans, Ionesco, Sartre, Camus*. Paris: José Corti, 1976.

———. *Huysmans devant la critique en France (1874–1960)*. Paris: Klincksieck, 1970.

Jakobson, Roman. *Essais de linguistique générale*. Tr. Nicolas Ruwet. Paris: Editions de Minuit, 1963. 209–48.

James, Henry. *The American Essays*. Ed. Leon Edel. New York: Vintage 1956.

———. "The Art of Fiction." *The American Tradition in Literature*. Ed. Sculley Bradley, Richmond Croom Beatty, and E. Hudson Long. Vol. 2. New York: W. W. Norton, 1962. 655–72.

———. *Critical Prefaces*. Ed. R. P. Blackmur. New York: Charles Scribner's Sons, 1934.

———. "Introduction." *Hubert Crackanthorpe: Last Studies*. London: William Heinemann, 1897. xviii–xix.

———. "Maupassant." *Partial Portraits*. New York: Macmillan, 1894. 243–87.

———. "The Story-Teller at Large: Mr. Henry Harland." *The American Essays*. Ed. Leon Edel. New York: Vintage, 1956.

Jasinski, René. "Le Sens des *Trois Contes*." *Essays in Honor of L. F. Solano*. Eds. Raymond J. Cormier and Urban T. Holmes. Chapel Hill: U of North Carolina P, 1970. 117–28.

Javorek, Henriette. "Vivant Denon's *Point de lendemain*." *Chimères* 23.1–2 (1996–97): 39–54.

Jung, Carl G. *Mysterium Coniunctionis: An Inquiry into the Separation and Synthesis of Psychic Opposites in Alchemy*. Trans. R. F. C. Hull. London: Routledge, 1963.

Kavanagh, Thomas M. *Enlightenment and the Shadows of Chance: The Novel and the Culture of Gambling in Eighteenth-Century France*. Baltimore, MD: Johns Hopkins UP, 1993.

———. "Whist, or the Aristocracy of Mystery: Barbey d'Aurevilly's 'Beneath the Cards in a Game of Whist'." *Dice, Cards, Wheels: A Different History of French Culture*. Philadelphia: U of Pennsylvania P, 2005. 150–67.

Kelly, Dorothy. "Balzac's 'L'Auberge rouge': On Reading an Ambiguous Text." *Symposium* 36 (1982): 30–44.

Knight, Diana. *Flaubert's Characters: The Language of Illusion*. Cambridge: Cambridge UP, 1995.

Kruse, Elaine M. "Divorce in Paris 1792–1804: Window on a Society in Crisis." Diss. U of Iowa, 1983.

La Varende, Jean de. *Flaubert par lui-même*. Paris: Seuil, 1967.

Larousse, Pierre. "Dilemme." *Le Grand Dictionnaire universelle*. Vol 8. 1866–90; rpt. Paris: Nimeo, 1990. 851–52.

Lasine, Stuart. "Matters of Life and Death: The Story of Elijah and the Widow's Son in Comparative Perspective." *Biblical Interpretation: A Journal of Contemporary Approaches* 12.2 (2004): 117–44.

Laubriet, Pierre. *Un Catéchisme esthétique: Le Chef-d'œuvre inconnu de Balzac* [In Appendix: a critical edition of two early versions of the story 201–39]. Paris: Didier, 1961. 9–200

Le Calvez, Eric. "Gobseck and Grandet: Semes, Themes, Intertext." *Romance Studies* 23 (1994): 43–60.

186   *Works Cited*

Le Corbeiller, Armand. *Les Diaboliques de Barbey d'Aurevilly*. Paris: Malfère, 1939.

Le Yaouanc, Moïse. *Nosographie de l'humanité Balzacienne*. Paris: Maloine, 1959.

Lebrun, François. "Les Débuts de la contraception." *L'Histoire* 63 (1984): 28–31.

Lee, Paula. "Death of a King." *Raritan* 24.1 (2005): 31–50.

Lehner, Ernst and Johanna. *Folklore and Symbolism of Flowers, Plants and Trees*. New York: Tudor, 1960.

Lessing, Gotthold Ephraim. *Lessing's Fables*. Trans. F. Storr. 2nd ed. London: Rivingtons, 1832.

———. "The Vision." *Fables and Epigrams*. Book 1. London: J. & H. L. Hunt, 1825. 1–2.

Lohafer, Susan, and Jo Ellyn Clarey, eds. *Short Story Theory at a Crossroads*. Baton Rouge: Louisiana State UP, 1989.

Loloi, Parvin. "The *One Thousand and One Nights* and Its Influence on English Short Fiction: Some Examples." *Tale, Novella, Short Story: Currents in Short Fiction*. Ed. Wolfgang Görtschacher and Holger Klein. Tübingen: Stazuffenburg Verlag, 2004. 5–16.

Louvel, Lilliane. "'Silence will speak'—Encoding the Short Story: for Brevity's Sake." *Tale, Novella, Short Story: Currents in Short Fiction*. Ed. Wolfgang Görtschacher and Holger Klein. Tübingen: Stauffenburg Verlag, 2004. 249–61.

Lukacs, Georg. *The Theory of the Novel*. Cambridge, MA: MIT P, 1971.

Lund, Hans Peter. *Gustave Flaubert, Trois Contes*. Paris: P. U. F., 1994.

Maingueneau, Dominique. "Signification du décor: L'Exemple de *Carmen*." *Romantisme* 12.38 (1982): 87–91.

Mallion, Jean, and Pierre Salomon, eds. *Théâtre de Clara Gazul, Romans et nouvelles*. Bibliothèque de la Pléiade. Paris: Gallimard, 1978.

Marsh, Leonard. "Of Walls and the Window: Charting Textual Markers in Flaubert's 'La Légende de saint Julien l'Hospitalier'." *Modern Language Studies* 30.1 (2000): 157–65.

Maupassant, Guy de. *Maupassant: Contes et nouvelles*. 2 vols. Bibliothèque de la Pléiade. Ed. Louis Forestier. Paris: Gallimard, 1974, 1979.

———. "Le Roman." *Romans*. Bibliothèque de la Pléiade. Paris: Gallimard, 1987. 703.–15.

Maury, L.-F. Alfred. *Essai sur les légendes pieuses du moyen-age*. Paris: Ladrange, 1843.

May, Charles E. "Checkhov and the Modern Short Story." *The New Short Story Theories*. Ed. Charles E. May. 199–217.

———. "Introduction: A Survey of Short Story Criticism in America." *Short Story Theories*. Ed. Charles E. May. Athens: Ohio UP, 1976. 3–12.

———, ed. *The New Short Story Theories*. Athens: Ohio UP, 1994.

———. "Prolegomenon to a Generic Study of the Short Story." *Studies in Short Fiction* 33 (1996): 461–73.

Mérimée, Prosper. *Carmen* (1845). *Romans et nouvelles*. Ed. Maurice Parturier. Vol. 2. Paris: Garnier, 1967. 339–409.

———. *Théâtre de Clara Gazu, Romans et nouvelles*. Bibliothèque de la Pléiade. Paris: Gallimard, 1978.

Works Cited 187

Monjaret, Anne. "De l'épingle à l'aiguille: L'Education des jeunes filles au fil des contes." *L'Homme* 173 (2005): 119–47.

Mordecai, Marcus. "What is an Initiation Story?" (1960). May 189–201.

Mortimer, Armine Kotin. "The Devious Second Story in Kleist's *Die Marquise von O...*" *The German Quarterly* 67.3 (Summer 1994): 293–303.

———. "Second Stories." *Short Story Theory at a Crossroads.*" Ed. Susan Lohafer and Jo Ellyn Clarey. Baton Rouge: Louisiana State UP, 1989.

———. "Second Stories: The Example of 'Mr. Know-All'." *Studies in Short Fiction* 25 (1988): 307–14.

———. "Secrets of Literature, Resistance to Meaning." *Confrontations: Politics and Aesthetics in Nineteenth-Century France.* Ed. Kathryn M. Grossman. Amsterdam: Rodopi, 2001. 55–66.

———. "Secrets of Literature, Resistance to Meaning." *Confrontations: Politics and Aesthetics in Nineteenth-Century France.* Eds. Kathryn M. Grossman, Michael E. Lane, Bénédicte Monicat and Willa Z, Silverman. Amsterdam: Rodopi, 2001. 55–66.

Naudin, Pierre. "L'Architecte et le romancier au siècle de Le Camus de Mézières et de Vivant Denon." *Travaux de littérature: Architectes et architecture dans la littérature française* 12 (1999): 63–70.

Neefs, Jacques. "Le Récit et l'édifice des croyances: *Trois Contes.*" *Flaubert: La Dimension du texte.* Ed. P. M. Wetherill. Manchester: Manchester UP, 1982. 121–40.

Niess, Robert J. "Two Manuscripts of Maupassant: 'Le Retour' and 'Le Champ des Oliviers'." *French Studies* 8.2 (1954): 149–57.

O'Conner, John R. "*Trois Contes* and the Figure of the Double Cone." *PMLA* 95 (1980): 812–26.

O'Connor (pseud. Michael O'Donovan), Frank. *The Lonely Voice: A Study of the Short Story.* Cleveland, OH: World Publishing, 1963.

O'Faolain, Sean. *The Short Story.* New York: Devin-Adair, 1951. 106–234.

Ohashi, Eri. "Analyse des manuscrits des *Trois Contes*: la transcendance des hommes, des lieux et des choses chez Flaubert." Littératures, Université Rennes, submitted Feb. 19, 2013. <https://tel.archives-ouvertes.fr/tel-00790321>.

Palacios, Conceptión, and Pedro Méndez. *La Représentation de l'histoire dans la nouvelle en langue française du XIXe siècle.* Paris: Classiques Garnier, 2016.

Panofsky, Erwin. "*Et in Arcadia ego*: Poussin and the Elegiac Tradition." *Meaning in the Visual Arts.* Anchor Books. Garden City, NY: Doubleday, 1955. 295–320.

Pascal, Jean-Noël. *Les Successeurs de La Fontaine au siècle des lumières (1715–1815).* New York: Peter Lang, 1995.

Pasco, Allan H. *Balzacian Montage:* Configuring La Comédie humaine. Toronto: U of Toronto P, 1991.

———. *Balzac, Literary Sociologist.* New York: Palgrave Macmillan, 2016.

———. "From Decadence in Huysmans and Barbey to Regeneration in Gide and Proust." *Dix-Neuf* 21.2–3 (2017): 192–203. doi:10.1080/14787318.2017.1386884.

188 Works Cited

Pasco, Allan H. *Inner Workings of the Novel: Studying a Genre*. New York: Palgrave Macmillan, 2010.

———. "Ironic Interference and Allusion: `Un Cœur simple'." *Allusion: A Literary Graft*. U of Toronto P, 1994; rpt. Charlottesville: Rookwood P, 2002. 22–38.

———. "Negative Representation in Huysmans' En rade." *Novel Configurations: A Study of French Fiction*. 2nd ed. Birmingham: Summa, 1994. 123–50.

———. *Revolutionary Love in Eighteenth- and Early Nineteenth-Century France*. Aldershot: Ashgate Publications, 2009.

———. "The Short Story: 'The Short of It'." *Style* 27.3 (1993): 242–44.

———. "Short Story Cycles." *Inner Workings of the Novel: Studying a Genre*. New York: Palgrave Macmillan, 2010. 35–50.

———. *Sick Heroes: French Society and Literature in the Romantic Age, 1750–1850*. Exeter: U of Exeter P, 1997.

———. "Subversive Structure in Gide's *L'Immoraliste*." *Novel Configurations: A Study of French Fiction*. 2nd ed. Birmingham, AL: Summa Publ. 1987. 99–122.

Paulson, William. "Pour une analyse dynamique de la variation textuelle: 'Le Chef-d'œuvre' trop connu." *Nineteenth-Century French Studies* 19.3 (1991): 404–16.

Persson, Karl Gunnar. *An Economic History of Europe: Knowledge, Institutions and Growth, 600 to the Present*. New York: Cambridge UP, 2010.

Peterson, Carla L. "The Trinity in Flaubert's *Trois Contes*: Deconstructing History." *French Forum* 8.3 (1983): 243–58.

Peterson, Thomas E. "'Le Dernier Coup de pinceau': Perception and Generality in 'Le Chef-d'Œuvre Inconnu'." *Romanic Review* 88.3 (1997): 385–407.

Petit, Jacques. "L'Enfant mort et la naissance du héros." *Revue des Lettres Modernes* 600–604 (1981): 67–83.

———. *Essais de lectures des* Diaboliques *de Barbey d'Aurevilly*. Paris: Lettres Modernes Minard, 1974.

———. "Note sur la structure des *Diaboliques*." *Revue des Lettres Modernes* 199–202 (1969): 85–89.

Philip, Michel H. "Le Satanisme des *Diaboliques*." *Etudes françaises* 4 (1968): 72–76.

Phillips, Roderick. *Family Breakdown in Late Eighteenth-Century France: Divorces in Rouen 1792–1803*. Oxford: Clarendon Press, 1980.

Pierce, Gillian B. "'Point de lendemain': Milan Kundera and the French Libertine Tradition." *Literature Interpretation Theory* 26.4 (2015): 298–317. doi:1i0.1080/10436928.2015.1092852.

Pinget, Robert. "Pseudo-Principes d'esthétique." Ricardou and Rossum-Guyon 2 vols. 311–24.

Poe, Edgar Allan. Rev. of *Twice-Told Tales*, by Nathaniel Hawthorn. May 44–51.

———. Review of *Twice-Told Tales*. *The Literature of the United States*. Vol. 1. Ed. Walter Blair, Theodore Hornberger, and Randall Stewart. Chicago: Scott, Foresman, 1953. 604–07.

Works Cited   189

Porter, Katherine Anne. *The Collected Essays and Occasional Writings of Katherine Anne Porter*. New York: Delacorte, 1970.

Powell, David A. "Word and Image in Balzac's 'Le Chef-d'œuvre inconnu'." *Interfaces* 29 (2009–10): 245–65.

Prince, Gerald. *A Grammar of Stories*. The Hague: Mouton, 1973.

Proust, Marcel. *A la recherche du temps perdu*. Ed. Jean-Yves Tadié. 4 vols. *Bibliothèque de la Pléiade*. Paris: Gallimard, 1987–89.

Przybos, Julia. "'Le Plus Bel Amour de Don Juan' or a Child's Phantom Pregnancy." *Notebook in Cultural Analysis* 2 (1985): 51–67.

Rabelais, François. *"A très illustre prince et révérendissime Monseigneur Odet, Cardinal de Chastillon" and "Aux lecteurs." Œuvres complètes*. Bibliothèque de la Pléiade. Paris: Gallimard, 1955.

———. *Le Tiers Livre des faites et dicts héroïques du bon Pantagruel. Œuvres complètes*. Eds. Jaccques Boulenger and Lucien Scheler. Bibliothèque de la Pléiade. Paris: N.R.F. 1962.

Rabinowitz, Peter J. "Singing for Myself: Carmen and the Rhetoric of Musical Resistance." *Audible Traces: Gender, Identity, and Music*. Ed. Elaine Barkin and Lydia Hamesley. Zürich and Los Angeles: Carciofoli Verlagshaus, 1999.

Raclot, Michèle. "L'Enfant mort." *Travaux de Littérature* 5 (1992): 249–55.

Raitt, Allan William. *Flaubert: Trois Contes*. London: Grant & Cutler, 1991.

Reid, Ian. "Destabilizing Frames for Story." *Short Story Theory at a Crossroads*. Ed. Susan Lohafer and Jo Ellyn Clarey. Baton Rouge: Louisiana State UP, 1989. 299–310.

———. *The Short Story*. Critical Idiom, No. 37. London: Methuen, 1977.

Restif de La Bretonne, Nicolas-Edme. *Le Palais royal*. 3 vols. 1790. Rpt. Geneva: Slatkine, 1988.

Ricardou, Jean, and Françoise van Rossum-Guyon, eds. *Nouveau Roman: Hier, aujourd'hui*. 2 vols. Paris: 10/18, 1972.

Ricœur, Paul. "Narrative Time," *Critical Inquiry* 7 (1980): 169–90.

Robb, Graham. *Victor Hugo*. New York: Norton, 1998.

Roberts, Thomas J. *When Is Something Fiction?* Carbondale: Southern Illinois UP, 1972.

Rogers, B. G. *The Novels and Stories of Barbey d'Aurevilly*. Geneva: Droz, 1967.

Ropars-Wuilleumier, Marie-Claire. "'Le Plus Bel Amour de Don Juan': Narration et signification." *Littérature* 9 (1973): 118–25.

Roudiez, Leon S. *French Fiction Today: A New Direction*. New Brunswick: Rutgers UP, 1972.

Rubin, David Lee. "Fable." *The Princeton Encyclopedia of Poetry and Poetics*. 4th ed. Ed. Roland Green, Stephen Cushman, and Associates. Princeton, NJ: Princeton UP, 2012. 476–77.

Sacchi, Sergio. "Carmen et le toréador." *Sport, lingua, letteratura francese*. Ed. Mariagrazia Margarito. Alessandria: Dell' Orso, 1991. 91–103.

Sachs, Murray. "Introduction." *The French Short Story in the Nineteenth Century*. New York: Oxford UP, 1969. 3–13.

Sainte Beuve, C.-A. "Florian (Fables illustrées)." *Causeries du lundi*. Vol. 3. Paris: Garnier, 1852. 229–48.

Saint-Pierre, Jacques-Bernardin-Henri de. *La Chaumière indienne*. Paris: B. Le Francq, 1791.

190   Works Cited

Savey-Casard, Paul. *Le Crime et la peine dans l'œuvre de Victor Hugo*. Paris: P. U. F., 1956.

———, éd. "Introduction." *Victor Hugo, Claude Gueux: Edition critique*. Paris: P. U. F., 1956. 9–86.

Schaeffer, Jean-Marie. *Qu'est-ce qu'un genre littéraire?* Paris: Seuil, 1989.

Scofield, Martin. *The Cambridge Introduction to the American Short Story*. Cambridge: Cambridge UP, 2006.

Séginger, Gisèle. "*A rebours* de Huysmans: la lévitation du sens." *Nineteenth-Century French Studies* 23.3–4 (1995): 479–87.

Seigel, Jerrold. *Bohemian Paris: Culture, Politics, and the Boundaries of Bourgeois Life, 1830–1930*. New York: Viking, 1986.

Seillan, Jean-Marie. "Les Dessous d'"Un Dilemme." *Bulletin de la Société J.-K. Huysmans* 98 (2005): 27–37.

Simond, Charles, éd. *Le Consulat—Le Premier Empire, La Restauration, La Vie parisienne au XIXe siècle: Paris de 1800 à 1900*, 2 vols. Paris: Plon, 1900. 1.564–66.

Smeets, Marc. *Huysmans l'inchangé: Histoire d'une conversion*. Amsterdam: Rodopi, 2003.

Soboul, Albert. *La Civilisation et la Révolution française*. 2 vols. Paris: Arthaud, 1970–83.

Solal, Jérôme. "Le Code qui tue: A propos d' 'Un Dilemme'." *Bulletin de la Société J.-K. Huysmans* 97 (2004): 37–52.

Solomon, Bill. "The Novel in Distress." *Novel: A Forum on Fiction* 43.1 (2010): 124–31.

Spoerri, Theophil. "Mérimée and the Short Story." *Yale French Studies* 4 (1949): 3–11.

Springer, Mary Doyle. *Forms of the Modern Novella*. Chicago, IL: U of Chicago P, 1976.

Stegner, Wallace. "Teaching the Short Story." *Davis Publications in English* 2 (Fall 1965): 11.

Steinhauer, Harry. "Towards a Definition of the Novella." *Seminar* 6 (1970): 154–74.

Stevenson, Robert Louis. Letter of Sept. 1891 to Sidney Colvin. *The Letters of Robert Louis Stevenson*. Vol. 3. Ed. Sidney Colvin. New York: Charles Scribner's Sons, 1911. 335–36.

Stow, John, and John Mottley. *A Survey of the Cities of London and Westminster, Borough of Southwark, and Parts Adjacent*. Vol. 1. London: T. Read, 1733. 70. Google Books. Web. 23 Nov. 2013.

Sullivan, Edward D. *Maupassant: The Short Stories*. London: Edward Arnold, 1962.

Swahn, Sigbrit. "'Le Chef-d'Œuvre Inconnu,' Récit Hoffmannesque de Balzac." *Studia Neophilologica* 76.2 (2004): 206–14.

Tessin, Carl Gustaf. *Briefe an einen jungen Prinzen von einem alten Manne*. Trans. from the Swedish by Johann D. Reichenbach. Vol. 1. Leipzig: Bernhard Christoph Breitkopf, 1756. 162–64. Google Books. Web. 23 Nov. 2013.

Théré, Christine. "Women and Birth Control in Eighteenth-Century France." *Eighteenth-Century Studies* 22.4 (1999): 552–64.

Thomas, Dylan. *Adventures in the Skin Trade and Other Stories*. New York: Signet, 1956.

Works Cited 191

Thomas, Shelly Purcell. "Thematic Progression in *Trois Contes*." *Romanic Review* 80.4 (1989): 541–47.

Tieghem, Philippe Van. "Les Prosateurs du XVIIe siècle." *Encyclopédie de la Pléiade*. Ed. Raymond Queneau. Vol. 3. Paris: Gallimard, 1958, 407–34.

Tilby, Michael. "Language and Sexuality in Mérimée's 'Carmen'." *Forum for Modern Language Study* 15 (1979): 255–63.

Todorov, Tzvetan. "La Grammaire du récit." *Langages* 12 (1968): 94–102.

Toqueville, Alexis de. *The Old Regime and the French Revolution*. Trans. Stuart Gilbert. Garden City, NY: Doubleday, 1955.

Torgovnick, Marianna. *Closure in the Novel*. Princeton, NJ: Princeton UP, 1981.

Tournier, Michel, éd. "Préface." *Trois Contes*. Folio. Paris: Gallimard, 1973. 8–23.

Tranouez, Pierre. *Fascination et narration dans l'œuvre de Barbey d'Aurevilly: la scène capital*. Paris: Lettres Modernes Minard, 1987.

Tynjanov, Jurij. "On Literary Evolution" (1927). *Readings in Russian Poetics: Formalist and Structuralist Views*. Eds. Ladislav Matejka and Krystyna Pomorska. Cambridge, MA: MIT P, 1971. 66–78.

Vassilev, Kris. "Histoire et fiction dans 'Le Dessous de cartes d'une partie de whist' de Barbey." *Neophilologus* 93.4 (2009): 581–601.

Vatan, Florence. "Lecture du merveilleux médiéval: Gustave Flaubert et Alfred Maury." *Savoirs en récits I, Flaubert: la politique, l'art, l'histoire*. Éd. Anne Herschberg Pierrot. Paris: PU de Vincennes, 2010. 87–107.

Verdier, Yvonne. "*Le Petit Chaperon rouge* dans la tradition orale." *Le Débat* 3 (1980): 31–61.

———. "*Le Petit Chaperon rouge* dans la tradition orale." *Coutume et destin. Thomas Hardy et autres essais*. Ed. Yvonne Verdier. Paris: Gallimard, 1995. 171–206.

Vial, André. *Guy de Maupassant et l'art du roman*. Paris: Nizet, 1954.

Viegnes, Michel. *L'Esthétique de la nouvelle française au vingtième siècle*. New York: Peter Lang, 1989.

Wain, John. "Remarks on the Short Story." *Les Cahiers de la Nouvelle: Journal of the Short Story in English* 2 (1984): 49–66.

Walker, Warren S. "From Raconteur to Writer: Oral Roots and Printed Leaves of Short Fiction." *The Teller and the Tale: Aspects of the Short Story*. Proceedings, Comparative Literature Symposium, 23–25 Jan. 1980. Lubboch: Texas Tech P, 1982. 13–26.

Walle, Etienne van de. *Motivations and Technology in the Decline of French Fertility*. Philadelphia: U of Pennsylvania P, 1980. 135–78.

Warnton, Edith. "Telling a Short Story." *The Writing of Fiction*. New York: Charles Scribner's Sons, 1925. 33–58.

Wellek, René. "Literary History." *Literary Scholarship: Its Aims and Methods*. Eds. Normon Foerster, John Calvin McGalliard, René Wellek, Austin Warren, Wilbur Schramm. Chapel Hill: U of North Carolina P, 1941.

Wellek, René, and Austin Warren. *Theory of Literature*. New York: Harcourt, Brace, 1949.

Wells, Byron R. "Objet/Volupté: Vivant Denon's *Point de lendemain*." *Romance Notes* 29.3 (1989): 203–08.

Wetherill, P.W., éd. "Introduction Générale." *Trois Contes*. By Gustave Flaubert. Paris: Classiques Garnier, 1988. 19–143.

192   Works Cited

Whyte, Peter. "'Le Chef-d'œuvre inconnu' de Balzac: esthétique et image." *Text(e) image*. Ed. Margret-Anne Hutton. Durham: U of Durham, 1999. 95–114.

Wilson, Elizabeth. *Bohemians: The Glamorous Outcasts*. New Brunswick, NJ: Rutgers UP, 2000.

Wölfflin, Heinrich. *Principles of Art History: The Problem of the Development of Style in Later Art*. Trans. from the 7th ed. (1929) M. D. Hottinger. New York: Dover, n.d.

Wood, Michael. "The Last Night of All." *PMLA* 122.5 (2007): 1394–402.

Wright, Austin M. "On Defining the Short Story: The Genre Question." Lohafer and Clarey 46–53.

Yonge, Charlotte. *History of Christian Names*. 1884; rpt. Detroit: Gale, 1966.

Ziegler, Robert. "Decadent Pathology or Naturalist Health: Literature at the Crossroads in Huysmans' 'Un Dilemme'." *Excavatio: Emile Zola and Naturalism* 12 (1999): 69–75.

———. *The Mirror of Divinity: The World and Creation in J.-K. Huysmans*. Newark: U of Delaware P, 2004.

Zola, Emile. "Alexis et Maupassant." *Œuvres complètes*. Ed. Henri Mitterand. Vol. 14. Paris: Cercle du Livre Précieux, 1962. 621–26.

Zumthor, Paul. "La Brièveté comme forme." *La Nouvelle: Formation, codification et rayonnement d'un genre médiéval* (Actes du Colloque International de Montréal—McGill University, 14–16 October 1982). Eds. Michelangelo Picone, et al. Montreal: Plato Academic P, 1983. 3–4.

———. *Essai de poétique medieval*. Paris: Seuil, 1972.

Index

Note: Page numbers followed by 'n' refer to endnotes.

abortion 64–65
Académie française 90
Adventures in the Skin Trade and Other Stories (Thomas) 10
aiguilles 150–52
The Aims of Interpretation (Hirsch) 15n8
A la recherche du temps perdu (Proust) 12, 177n9
allusion 101, 102, 143–45, 169, 171–75
ambiguity xii, 30–33, 134, 144, 161
analogy 67–70
Anatomy of the Novella: The European Tale Collection from Boccaccio and Chaucer to Cervantes (Clements and Gibaldi) 14n5
A rebours (Huysmans) 35–39, 47
"L'Auberge rouge" ('The Red Inn' Balzac) 131, 134, 135–45, 146n7, 165, 173–75
A vau-l'eau (Huysmans) 35–36
"L'Aveu" (Maupassant) 149–50
Ashliman, D. L. 108n24

Baldeshweiler, Eileen 16n17
Baldick, Robert 39, 49nn7–8
Baltzell, James 127n1
Balzac, Honoré de 6, 46, 63, 90, 91, 108n28, 110, 127n1, 131–45, 145nn2–5, 146n7, 150, 163n11, 168, 173–76
Banville, Théodore de 130n28
Barbey d'Aurevilly, Jules 51–70, 70n1, 90, 110, 144, 167, 168, 171, 172
Bates, H. E. 1, 14n4

Baudelaire, Charles 34n15, 97, 107n16, 108n22, 168, 169, 177, 177n5
Beck, William J. 113–14, 118, 124, 126, 128n5, 128n7, 128n11, 130n30
Bernard, Claudie 103, 108n27
Berthier, Philippe 52, 55, 61, 70nn11–12, 71n14, 21
Biaisi, Pierre-Marc de 130n31
Bizet, Georges 72, 74, 75, 77, 79, 86
Bloy, Léon 38
Boccaccio, Giovanni 4
"Boule de suif" (Maupassant) 150
Le Bourgeois gentilhomme (Molière) 43
Bourgeois, Bertrand 49n9
Bourget, Paul 34n15
Bowen, Elisabeth 1, 14n3
Brereton, Geoffrey 1, 14n5
Bricout, Bernadette 151, 162n6, 162n8
"the broad way of sentiment" 27
Brombert, Victor 107n4, 107n12
Broussais, F. J. V. 140
Brown, Suzanne Hunter 15n17, 32n2

Camus, Albert 10
Carlson, Maria xiii
"Carmen" (Mérimée) 72–86, 87n6, 88n12, 89n22, 89n24, 167, 172
Castex, Pierre-Georges 131
Castries, René de la Croix de 40
Catholic Church 21, 57
Caws, Mary Ann 72
Céard, Henry 38
"Ce Cochon de Morin" (Maupassant) 12

194   Index

Cent Nouvelles Nouvelles (1462) 6
"Le Champ d'oliviers" (Maupassant 1890) 151–61, 175
Charpentier, André 88n7
Cheever, John 16n23
"Le Chef-d'œuvre inconnu" (Balzac) *see* "Gillette"
Chekhov, Anton 8n27, 12
Christianity 113, 121, 122, 124–7, 171
La Civilisation et la Révolution française (Soboul) 108n28
civilization 2, 4, 83, 126, 127
"Claude Gueux" (Hugo) 90–106, 107n19, 166, 167, 169
Clements, Robert J. 1, 14n5
close reading ix
closure xii–xiii, 131–45, 147–50, 147n6, 174
Closure in the Novel (Torgovnick) 87n4
"Un Cœur simple" (Flaubert, Beck) 113, 114, 118, 124, 126, 128n5, 128n11, 130n30
Cogman, P. W. M. 76–78, 111, 128n3, 160–61, 163n11
Comeau, Paul T. 108n28
La Comédie humaine (Balzac) 131, 132, 173
Les Confessions (Rousseau) 5–6
"Confessions d'une femme" (Maupassant) 148
connotation 21, 38, 49n16
conte 16n20
Corbière-Gille, Gisle 52
Cornell, Kenneth 176
Cortes, Miguel 74
Cromwell (Hugo) 92, 93, 107n8
Cropper, Corry L. xiii, 74–5, 88n13, 88n14
Crouzet, Michel 56
cycle 121–27
Culler, Jonathan D. 19

"Death of a King" (Lee) 108n24
The Death of Sardanapalus (Delacroix) 54
La Débacle (Zola) 35
Debray-Genette, Raymonde 113, 124
Definitions, short story: artistically designed, short, prose fiction x, 5, 7, 8, 10, 13–14, 19, 111, 164, 176
Delacroix 54, 70n13
Delon, Michel 30, 33n6
Demers, Jeanne 16n21

de Negri, Enrico 15n13
Denon, Vivant 18–34, 45, 90, 134, 144, 165, 170, 175
denotation 21, 42–44
Le Dernier Jour d'un condamné (Hugo) 92, 96, 99, 109n30
Descaves, Lucien 38
"Le Dessous de cartes" (Barbey) 51–70, 172
Les Diaboliques (Barbey d'Aurevilly) 51–70, 70n1, 110, 171
Dickens, Charles 7–8, 16n24
Diderot, Denis 22–23, 33n9
"Un Dilemme" (Huysmans) 35, 39–48, 49n9, 49n10, 50n18, 168, 170
Discours sur la poésie (Hugo) 94
discrimination 4, 5
Le Divorce (Desfontaines) 23
Dominican 76
Don José Lizarrabengoa 74–84, 86
"La Dot" (Maupassant) 150

Ejxenbaum, B. M. 20, 32n5
Ellison, David R. 73, 74, 87n6
Encyclopédie (Diderot) 22–3
Engstrom, Alfred G. 7n20, 16
"L'Enjeu" (Villiers) 29
Enlightenment and the Shadows of Chance: The Novel and the Culture of Gambling in Eighteenth-Century France (Kavanagh) 33n12
En rade (Huysmans) 36–39, 47
"Les Epingles" (Maupassant) xii, 150–53
Erlich, Victor 10, 16n29
Essai sur les légendes pieuses du moyen-âge (Maury) 121, 128n10
Eugenides, Jeffrey 13
étymology 82
Eugen Onegin (Pushkin) 9

fable 90–102, 104–05, 106nn1,3, 107n15
fabliaux 9, 16n29
Fagley, Robert M. 162n10
Family Breakdown in Late Eighteenth-Century France: Divorces in Rouen 1792–1803 (Phillips) 33n7
Félicité, *see* "Un Cœur simple"
Fécondité (Zola) 63
La Femme de trente ans (Balzac) 174
fiction 5–7, 35, 37, 38
Fielding, Henry 1

Le Figaro 157–59
Flaubert, Gustave 8, 38, 91, 110–27, 128n10, 129n20, 130n26, 130n30, 130n33, 166, 167, 173
Les Fleurs du mal (Baudelaire) 51
"La Folle" 6, 148
Forestier, Louis 158, 162n4
Forms of the Modern Novella (Springer) 14n3
Forster, E. M. 10–11, 17n32
frame 110–27
France, Anatole 8
Frank, Joseph 6, 15n17, 73, 129n19
Friedman, Norman 15n8
Frye, Northrop 8

Ganz, Eric 146n5
Gautier, Théophile ("Jettatura") 11
Géal, François 88n16, 89n25
Genette, Gérard 14n6
genre 1–10, 13–14, 14n6, 15n17, 19, 23, 29, 35, 38, 48, 73, 84, 85, 90–106, 110, 111, 127, 127n1, 131, 147, 150, 164–69, 172, 176
George, Albert J. 16n21
Germinal (Zola) 35
Giard, Anne 52
Gibaldi, Joseph 1, 14n5
Gide, André 10, 177n9
"Gillette" ('Le Chef d'œuvre inconnu' Balzac) xii, 131–35, 145–46n5, 173, 175, 176
Girouettes (Weathervanes) 22
Gobineau, Arthur 9
"Gobseck" (Le Calvez) 131–32, 134, 144, 145n2, 145n3
Godard, Jean-Luc 4
Godenne, René 73
Goethe 143–45
Gould, Evlyn 87n6
Gracq, Julien 52
grande finale 30
Grelé, Eugène 69, 71n27
Grossman, Kathryn xiii, 101-01, 107n12
Guilleragues, Gabrielle de 6
Guise, René 132, 145n5
Gullason, Thomas A. 1, 14n2

Halévy, Ludovic 74
Hamrick, L. Cassandra 127n1
Hawthorne, Nathaniel ("Young Goodman Brown") 7
Hecht, Jacqueline 71n24

Hemingway, Ernest 19, 20, 32n3
Hennique, Léon 38
Henry, O. 8
Heptaméron (Marguerite de Navarre) 72, 110, 169
Hermann und Dorothea (Gœthe) 143, 174
Hernani 93
"Hérodias" 117–20, 124, 128n5, 130n26
Hesse, Douglas 15n12
Hirsch, E. D., Jr. 2–3, 15n8
Histoire des treize (Balzac) 110
History of the Peloponnesian War 8
Hoffmann, E. T. A. 135
Holy Spirit 57, 110–18, 121, 126, 127
"Le Horla" (Maupassant) 19, 150, 165
Horrocks, Gillian 79
Houppermans, Sjef 33n11
Hugo, V. 90–106, 106n1, 106n2, 106n3, 107n12, 107n19, 108n22, 108n24, 108n28, 109n30, 110, 164, 167, 172, 177n1
humanity 19, 39, 42, 45, 122, 127, 129n15
Huysmans, J.-K. 35–50, 48n2, 48n4, 49n7, 49n9, 49n10, 90, 91, 168, 170, 171, 177n6

"image structure" 6, 48–73, 118, 129–45, 147–61
impotence 54–55, 62, 70–71n13
infanticide 71nn24–25
Ingram, Forest L. 34n15
Iaokanann (John the Baptist) 120–27
Israel-Pelletier, Aimée 119
Issacharoff, Michael 49n, 111–12, 120

Jacobus de Voragine 8
Jakobson, Roman 73, 88n10
James, Henry 13, 15n17, 17n31, 17n3820, 147, 162n3, 166, 177n3
Jaucourt, Chevalier de 23
Javorek, Henriette 27
Jesus 57, 118–26
Job 4
"Le Jongleur de Notre-Dame" (France) 8
Judeo-Christian culture 141
Julien l'Hospitalier, Saint 113–17, 123
Jung, Carl G. 108n22

196 Index

Karkoël, Marmor de 58–60, 63–67, 69, 171
Kavanagh, Thomas 24, 33n12, 71n19
Kerrigan, Jennifer 13
Kilchenmann, Ruth J. 8
Kruse, Elaine M. 33n7
Kurzgeschichte 10

Là-bas (Huysmans) 37, 39, 47, 49n7
Lambois, M. 39–47, 50n16, 170
Lasine, Stuart 114–15, 129n15
La Varende, Jean de 127
"L'Aveu" (1884) 149
L'Ecole des femmes (Molière) 169–70
Le Corbeiller, Armand 52, 61, 70n12
Lee, Paula 108n24
Legenda aurea (Jacobus de Voragine) 8
"La Légende de Saint Julien l'Hospitalier" (Flaubert) 8, 113–17, 118, 119, 130n30
"L'Enjeu" (Villiers de l'Isle-Adam) 29
Le Ponsart, Maître 39–47, 50n16, 170
Leroux, Pierre 96
Lessing, Gotthold Ephraim 107nn13–4
"The Lesson of the Master" (James) 17n31, 20
Lettres de la religieuse portugaise (Anonymous) 6
lexicographers 3
The Life of J.-K. Huysmans (Baldick) 49n7
linguistic signs 3
lion and the dog 101–02
"Le Lit" (Maupassant) 11
Littérature et philosophie mêlées (Hugo) 92–94
Little Red Riding Hood 152
Loulou 114, 127
Louvel, Lilliane 11, 17n35
Lucrèce Borgia (Hugo) 92, 94
Lukacs, Georg 16n17

Madame Bovary 51, 110, 113
Madame Dampyré (Gyp) 37–38
"Madame Parisse" (Maupassant) 147, 162n4
Mademoiselle de Maupin (Gautier) 97
"La Main" (Maupassant) 148, 165
La Maison Tellier (Maupassant) 147
Mallarmé, Stéphane 35, 37, 38, 161, 176

Marcus, Mordecai 16n17
Marguerite de Navarre 1, 6, 72, 110, 169
Le Mariage de Figaro (Beaumarchais) 23
"Le Mariage du lieutenant Laré" (Maupassant) 18
Mary, Virgin 56–57, 112
masterpiece 5, 6, 8, 19, 20, 32, 36, 161, 164, 165–68, 176–77
Matters of Life and Death: The Story of Elijah and the Widow's Son in Comparative Perspective (Lasine) 129n15
Matthews, Brander 8
Maupassant, Guy de 6, 11, 12, 16n25, 18, 19, 147–61, 162n1, 162n5, 166–68, 174–76
Maury, L.-F. Alfred 112–27, 128n10
May, Charles E. 1, 14n2
Meilhac, Henri 74
Meininger, Anne-Marie 140, 146n10
Méndez, Pedro 14
Mérimée, Prosper 72–87, 87n6, 110, 172
"Minuet" (Maupassant) 6
Les Misérables (Hugo) 101
The Modern Short Story: A Critical Survey (Bates) 14n4
Les Mœurs (Pigault-Lebrun) 23
Molière 30, 32, 43, 54, 131, 169–71, 175
Monjaret, Anne 152–53
Monsieur D. 98–100, 102, 105, 106
Mortimer, Armine Kotin 86, 89n27, 111, 128n4, 134, 146n6
Mysterium Coniunctionis: An Inquiry into the Separation and Synthesis of Psychic Opposites in Alchemy (Jung) 108n22

Nana (Zola) 35
Naudin, Pierre 28, 34n14
needles *(la voie des aiguilles)* 152
Niess, Robert J. 153, 162n9
nouvelle 1, 7, 16n21
Novellinos 9

O. Henry 8
O'Connor, Frank 6n17
Ohashi, Eri 128n2
onomastics 41–41, 49nn15–16, 98–99, 107n18
overture 146n6

Index 197

Palacios, Concepción 14
Parturier, Maurice 82, 87n6, 89n21, 89n22
"La Parure" (Maupassant) 148
Pasco, Allan H. 14n1, 15n17, 36, 48n1, 48n3, 48n6, 87n5, 107n21, 109n29, 128n11
Le Père Goriot 135
Persson, Karl Gunnar 108n28
Peterson, Carla L. 118
Peterson, Thomas E. 5, 15n14
Petit, Jacques 51, 52, 57, 61–62, 70n1, 70n13, 71n25
Phillips, Roderick 33n7
philosophes 23
Pierce, Gillian B. 34n12
"La Pierre qui pousse" (Camus) 19
Pinget, Robert 15n17
"Le Plus Bel Amour de don Juan" 52–58, 61, 67, 68, 168, 171
Poe, Edgar Allan 11, 17n36, 74, 166, 177n4
"Point de lendemain" (Denon) 20–24, 30–32, 32–33n6, 45, 90, 134, 135, 165, 169, 175
Porter, Katherine Anne 12, 14n4
post-structuralism 2
Poussin 133–34
Powell, David A. 146n5
Powers, Richard 16n27
primogeniture 63–64
Prince, Gerald 6
"Le Protecteur" (Maupassant) 147
Proust, Marcel 12, 38, 161, 163n12, 177n9
Przybos, Julia 56–57, 71n17
Pushkin, Alexander (*Eugen Onegin*) 9

Rabelais, François 23, 33n10, 73, 135, 140–44, 146n11, 174
Rabelaisian model 141
Rabinowitz, Peter J. 89n23
La Rabouilleuse (Balzac) 63
reader ix, 67–68, 177n9
Realism 37, 38
"recapitulation" 92
Reid, Ian 7, 16n21, 87n4
Restif de La Bretonne, Nicolas-Edme 22, 33n8
"La Retraite de Monsieur Bougran" (Huysmans) 39
Richepin, Jean 38
Robbe-Grillet, A. 6, 12
Roberts, Thomas J. 5, 15n15

Rogers, B. G. 52, 61
Romany language 82
Roudiez, Leon S. 4, 15n11
Le Rouge et le noir (Stendhal) 43, 73
Rousseau, Jean-Jacques 5–6
Russian Formalism: History—Doctrine (Erlich) 16n29

Sacchi, Sergio 89n24
Sachs, Murray 7, 16n19
Sainte-Beuve 92, 96
Salomé 1
"Sans lendemain" 48, 18–34
Saroyan, William 11
Sardanapalus 54
Satan 70n12
Savey-Casard, Paul 98–99, 105, 107n19–20
Schaeffer, Walter 14n6
Scott, Walter 56, 135
Sedgewick, Ellery 8
Seigle, Jerrold 87n6
shadow drama 105–06
"The Short Happy Life of Francis Macomber" (Hemingway) 19
short story: ambiguity xi, 87n6; artistic 166–67; brevity ix, 10–12, 86, 168; closure xii–xiii, 87n4; definition x, 2, 5, 7, 8, 10, 13–14, 19, 111, 164, 176; economy xiii; fiction 5–7, 35, 37, 38, 169; frame 72–84, 87n4; genre xi–xii, 2, 14n5, 16n21, 90–106, 147 (*see also* genre); history of 1–2; image x, 6, 37, 86, 171; masterpieces 6, 165–67, 176; modern 72, 87nn1–3, 88n7; narration 38, 84; prose 168; reputation 127n1; sequence x–xi, 20, 48–70, 145
Sierra-Leone, duchess de 52, 55, 56, 58
Smeets, Marc 49n9
Soboul, Albert 108n28
society 4, 21, 22, 24, 31, 33n7, 35, 38, 40, 47, 59, 62, 72, 76, 77, 81, 83, 85, 90–106, 116, 117, 128n5, 131, 132, 145, 148, 151, 157, 160, 170, 171
Soirées de Médan (Zola) 36
Solal, Jérôme 40, 49n12, 49n15, 49n16
Sollers, Philippe 4
Sophie's Choice (Styron) 46
"spatial form" 6, 129n19
spiritualistic naturalism 37, 47
Spoerri, Theophil 72

198   Index

Springer, Mary Doyle 1, 14n3
Stasseville, Madame de 59–67,
171, 172
Stegner, Wallace 34n15
Steinhauer, Harry 157
Stephens, Bradley xiii
Steinhauer, Harry 2, 15n7
Stevenson, Robert Louis 32n5
Styron, William (*Sophie's Choice*) 46
*Supplément au voyage de
Bougainville, ou Dialogue entre A
et B.* (Diderot) 22
symbol 103–04, 108n23
Swahn, Sigbrit 146n5

Tharsis, Chevalier de 58, 61, 63
Thomas, Dylan 10, 17n30
Thomas, Shelly Purcell 130n26
Thucydides (*History of the
Peloponnesian War*)
Tieck, Ludwig 8
Tilby, Michael 88n12
Todorov, Tzvetan 6, 16n18
"Tomboctou" (Maupassant) 148
"Tom Thumb" (Perrault) 8
Torgovnick, Marianna 72, 87n4
trinitarian cycle 118–21
Trois Contes (Flaubert) 38, 107–27,
128n2, 128n8, 128n10, 129n15,
130n26, 130n29, 166
Tynjanov, Jurij 3–4, 15n10

uncertainty 21–5, 29, 31, 134, 135,
139, 143, 145, 165, 170, 174

Van Tieghem, Philippe 6n16
Vassilev, Kris 71n19
"La Vénus d'Ille" (Mérimée)
A vau-l'eau (Huysmans) 35–7
Verdier, Yvonne 151–52, 162n5,
162n7, 162n8
Vian, Boris ("Le Rappel") 7
la Vierge Marie (see, Mary)
56–57, 112
Villèle, Jean-Baptiste 63, 171
Villiers de l'Isle-Adam, Auguste
("L'Enjeu") 18
la voie des aiguilles 150–52
la voie des épingles 150–52

Walker, Warren S 14n5
Warren, Austin 15n15
Wellek, René 9n28, 15n15, 16n28
Wharton, Edith 147, 162n2, 165, 172,
177n4
When Is Something Fiction? (Roberts)
15n15
*The Widening Gyre: Crisis and
Mastery in Modern Literature*
(Frank) 129n19
Wölfflin, Heinrich 3, 15n9
Women's Day 8
Wright, Austin M 14n6

Ziegler, Robert 49n7, 50n18
Zola, Emile 16n25, 35–37, 63, 91,
147, 162n1
Zumthor, Paul 11, 17n33, 17n34,
18, 32n1

Printed in the United States
by Baker & Taylor Publisher Services